THEME OF COMPASSION
IN THE NOVELS OF BERNARD MALAMUD

THEME OF COMPASSION
IN THE NOVELS OF
BERNARD MALAMUD

M. RAJAGOPALACHARI
Department of English
Kakatiya University

Distributed By
ADVENT BOOKS
141 East 44 Street
New York, NY 10017

PRESTIGE BOOKS
NEW DELHI

ISBN 81-85218-02-1

First Published: 1988

Published by:
Prestige Books
3/28, East Patel Nagar
New Delhi 110 008
Phone: 5710787

Printed by:
Creative Printers
at Pal Mohan Process
W.Z. 130-A, Naraina
New Delhi 110 028

CONTENTS

Preface ... 7

1. Contexts of Compassion ... 11

2. Two Lives of Roy: *The Natural* ... 37

3. "I Suffer for You": *The Assistant* ... 54

4. Levin's Burden: *A New Life* ... 76

5. Grace under Pressure: *The Fixer* ... 95

6. Art is Not Life: *Pictures of Fidelman* ... 125

7. *Hab Rachmones*: *The Tenants* ... 152

8. To Kitty with Love: *Dubin's Lives* ... 170

9. After the Second Flood: *God's Grace* ... 183

10. In Defense of the Human; *The Magic Barrel, Idiots First* and *Rembrandt's Hat* ... 191

11. Conclusion ... 206

Bibliography ... 208

Index ... 219

To My Parents
with love

PREFACE

   In the post-world-war period of bad faith and nihilism, the Jew emerged as a symbol of "conscience" and compassion in American-Jewish fiction. The historic rootlessness and the Holocaust inflicted on the Jews have given the figure of Jew the role of "victim" as against the role of rebel assumed by the black in black fiction. But the Jewish tradition has also taught the Jew the meaning of suffering in compassion. William Freedman among others remarks that "Clearly the principal emotion, indeed the principal virtue, espoused in Jewish fiction is compassion."[1] Irving Malin's *Jews and Americans*, Leslie and Joyce Field's *Bernard Malamud and the Critics*, Sansford Pinsker's *The Schlemiel as Metaphor* stress the humanism of contemporary Jewish-American literature. Writers like Saul Bellow, Bernard Malamud, J.D. Salinger, Isaac Bashevis Singer in mirroring the modern life of complexity and commotion have evinced a profound moral vision based on compassion in their works. While sharing the deep concern of other Jewish novelists for the predicament of modern man, Malamud goes a little further and asserts that compassion alone redeems modern man. Chastened by suffering, his characters mellow under its cathartic effect. Compassion is not just a strain as in other Jewish writers but it is the ethos of Malamud's moral vision. Further Malamud's preoccupation with the theme of compassion is so consistent in his work that it merits a full-length study.

Sick of the "deceitful devaluation of man" in the present-day world, Malamud affirms everything that is human. He explains the credo of his philosophy as follows:

My work, all of it, is an idea of dedication to the human. That's basic to every book. If you don't respect man, you cannot respect my work. I'm in defense of the human.[2]

This intense reverence for man and his dignity is integral to Malamud's moral vision. Literature for him has a purpose—"to make some lives better."[3] He wants to bring commitment into literature and says "Art must interpret, or it is mindless."[4] He goes on: "To preserve itself it must, in a variety of subtle ways, conserve the artist through sanctifying human life and freedom."[5] He thinks the writer's most important task is "to recapture his image as human being as each of us in his secret heart knows it to be and as history and literature have from the beginning revealed it," besides imagining "a better world for men the while he shows us, in all its ugliness and beauty, the possibilities of this."[6] The anguish for "a new life" of better human relationships is evident in his assertion of Camus' statement: "The purpose of the writer is to keep civilization from destroying itself."[7] This compassionate vision of Malamud informs all his work. Although Malamud presents the tragic underground of man, he does not like the categorization of his fiction as that of victims of *schlemiels*. He is interested in bringing out "man's hidden strength" seen in "the resources of the spirit."[8] Compassion provides man with this "hidden strength." The stubborn Yakov Bok (*The Fixer*), the complacent Morris Bober (*The Assistant*) or the flippant Seymour Levin (*A New Life*)—although losers—evince extraordinary tenacity to suffer on account of their compassion. Morally and spiritually they outgrow their victim-fate. Compassion remains the quintessential ethos of Malamud's moral vision in his entire work.

Although there is a large body of critical scholarship on Malamud, only sporadic references to the ubiquitous theme of compassion could be found. Mention may be made of critics like Granville Hicks, Ihab Hassan, H.E. Francis, Ben Siegel,

Lois Symons Lewin. Much of the criticism is addressed to the analysis of suffering. Suffering for Malamud becomes nihilistic and corrosive if it is not endowed with compassion. An in-depth study of this significant theme of compassion in the work of Malamud deserves to be made. The present study seeks to show how compassion is integral to Malamud's world-view in his fiction.

M. Rajagopalachari

NOTES

1. William Freedman, "American Jewish Fiction: So What's the Big Deal?" *Chicago Review* 19.1 (1966): 90-107.
2. Haskel Frankel, "Interview with Bernard Malamud," *Saturday Review* 10 September 1966: 40.
3. Ralph Tyler, "A Talk with the Novelist," *The New York Times Book Review* 18 February 1979: 34.
4. Bernard Malamud, "Speaking of Books: Theme, Content and the 'New Novel'," *New York Times Book Review* 26 March 1967: 29.
5. Malamud, "Speaking of Books," 29.
6. Bernard Malamud, "The Writer's Task." *Writing in America*, ed. John Fischer and Robert B. Silvers (New Brunswick, N.J.: Rutgers Univ. Press, 1960) 173.
7. Quoted in Ihab Hassan, "The Hopes of Man," *New York Times Book Review* 13 October 1963: 5.
8. Quoted in W.J. Handy, "The Malamud Hero: A Quest for Existence," *The Fiction of Bernard Malamud*, ed. Richard Astro and Jackson J. Benson (Corvallis: Oregon State Univ. Press, 1977) 65.

Acknowledgements

I am grateful to my teacher Dr. S. Laxmana Murthy, Professor of English, Kakatiya University for his affectionate advice and meticulous care in shaping this study. He has been an unfailing source of inspiration to me.

I remember with gratitude the late Professor H.N.L. Sastry who guided me during the early stages of research.

I thank Professor K. Venkata Ramiah, former Vice-Chancellor of Kakatiya University and Professor K. Venkata-chari of A.P. Open University for their constant encouragement. My thanks are due to Prof. William Mulder, former Director of American Studies Research Centre, Hyderabad, whose perceptive remarks on several chapters provided the necessary fillip to my work. He has also been kind to sanction the Teachers' Research Grant twice to enable me to spend a few months at the ASRC collecting the relevant research material on Malamud.

I thank the University Grants Commission for providing me partial financial assistance for the publication of doctoral dissertation. I am thankful to Prof. T. Vasudev, Vice-Chancellor and Prof. Dinker Sirdeshmukh, Coordinating Officer (UGC Unit) of Kakatiya University who have helped me greatly in this regard.

I am highly obliged to Dr. R.K. Dhawan of Delhi University for his kind help and advice.

I am thankful to M/s Prestige Books who have come forward to bring out the book neatly and promptly.

M. RAJAGOPALACHARI

1

CONTEXTS OF COMPASSION

"We are lonely. . . . We've learnt to pity one another for being alone. And we've learnt that nothing remains to be discovered except compassion."

Jacob Bronowski, *The Face of Violence: An Essay with a Play* (Cleveland: World, 1967), 161-162

The shocking awareness of the widening gulf between what man is and what he ought to be has prompted the Jewish writer to think in terms of moral regeneration and to evolve an idea of new life based on compassion, love and humanism. Mark Schechner observes that "the horror of the recent past stands behind all postwar Jewish-American fiction."[1] Novelists like Bernard Malamud, Saul Bellow, J.D. Salinger, Isaac Bashevis Singer project a profound moral vision in their works and take a compassionate view of suffering of man as seen in the Jewish personae. The Jew in recent literature has emerged as "a symbol of conscience—outwardly, as a function of his persecution which reached its climax in the Holocaust, and inwardly, as a function of his religious character."[2] Jewish history with

its untold human suffering and Jewish tradition with its emphasis on humanism have added a poignant touch to Jewish
writing. Suffering and compassion have been integral to Jewish
history and their way of life. An understanding of the history
and tradition of Jews will, therefore, provide insights into
Jewish-American fiction.

II

The history of Jews, the so-called "chosen people of God,"
reveals that they have always been "chosen" either for persecution or discrimination. The horrendous blood-bath in Germany,
the organized killing in the shape of pogroms in Russia, depri-
vation of rights in Rumania, political oppression and religious
persecution in other countries have compelled the Jews to flee
from their own homelands to different places like nomads in a
state of unsettlement and unrest. Until 1948, they had no country
of their own. They remained slaves in Egypt and "dwelt among
the Babylonians, lived in the Hellenic world, stored at the
bier of the Roman empire, flourished in the Mohammedan
civilization, emerged from a twelve-hundred-year darkness
known as the Middle Ages, and rose to new intellectual
heights in modern times."[3] Despite that the Jews are a mino-
rity race always oppressed by the majority, they have evinced
an extraordinary resilience and tenacity to maintain their ethnic
identity successfully in their arduous struggle for survival.
Drifted though by the forces of inhumanity, they are not
disintegrated as a race.

The secret of this astonishing success of Jews, however,
could be traced to their tradition—a "tradition of mutual
responsibility—of the responsibility of the Jew for the other,
of the individual Jewish collectivity, of the Jewish community
for the single Jew in distress, of the better-situated Jew for the
under-privileged one."[4] Floating in the same boat of travails,
the Jews could take a compassionate view of one another.
Every Jew regarded himself as his brother's keeper. This bibli-
cal spirit was behind many Jewish societies and communities.
Constant suffering has fostered the values of compassion and

charity. They gave support to the needy brethren—not Jews but also non-Jews. Max I. Dimont explains the Jewish spirit:

> No matter how poor a Jew is, he always feels there is someone poorer than he, and a Jew living on charity sees nothing incongruous in giving some of his charity money as charity to some one else.[5]

Some sociologists and historians hold that this "mutual dependence of the Jews was strengthened solely as a result of the persecution and discrimination to which the Jews were subjected by the outside world."[6] Bezalel Sherman points out that the Nazi catastrophe reinforced the community bonds among the Jews of different places and strengthened the urge to "belong" wherever they are geographically.[7]

In America the Jews suffered the same disabilities as the other immigrant groups. But ever since their first settlement in that country, they have resisted the tyranny of the majority. Resistance evoked "the mistrust of the majority and tightened the internal cohesion of the Jewish community."[8] Suffering has chastened the Jews and acted as a cohesive force of union and solidarity. Their four-thousand-year history has taught the Jews not only suffering but also compassion as a way of life.

Although isolation and assimilation for the Jews in America have become concomitants rather than alternatives, many of the Jewish intellectuals today view Judaism in its quintessential form of struggle for universal justice and human brotherhood and not as a ritual-based religion. They, however, seem to take a "non-religious pride" in their "family tradition."[9]

The Jewish tradition as represented by the old prophets like Amos and Hosea too emphasises more on universal justice, love and compassion as cardinal principles of moral life than on the ritual. The prophets have discovered the meaning of religion in "a life of righteousness, mercy and justice, and asserted that *what was pleasing to God was a heart of compassion.*"[10] (Italics mine) Their emphasis is on man's imitation of the main qualities that characterize God: "justice and love (*rahamim*)." They have asserted that the people of Israel are chosen to exemplify an ethical life. Amos exhorts: "But let justice roll down like waters, righteousness like an everflowing stream."[11] (5:24) Jewish philosopher Philo held that Judaism was "the instrument which enabled man to achieve moral perfection and the Torah was the path to union with God."[13] According to the commentary on Exodus of the Talmudist Rabbi Eleazer of Modiim, a Jew is accounted to have fulfilled the Torah if he "transacts his business honestly and is pleasing to his fellowmen."[14] Asked by a pagan, the great Hillel is said to have explained the Torah as "Do not do unto others what you would not want to be done unto you. This is the essence, and the rest is commentary; go and learn." (Shabbat, 31a) In the Jewish view, man is born with the capacity to sin, but he can return and redeem himself by his own effort. The possibility of redemption is in his own hands.

Though the God of the Old Testament is a jealous God demanding that His people worship Him and Him alone, he is also a righteous, loving and merciful God who commands men to behave with brotherly love and show compassion for the oppressed.

'Thou shall love the Lord thy God with all thy heart and thy neighbor as thyself.'
'Cease to do evil, learn to do well, seek judgment, relieve the oppressed, judge the fatherless, plead for the widow.... What doth the Lord require of thee but to do justly, and to love mercy, and to walk humbly with thy God.' (Micah 6:8)

God in the Bible is a manifestation of justice and compassion. While the concept of justice is emphasised in a few older parts of the Bible, the concept of God's love and compassion abounds in the prophetic literature.[15]

Erich Fromm in his radical interpretation of the Old Testament traces the universalism in Jewish tradition. Fromm believes that the Old Testament recounts "a remarkable evolution from primitive authoritarianism and clannishness to the idea of the radical freedom of man and the brotherhood of all men."[16] He explains that the first covenant in the Old Testament is one between God and mankind and not between God

and the Hebrew tribe. "The history of the Hebrews is conceived as only a part of the history of man; the principle of
"reverence for life" precedes all specific premises to one particular tribe or nation."[17]

The religious movement of Hasidism which seized the
Eastern European Jewry in the middle of the 18th century
condemns "self-intending" or selfish pursuit of one's own
salvation, and insists on living for others. Martin Buber explains the pursuit of Hasidism as

> To begin with oneself, but not to end with oneself; to start
> from oneself, but not to aim at oneself, to comprehend one-
> self, but not to be preoccupied with oneself.[18]

Buber holds that one of the main points of divergence between
Christianity and Judaism is that while the former makes each
man's salvation his highest aim, the latter believes that "no
soul has its object in itself, in its own salvation," but in those
of others.[19]

The Sabbath and Festival Prayer Book, which the Jews use
in most of the synagogues today, defines the Jew as a figure of
compassion. One of the prayers reads: "I am a Jew because in
all places where there are tears and suffering the Jew
weeps."[20] The Jewish belief that suffering is a means of
compassion informs the prayer before Kaddish (the Jewish
prayer of mourning): "Give us insight in this hour of grief,
that from the depths of suffering may come a deepened sympathy for all who are bereaved, that we may feel the heart-break
of our fellowmen and find our strength in helping them."[21]

Thus a struggle for new order of life with compassion as its
cardinal principle seems to characterize Jewish tradition
supported by their history. Although the preoccupation with
compassion is not something felt by the Jews alone, it acquires
a unique connotation for them in the context of their tragic
history. The affirmation of human values in the wasteland
world has been emphasised by creative writers in general.
While reflecting the disorder, defeat and despair of the day, the
writer has to face the moral question, the essence of which
according to Bellow is—"In what form shall life be justified ?"[22]
Bellow further asserts that the moral function of a writer

cannot be divorced from art.[23] The conscientious writer cannot
be content with just mirroring the times. He feels the need to
suggest or instruct, however slyly it may be, without inviting
upon himself the risk of being a propagandist. Bernard
Malamud, quoting Albert Camus, says: "The purpose of the
writer is to keep civilization from destroying itself."[24] Being
"civilized" implies a sense of fellow-feeling and compassion
the lack of which is the rootcause of all problems in the
modern world. Man, Faulkner believes, will endure and pre-
vail because he has "a spirit capable of compassion and
sacrifice and endurance."[25] Jacob Bronowski makes a very
perceptive comment in his book *The Face of Violence: An
Essay with a Play*:

> We are all lonely. . . . We've learnt to pity one another for
> being alone. And we've learnt that *nothing remains to be
> discovered except compassion.*[26] (Italics mine)

Whether one learns to pity in the spirit of compassion or not,
one realises its inescapable need.

III

Compassion provides man with a comprehensive view of
life. It calls for inter-personal responsibility underscored by
love, authentic empathy and intense understanding. The
meaning of compassion could be discovered not in isolation or
alienation but in a feeling of community that one's fate is tied
up with others in pain and pleasure. The term "compassion"
has its etymological roots in the French and Latin expression
compassio which means "to suffer with." Rollo May, a psycho-
therapist, aptly illustrates the tenets of compassion in *The
Power and Innocence*. He defines compassion as follows:

> Compassion is the name of that form of love which is based
> on our knowing and understanding eath other. Compassion
> is the awareness that we are all in the same boat and that
> we all shall either sink or swim together. Compassion
> arises from the recognition of community. It realizes that
> all men and women are brothers and sisters, even though a
> disciplining of our own instincts is necessary for us even to
> begin to carry out that belief in our actions.[27]

Compassion carries with it a sense of community and frater-
nity. R.W.B. Lewis finds the echo of compassion in "human
companionship" and the idea of sharing the pain of others.[28]
Compassion recognizes the fallibility of man. Everyone has his
lacunae and failures. It is these common failures, weaknesses
and sufferings that make one feel a tie with another and experience what Henry James calls a "tragic fellowship" with
suffering humanity. The "human" element in man with its
"struggles between fulfillment and non-fulfillment" makes him
feel a mutual responsibility.[29] This is spontaneous and "a
willingly assumed responsibility for our fellowmen and
women."[30] Compassion is thus a balance set between individuality and a new sense of solidarity. It combines in itself "the
consciousness of the individual" and "the elements of interpersonal responsibility"—the sources of all ethics.[31] Edmund
Fuller comments:

> What is compassion, anyhow? It means the sharing of a
> sorrow, a pity and sympathy, a desire to help—feeling
> another's pain or plight as if it were one's own, seeing
> 'those in chains as bound with them.' It applies to a man's
> moral as well as material or physical breakdown. In the
> moral realm it recognizes the sharing of all human guilt,
> the potentiality of evil in the most blameless, the element
> which the Christian calls original sin and the analysts call
> the Id.[32]

Fuller links compassion with a sense of morality since this
alone makes one capable of distinguishing the good from the
bad. He asserts: "No valid compassion can exist without a
moral framework."[33]

Love becomes "a possible impossibility" (to quote Reinhold
Niebuhr's phrase) evidenced in the case of loving one's
enemies. But compassion is within the reach of the human
agent since it is born of understanding. May explains:

> Understanding, in contrast to ideal love, is a human possi-
> bility—understanding for our enemies as well as our friends.
> There is in understanding the beginnings of compassion, of
> pity and of charity.[34]

Compassion emerges from understanding and is sustained in
the act of suffering.

Martin Buber speaks of two forms of existence: the I-It,
which is a subject-object relationship and the I-Thou, which is an
interpersonal relationship. He further asserts that a man defines
himself in his relation with others and that wholeness, integra-
tion of personality, depends on eschewing the I-It impersonal
for the I-Thou: "Entering into relation is an act of the whole—
it is in fact *the* act by which we constitute ourselves as
human. . . ."[35] Buber believes that the essence of man can
be grasped "by beginning neither with the individual nor with
the collectivity, but only with the reality of the mutual relation
between man and man."[36] It is only compassion which brings
about a whole I-Thou relationship. In this sense compassion
becomes an act of humanism and shares with it the concern
for the dignity of man. Erich Fromm says that one can be
related to the "human core" of another only through love, and
that the unfolding of the human in man is chiefly through
human solidarity.[37] Compassion comes out of the conviction
that "nothing human is foreign to me."[38] It may be defined as
"the capacity to sense injustice and take a stand against it in
the form of I-will-be-destroyed-rather-than-submit."[39] Ultimately it is one's capacity for empathy that makes one compassionate.

IV

These tenets of compassion are the the bed-rock of the
Jewish ethical code, what J.C. Landis calls the code of *mentshlekhkayt*. Rooted in the ancient Jewish Law, the code has
become an integral part of the *shtetl* culture of Eastern Europe
emphasising the sense of community and felt responsibility for
the fellow-being. Knopp writes:

> *Mentshlekhkayt* also encompasses the very strong sense of
> community that has traditionally been a feature of Jewish
> life. The paramount characteristic of this community feeling
> is the moral imperative of man's responsibility to his fellow
> man.[40]

Like compassion, the code also recognises the 'human" element in man—the presence of opposing tendencies toward good and evil within man. But it has an "implicit faith in the moral significance of man's actions, the faith that man has the power within him to effect changes in the world for good or for ill, and that he has the obligation to apply this power in the cause of good."[41] The code is pragmatic and chooses to concern itself with the living condition of man rather than the salvation of his soul. The redemption is sought here—in this world itself—in an ethical uprightness. The code is in agreement with the traditional Jewish view of Messianic redemption as "a hope for an earthly paradise of love and learning, (and) a Utopian vision of a region of social justice and decency."[42] In a world of chaos and suffering, the morality of *mentshlekhkayt* becomes "a compensation for suffering or a mitigation of it."

V

As the quintessential spirit of Jewish humanism, compassion has shaped the imagination of many a Jewish writer. Referring to Singer, Wiesel, Malamud and Roth, Knopp points out:

All of them in their concern for other men, in their compassion and emphasis upon right and moral action, are responding to the principal tenets of *Mentshlekhkayt* and thus to a uniquely Jewish view of the world.[44]

Knopp has examined how *mentshlekhkayt* is put on trial in the works of Isaac Bashevis Singer, Nelly Sachs, Andre Schwaz-Bart, Elie Wiesel, Bernard Malamud and Saul Bellow. Theodore Solotaroff traces the process of moral development in Bellow, Rosenfeld, Malamud, Gold and Roth and asserts that these writers delineate "life's losers and victims with deep compassion," and guard "their pity from the sentimentality."[45] In Saul Bellow compassion becomes a subtle form of expression of his affirmative vision with its distrust of the cult of the ego. The moral problem of the writer, Bellow feels, is to find ways to break the isolation of the self. He asserts further that if the writer can convince his readers "that the existence of others is a reality, he can then proceed to higher moral questions, questions of justice, questions of duty, of honour."[46] A struggle to overcome egotism with universal love characterises the ordeal of Bellow's protagonists. Joseph in *The Dangling Man* fails in his attempt to find answer to the vital question of "How should a good man live: what ought he to do ?"[47]

He realises he "had not done well alone" and considers the possibility of establishing a "colony of the spirit" devoid of spite and rancour. Tommy Wilhelm of *Seize the Day* breaks the shell of self-glorification to affirm his bond with all men. He realises the paradox of human existence that man is alone and yet is a part of the greater entity than himself. Augie's refusal to resort to machiavellian strategies in life and his readiness to establish a home for orphans, and Henderson's plans to adopt a homeless boy with whom he returned from Africa—stress the obligation of man to man. Herzog under the strain and stress of life drifted away by pride and evil learns the values of love, compassion and togetherness. He decides not to kill his ex-wife's paramour after watching him bathe his daughter and acknowledges that "Man liveth not by self alone, but in his brother's face."[48] He confesses that "subjective monstrosity" must be corrected by a feeling of community and brotherhood which makes one human. Sammler sees no end to suffering as long as there is no ethical life. To him "contemporaneity" is synonymous with "lawlessness." Despising man's hunger to land on the moon, he pleads for a rationale of having "justice on this planet first."[49] He considers the degenerating trends of individualism as the root cause of discontent of the day. He cultivates a disinterestedness but does not become a misanthrope. Like that of Herzog's, his affirmation lies in a personal ethic sanctified by a faith in God. Citrine and Leventhal of *Humboldt's Gift* and *The Victim* also give unmistakable evidence of their love for mankind in their realisation of inter-personal responsibility. Bellow's achievement, thus, could be summed up as the pursuit of an idea of order in "the contending forces of his fiction—life and death, optimism and despair, reason and feeling, self and brotherhood."[50]

J.D. Salinger's fiction presents the struggle of a conscientious man in a conscienceless world. He depicts the epic "journey of the human spirit through the illusions of the material world to the transcendent spiritual oneness beyond."[51] His Holden Caulfield of *The Catcher in the Rye* in fact has emerged as the representative of "an adolescent America uncertainly searching for the lost garden, suspicious of alien or intimate entanglements, reluctant to encounter the horrors of reality."[52] Holden presents the picture of a man torn between the conflicting impulses of withdrawal from the "phony" world and search for responsive relationship with people. In his quest to preserve innocence, he finds himself a neurotic misfit in the world. His painful odyssey through life makes him realise the futility of his ambition to "catch everybody if they start to go over the cliff." Holden himself is little conscious of his own fall from the cliff when he runs away from home and his master Antolini, and dreams of finding a peaceful retreat for himself. He fails to find such retreat in a world ridden with obscenity because such a world does not exist here. He is, however, saved from his further fall at the end by his sister Phoebe who had readily offered to go with him into exile. He is redeemed in his choice to live and stay with his sister. He feels happy watching his sister ride round and round on the carrousel in the midst of a drenching rain. After this he begins "missing" everybody he has told about—including those who had beaten and hurt him. This speaks for the love he bore within for others. He realises that "if you are aware of the human comedy, you must love individual human beings."[53] Holden's journey is a movement "from innocence to knowledge, from self-ignorance to self-awareness, from isolation to involvement."[54] This love of life and individual human beings makes him compassionate, and redeems.

Much of Philip Roth's fiction appears to be steeped in obscenity, sex and eroticism and a psychological study of eccentrics, misfits and marginal neurotics. But it is also concerned with "the conflict between moral superiority and worldly imperfection."[55] His early fiction presents "mad crusaders" who attempt to reform their neighbours at the cost of their own lives.[56] Roth sees the task of the Jewish novelist "not to forge in the smithy of his soul the uncreated conscience of his race, but to find inspiration in a conscience that has been created and undone a hundred times over in this century alone."[57] In *Letting Go*, Roth portrays an interesting character in Gabe Wallach who "tries to help out in other people's affairs without fully committing himself to anyone or anything."[58] This lack of involvement fails Gabe in his relations with Marge Howells, Martha Regenhart and Libby Herzy. *When She Was Good* presents the struggle of a woman obsessed with truth and righteousness against a world of mediocrity. She, however, fails in life because of her inability to moderate her values in the face of human weaknesses including hers. *Portnoy's Complaint* depicts Alexander Portnoy's vain attempts to improve others without his involvement which ultimately makes him a hero of sex and masturbation. Referring to the obscene language of Portnoy, Roth complains "that's the way people talk."[59] *Our Gang* is a political satire of Swiftian proportions on the ambitions of evil politicians. Dixon of the novel, a caricature of Richard Nixon, campaigns in Hell and tries to prove that he has outlasted Satan as far as evil is concerned.

Isaac Bashevis Singer, a Yiddish writer, presents a gloomy and pessimistic view of the world and dark forces that govern man's life. He gives a supernatural touch to his fiction by his flair for devils, imps and demons. But the supernatural in his fiction becomes "primarily an extension of the problematic morality of this world."[60] The devils symbolize for him the world—"human beings and human behaviour."[61] With his staunch belief in God, Singer presents the eternal moral problem seen in the conflict between good and evil although good in the process does not always triumph over evil. In fact he says that "any writer who does not think in terms of good and evil cannot go very far in his writing."[62] He suggests that his characters are not "morality tales" but narratives "constructed around a moral point of view."[63] His characters, like those of Malamud, stress the importance of endurance despite suffering and disappointment without losing their love of life. Singer exposes the futility of philosophical abstractions and isms with existential finality and emphasises man's essentially tragic fate. He seems to believe that "if compassion . . . is missing, piety, asceticism, and intellectualism are useless."[64]

The value of compassion is better exemplified by Singer in *The Family Moskat*, his first novel to appear in English. Asa Heshel Bannet in the novel represents the moral and spiritual decay of the Poland's Jewry. In his pursuit of a university degree, divine truth and earthly happiness, he grows cynical. Unable to confront the problems of life, he retreats both from his family and self, and nurses the illusion of shielding individuality. With an uncanny knack for survival, he escapes death in the midst of pogroms, war and hunger. Yet at the end, he refuses to escape from Warsaw and rejoins his family and friends to accept the common fate of death that awaits them in the shape of Nazis. It is in this act of courage and compassion—to suffer *with* and not by himself—that Asa finds his redemption.

Singer's subsequent novels—*Satan in Goray, The Magician of Lublin, The Slave*—all represent "man's urge toward the sacred and yielding to the profane."[65] In *The Manor*, Singer approves neither of Calman Jacoby's retreat into private synagogue nor of Ezriel Babad's pursuit of science. He seems to suggest as Ezriel realises in the novel that science offers no more "truth" or certainty than does religious faith unless one has a sense of responsibility and love for fellow-beings. Singer thus "strives for those acts of revelation that catch his proud, lustful, deluded little people at points of great stress, acts that cut through the banalities of religion, culture, and setting to expose their common substance across the generations."[66]

VI

Bernard Malamud shares Bellow's affirmative vision, Roth's psychological and moral concerns and Salinger's quest for meaningful human relations. If his novels are not so intellectual as those of Bellow, they are not any the less evocative of moral response. He imbibes the fervent moral vision of Singer and his humanist concerns but not his supernaturalism. He seems to believe with him that "you are a good man if you don't make people suffer. This is the only measure; there is no other measure."[67] His measure of humanness, however, is not complacent with not making others suffer. It extends further and seeks meaning of existence in suffering for

others as Morris Bober in *The Assistant* tells Frank Alpine:
"I suffer for you."[68] Here he echoes Elie Wiesel's formulation:
"I suffer, therefore you are."[69] Like Camus and Silone, Malamud finds the answer to the abysmal sense of hopelessness or
non-existence in companionship and compassion. The ideal of
compassion in Camus lies in "solidarity with the vanquis-
hed."[70] As R.W.B. Lewis points out, the ideal of compassion
and the ambition to be a man *are* the ingredients of the one
really authentic mode of sainthood in the contemporary
world.[71] Malamud's protagonists become saints in this sense
not because there is something divine about them but because
they primarily strive to be men in the real sense of the word.
Their sanctity lies not in private communion with God but in
communion and involvement with fellowmen so as to understand and share their suffering.

While sharing the deep concern of other Jewish novelists
for the predicament of modern man, Malamud goes a little
further and asserts that compassion alone redeems modern
man. Suffering chastens his characters. The characters mellow
under its cathartic effect. From senseless suffering they move
to suffering for others. Suffering acquires meaning in relation
to compassion. Malamud shows a deeper awareness of the
cathartic value of suffering and compassion, and deals with
the theme of compassion more effectively and expansively than
any other Jewish-American novelist. Compassion is not just a
strain as in the case of other Jewish writers but the ethos of
Malamud's moral vision. Further, Malamud's preoccupation
with the theme of compassion is so consistent in his work that
it merits a full-length study.

VII

Unlike Bellow, Malamud agrees that Jewishness has been
a source of his moral and imaginative sustenance. He pro-
claims:

I am an American, I'm a Jew, and I write for all men. . . .
I write about Jews, when I write about Jews, because they

set my imagination going. I know something about their history, the quality of their experience and belief, and of their
literature though not as much as I would like. Like many
writers I'm influenced especially by the Bible, both Testa-
ments. I respond in particular to the East European immi-
grants of my father's and mother's generation.[72]

The suffering of Jews including the tragedy of destruction of
six million Jews has cast a distinct stamp on the sensitive mind
of Malamud and he feels the need on the part of a writer to
"cry" about it.[73] He also asserts that "Jews are absolutely the
very stuff of drama."[74] Despite these assertions, Malamud in
his work transcends the regionalism and ethnic barriers in his
depiction of human suffering and complexity of life. Except
Roy Hobbs and Frank Alpine (who at the end becomes a Jew),
all the protagonists of his novels are Jews. Yet Malamud is
not interested in evoking the authentic portrayal of a contemporary Jew like Philip Roth. Roth complains that Malamud
has not shown "specific interest in the anxieties and dilemmas
and corruptions of the modern American Jews, the Jew we
think of as characteristic of our times" and that his people live
in "a timeless depression and a placeless Lower East-side."[75]
It is true that Malamud does not give much importance to the
vivid portrayal of Jewish life and setting, but it need not be
viewed as a disadvantage. Malamud is not interested in the
superficialities of Jewish life; rather his interest lies in capturing the spirit of Jewish life and moral experience seen in
suffering and compassion. From this ethos of Jewish experience, he moves on to probe the human misery in general. The
grim and tragic struggle of a Jew for a life of love and compassion could be the struggle of any man in the twentieth
century. Malamud himself confesses that "Personally I handle
the Jew as universal man. Every man is a Jew though he may
not know it. The Jewish drama is a . . . symbol of the fight
for existence in the highest possible terms. Jewish history is
God's gift of drama."[76] The heroes of Malamud, mostly Jews,
thus become "the symbols of struggling humanity, partaking
in its ambiguous fate."[77] Everyone becomes a Jew in tasting
the bitterness of life. Perhaps this is what Malamud meant by

his statement: "All men are Jews" or as a character in his story "Angel Levin" says: "Believe me, there are Jews everywhere."[78] Jewishness to Malamud, as Robert Alter and Theodore Solotaroff point out, is "an ethical symbol"—a moral stance or a type of metaphor "for the tragic human condition and for a code of personal morality."[79] From the thick concreteness of Jewish moral experience, Malamud like Roth gets at "the dilemmas and decisions of the heart generally."[80] This gives a universal significance to Malamud's handling of the Jew who is as real as any man. At the same time Malamud's Jews are more than mere types or metaphors.

Essentially a humanist, Malamud views Judaism as "another source of humanism."[81] He is very much concerned about the degradation and loss of human dignity in the modern world. In his acceptance address of the National Book Award for *The Magic Barrel*, Malamud reveals his anguish at the "deceitful devaluation of man."

> I am quite tired of the colossally deceitful devaluation of man in this day; for whatever explanation: that life is cheap amid a prevalence of wars; or because we are dragged by totalitarian successes into a sneaking belief in their dehumanizing processes; or tricked beyond self-respect by the values of the creators of our own thing-ridden society; ... or because having invented the means of his extinction, man values himself less for it and lives in daily dread that he will in a fit of passion, or pique or absent-mindedness, achieve his end. Whatever the reason, his fall from grace in his eyes is betrayed in the words he has invented to describe himself as he is now: fragmented, abbreviated, other-directed, organisational, anonymous man, a victim, in the words that are used to describe him, of a kind of syndech-dochic irony, the part for the whole. The devaluation exists because he accepts it without protest.[82]

Spurning this gloomy state of affairs in the modern world, Malamud has faith in humanity. He strikes a note of affirmation in his belief that "we will not destroy each other . . .

we will live on."[83] The world-view projected by Malamud in his work is thus qualified by a moral vision.

In his interview with Haskel Frankel, Malamud explains the credo of his philosophy as follows:

> My work, all of it, is an idea of dedication to the human. That's basic to every book. If you don't respect man, you cannot respect my work. I'm in defense of the human.[84]

This intense reverence for man and his dignity informs his vision. It is in defense of the human that his fiction prescribes the value of compassion revealing "what it is to be human, to be humane."[85] Art for Malamud tends toward morality, and morality in his own words, "begins with an awareness of the sanctity of one's life, hence the lives of others—even Hitler's to begin with—the sheer privilege of being in this miraculous cosmos, and trying to figure out why."[86] He believes that art celebrates life and gives us our measure. Malamud's compassionate vision does not exclude even villains like Hitler.

Malamud's response to the human condition is sensitive and is born of a compassionate understanding. Life for him is a drama of moral issues while words like conscience, responsibility, love, suffering and compassion have implicit value. He recognizes that man is a compound of good and bad, and yet has the potentiality to change for the better. His interest in fiction is on man "in the process of changing his fate, his life.[87] In his interview with Joseph Wershba, he describes his fiction as telling the story of personality fulfilling itself.[88] Malamud's protagonists struggle for a "new life" whatever be their guilt-ridden past. Suffering and compassion become instrumental to this process of transformation to new life.

In their quest for "new life," Malamud's protagonists do not just limit themselves to the struggle for survival in the "naturalistic world" as do the protagonists of Theodore Dreiser, but enter into human relationships and live in a "world of interpersonal relationships which the existentialist psychoanalyst Ludwig Binswanger calls 'Mit-welt,' literally 'with-world'."[89] Although they appear to be *schlemiels* destined to fail and lose, they are not just passive victims of fate and circumstances without any capacity to resist or change. They have the spiritual strength within. In fact Malamud himself disapproves of reading his fiction as "writing about losers" and states in an interview in *The National Observer* that

> One of my most important themes is a man's hidden strength. I am very much interested in the resources of the spirit, the strength people don't know they have until they are confronted with a crisis.[90]

This inner spiritual strength of characters comes out of their compassion. Compassion in Roy Hobbs of *The Natural* dawns very late in the form of his understanding the feeling and love of Iris Lemon, but it gives him strength to throw the corrupt compact with Judge Goodwill Banner. It also makes him prepared for further suffering. In *The Assistant* Morris Bober is compassion-incarnate and lives and dies for others in the midst of crushing suffering. Frank Alpine, his gentile assistant, takes the role of Morris Bober after his death and works day and night out of compassion and love for the Bober family. Compassion in Seymour Levin of *A New Life* gives him strength to give up his job and shoulder the responsibility of Pauline Gilley and her adopted children. Suffering chastens Yakov Bok of *The Fixer* who ultimately decides to suffer for the sake of his race, and does not yield to the tempting offers of release by the Tsarist officials despite inhuman torture. Fidelman's inability to understand the relation between art and life, and the values of love and compassion lead him to failure as painter and historian. Harry Lesser and Willie Spearmint of *The Tenants* fail as writers due to lack of compassion and love, and seek to destroy each other at the end. Dubin in *Dubin's Lives* is torn with the conflict between his obligation for wife and lust for a promiscuous girl. Ultimately obligation wins over lust. In *God's Grace* Cohn realises the value of compassion in the context of extinction of human life. He desperately struggles to infuse a sense of community into animals and becomes a victim of their hatred in the process.

VIII

Although there is a large body of critical scholarship on Malamud, we could find only sporadic references to this theme of compassion which as the underlying principle of his humanistic vision permeates his entire creative output. Granville Hicks points out that Malamud, greatly troubled by the depreciation of the human in modern times, believes that "the human must be protected, and the note he sounds again and again is compassion."[91] Alfred Kazin remarks that Malamud in capturing the "strangeness" of Jewish life brilliantly, "relies on compassion, not on the covenant."[92] Francis comments on the humanism and compassion as follows:

> . . . it is compassion, not theology, which allies his Christian and Jewish characters. Malamud's own humanity can be felt in them as they sympathize with each other in their tragedy. And his own deep compassion is felt through his characters as they cry out, like Ida in her despair, 'Why do I cry ? I cry for the world, I cry for my life that it went away wasted. I cry for you [93]

Ihab Hassan perceives the "voice of conscience" in Malamud.[94] Joseph Featherstone considers Malamud's novels "parables of possible regeneration of the self."[95] Leslie Fiedler finds Malamud more metaphysical and richly inventive than most of his colleagues.[96] Jonathan Baumbach finds Malamud exploring the possibilities of heroism in making "moral art of the self."[97] Peter L. Hays says that Malamud's protagonists emerge as "secular saints" from "the hellish depths of human misery" with courage, compassion and humanity.[98] Landis finds in Malamud "the evolution of man into *mentsch*, the slow, painful discovery of the ways of *mentshlekhkayt*."[99] Ben Siegel comments that each of Malamud's works is "a moral critique" which reveals his "ironic and yet compassionate insight into the dark dilemma" of modern life.[100] Sandy Cohen analysing the theme of "self-transcendence" in Malamud comments that Malamudian protagonists through trial by love and suffering transform their basic drives "from *eros* to *caritas*."[101] Robert Ducharme in

his study of the first four novels of Malamud finds a gradual
emergence of the theme of responsibility as a conflicting idea
to the theme of suffering.[102] Lois Symons Lewin asserts that
the idea that "suffering is the necessary condition of compassion, that it is a way of reaching God" is dominant in the
fiction of Malamud.[103]

The critics have viewed compassion in Malamud as infor-
ming his moral vision. It is not just a note found here and there
but a theme consistently portrayed in all his novels. The aspect
of suffering which is largely commented upon acquires meaning
and significance only in relation to compassion. An in-
depth study of this significant theme of compassion in the
work of Malamud deserves to be made. The present study is an
effort in this direction and seeks to show how compassion is
integral to Malamud's world-view in his eight novels and three
collections of short stories.

NOTES

1. Mark Schechner, "Jewish Writers," *Harvard Guide to
   Contemporary American Fiction*, ed. Daniel Hoffman
   (Cambridge, Mass.: Harvard Univ. Press, 1979) 196.

2. Jackson J. Benson, "An Introduction: Bernard Malamud
   and the Haunting America," *The Fiction of Bernard
   Malamud*, eds. Richard Astro and Jackson J. Benson
   (Corvallis: Oregon State Univ. Press, 1977) 29.

3. Max I. Dimont, *Jews, God and History* (New York:
   Signet Books, 1964) 15.

4. C. Bezalel Sherman, *The Jew within American Society:
   A Study in Ethnic Individuality* (Detroit: Wayne State
   Univ. Press, 1961) 134.

5. Dimont 124.
6. Sherman 135.
7. Sherman 211.
8. Sherman 58.
9. See "Jewishness and the Younger Intellectuals: A Symposium," *Commentary* 31.4 April 1961: 306-359.

10. Eugene G. Bewkes, Howard B. Jefferson et al. *The Western Heritage of Faith and Reason* (New York: Harper and Row, 1963) 55.

11. Quoted in Bewkes et al., 57.

12. Dimont 42.

13. Dimont 117.

14. See S.S. Cohen, *Judaism: A Way of Life* (New York: 1962) 102.

15. See Erich Fromm, *You Shall be as Gods: A Radical Interpretation of the Old Testament and its Tradition* (New York: Holt, Rinehart and Winston, 1967) 185-86.

16. Fromm 6-7.

17. Fromm 25.

18. Martin Buber, *The Way of Man According to the Teaching of Hasidism* (Secaucus, New Jersey: The Citadel Press, 1973) 31-32.

19. Martin Buber, *The Way*, 33-34.

20. *Sabbath and Festival Prayer Book*, Rabbinical Assembly of America and the United Synagogue of America (n.p., 1946) 304.

21. *Sabbath* 38.

22. Saul Bellow, "The Writer as Moralist," *The Atlantic Monthly* 211.3 March 1973: 62.

23. Bellow, "The Writer as Moralist," 62.

24. Quoted in Ihab Hassan, "The Hopes of Man," *New York Times Book Review* 13 October 1963: 5.

25. William Faulkner, "The Stockhome Address," in *William Faulkner: Three Decades of Criticism*, eds. Frederic J. Hoffman and Olga W. Vickery (New York and Burlingame: Harcourt, Braces World,1963) 348.

26. Jacob Bronowski, *The Face of Violence: An Essay with a Play* (Cleveland: World, 1967) 161-62.

27. Rollo May, *Power and Innocence: A Search for the Sources of Violence* (New York: W.W. Norton, 1972) 251.

28. R.W.B. Lewis, *The Picaresque Saint: Representative Figures in Contemporary Fiction* (Philadelphia and New York: J.B. Lippincott, 1959) 29.

29. Rollo May 251.

30. Rollo May 258.

31. Rollo May 254.

32. Edmund Fuller, "New Compassion in the American Novel," *Five Approaches of Literary Criticism*, ed. Wilbur Scott (New York and London: Collier Macmillan, 1974) 58.

33. Fuller 61.

34. Rollo May 258.

35. See Maurice B. Friedman, *Martin Buber: The Life of Dialogue* (London, 1955) 83.

36. Martin Buber, Foreword, *Between Man and Man* (New York: Macmillan, 1975) xi.

37. Erich Fromm, *Man for Himself: An Enquiry into the Psychology of Ethics* (New York: Holt, 1947) 100-01.

38. Rollo May 252.

39. Rollo May 220.

40. Josephine Zadovsky Knopp, *The Trial of Judaism in Contemporary Jewish Writing* (Chicago: Univ. of Illinois Press, 1975) 7.

41. Knopp 7.

42. J.C. Landis, "Reflections on American Jewish Writers," *Jewish Book Annual* 25 (1967-68): 114.

43. J.C. Landis, *The Dybbuk and Other Great Yiddish Plays* (New York: 1966) 5.

44. Knopp 16.

45. Theodore Solotaroff, "Roth and the Jewish Moralists," *Chicago Review* 13.4 Winter 1959: 96.

46. Saul Bellow, "Writers and Morals," 15, an unpublished paper preserved at the Joseph Regenstein Library, University of Chicago. Quoted in Chirantan Kulshrestha, *Saul Bellow: The Problem of Affirmation* (New Delhi; Arnold Heinemann, 1978) 42.

47. Saul Bellow, *The Dangling Man* (New York: Vanguard, 1944) 39.

48. Saul Bellow, *Herzog* (New York: Viking Press, 1964) 273.

49. Saul Bellow, *Mr. Sammler's Planet* (New York: Viking Press, 1970) 237.

50. Chester E. Eisinger, "Saul Bellow," *The Contemporary Novelists*, ed. James Vinson (London: St. James Press, 1976) 126.

51. Warren French, "J.D. Salinger," *Dictionary of Literary Biography*, 4 vols. eds. Jeffrey Helterman and Richard Layman (Detroit, Michigan: A Bruccoli Clark Book, 1978) 2:435.

52. James E. Miller, Jr., *J.D. Salinger* (Minneapolis: Univ. of Minnesota Press, 1968) 5.

53. Fredrick L. Gwynn and Joseph L. Blotner, *The Fiction of J.D. Salinger* (Pittsburgh, Pa.: Univ. of Pittsburgh Press, 1964) 31.

54. Miller, Jr. 12.

55. Irving Malin, "Mad Crusader," *Progressive* 31 July 1967: 34.

56. Malin 34.

57. Philip Roth, *Reading Myself and Others* (New York: Farrar, Straus and Giroux, 1975) 246.

58. Jeffrey Helterman, "Philip Roth," *Dictionary of Literary Biography* 2: 25-26.

59. George Plimpton, "Philip Roth's Exact Intent," *New York Times Book Review* 23 Feb. 1969: 23.

60. Michael Fixler, "The Redeemer: Themes in the fiction of Isaac Bashevis Singer," *The Kenyon Review* 26 Spring 1964: 372.

61. Joel Blocker and Richard Elman, "An Interview with Isaac Bashevis Singer," *Commentary* 36 Nov. 1963: 371.

62. Blocker et al 372.

63. *Loc. cit.*

64. Ben Siegel, *Isaac Bashevis Singer* (Minneapolis: Univ. of Minnesota Press, 1969) 25.

65. Ben Siegel, *Singer* 16.

66. Siegel 44.

67. Cyrena N. Pondrom, "Isaac Bashevis Singer: An Inter-
    view, Part II," *Contemporary Literature* 10 Summer
    1969: 336.

68. Bernard Malamud, *The Assistant* (Harmondsworth:
    Penguin Books, 1975) 113.

69. Elie Wiesel, *The Town Beyond the Wall* (New York:
    1968) 100.

70. R.W.B. Lewis 101.

71. *Loc. cit.*

72. Daniel Stern, "Art of Fiction LII: Bernard Malamud,"
    The Paris Review 16.61 Spring 1975: 56.

73. See Joseph Wershba, "Not Horror but 'Sadness'," *New
    York Post* 14 Sept. 1958: M2 Interview.

74. See Marjorie Dent Candee, ed., *Current Biography
    Year-Book,* 1958 (New York: 1958) 272.

75. Philip Roth, "Writing American Fiction," *Commentary*
    31.3 March 1961: 229.

76. Leslie Field and Joyce Field, "Malamud, Mercy, and
    Menschlechkeit," *Bernard Malamud: A Collection of
    Critical Essays,* eds. Leslie Field and Joyce Field
    (Englewood Cliffs, N.J.: Prentice-Hall, 1974) 7.

77. Ihab Hassan, "Bernard Malamud," 876.

78. Bernard Malamud, *The Magic Barrel* (New York:
    Farrar, Straus, Cudahy, 1958) 56.

79. See Robert Alter, "Jewishness as Metaphor," 29-42 and
    Theodore Solotaroff, "The Old Life and the New,"
    235-48 in *Bernard Malamud and the Critics,* eds. Leslie
    A. Field and Joyce W. Field (New York: New York
    Univ. Press, 1970).

80. Theodore Solotaroff, "Roth and the Jewish Moralists,"
    90.

81. In his letter to Sidney Richman (12 May 1963), Mala-
    mud says: "I considered Judaism, once I got to know
    about it through reading, as another source of huma-
    nism. The first being Western Literature and history

from the Greeks on." Sidney Richman, *Bernard Malamud* (New York: Twayne Publisbers, 1966) 29.

82. Quoted in Granville Hicks, "His Hopes on the Human Heart," *Saturday Review* 12 Oct. 1963: 32.

83. Ihab Hassan, "The Hopes of Man," 5.

84. Haskel Frankel, "Interview with Bernard Malamud," *Saturday Review* 10 Sept. 1966: 40.

85. Philip Roth, "Writing American Fiction," 229.

86. Daniel Stern 51.

87. Quoted in Granville Hicks 32.

88. Joseph Wershba, "Close up," *New York Post Magazine* 14 Sept. 1958.

89. W.J. Handy, "The Malamud Hero: A Quest for Existence," *The Fiction of Bernard Malamud* 67.

90. Quoted in W.J. Handy 65.

91. Granville Hicks 32.

92. Alfred Kazin, "The Magic and the Dread," *On Contemporary Literature*, ed. Richard Kostelanetz (New York: Avon Books, 1964) 440.

93. H.E. Francis, "Bernard Malamud's Every Man," *Midstream* 7.1 Winter 1961: 96.

94. Ihab Hassan, "The Hopes of Man," 5.

95. Joseph Featherstone, "Bernard Malamud," *Atlantic* 219.3 March 1967: 96.

96. Leslie A. Fiedler, "The Breakthrough: The American Jewish Novelist and the Fictional Image of the Jew," *Recent American Fiction: Some Critical Views*, ed. Joseph J. Waldmeir (Boston: Houghton Mifflin, 1963) 106.

97. Jonathan Baumbach, "Malamud's Heroes," *Commonweal* 85.1. 7 Oct. 1966: 97-99.

98. Peter L. Hays, "The Complex Pattern of Redemption," *Bernard Malamud and the Critics* 219.

99. J.C. Landis, "Reflections on American Jewish Writers," 146.

100. Ben Siegel, "Victims in Motion: The Sad and Bitter Clowns," *Bernard Malamud and the Critics* 203-14.

101. Sandy Cohen, *Bernard Malamud and the Trial by Love* (Amsterdam: Rodopi N.V., 1974).

102. Robert Ducharme, *Art and Idea in the Novels of Bernard Malamud: Toward The Fixer* (The Hauge, Paris: Mouton, 1974).

103. Lois Symons Lewin, *The Theme of Suffering in the Work of Bernard Malamud and Saul Bellow*, Diss. Univ. of Pittsburgh, Ph. D., 1967; Microfilm: 2.

2

TWO LIVES OF ROY: *THE NATURAL*

*"We have two lives, Roy, the life we learn with and
the life we live with after that. Suffering is what
brings us toward happiness."*

*The Natural** is Malamud's first and the only non-Jewish
novel. It is the story of Roy Hobbs, an untrained, natural
baseball player, and his crucial rise and fall. Most of the
incidents in the book are traced to be grounded in historically
accurate facts such as shooting of Eddie Waitkus in 1949,
Babe Ruth's stomach illness of 1925, the throwing of a crucial
game by the White Sox in 1919. The novel attempts the imaginative transformation of history into myth—the myth of "the
everlastingly crucial story of man,"[1] and in the process becomes
a curious mixture of myth, fantasy, symbolism and realism. In
portraying Roy's quest for heroism in baseball, Malamud has
drawn on folklore of Baseball, the pastoral, Arthurian legend,
Jungian psychology and Homeric epic. These elements have
been analysed by critics like Leslie Fiedler, Norman Podhoretz,
James Mellard, Earl Wasserman and Robert Ducharme. Peter

*Bernard Malamud, *The Natural* (Harmondsworth: Penguin Books
1973). All subsequent references with page numbers in parentheses are to
this edition.

Hays examines Malamud's work including *The Natural* from
the perspective of medieval literature, specifically Chretien de
Troye's "Lancelot, or The Knight of the Cart."[2] By drawing
his material on various sources, Malamud has set his novel "in
a region that is both real and mythic, particular and universal,
ludicrous melodrama and spiritual probing—Ring Lardner and
Jung."[3] Despite the impressive experiment in combining the
disparate elements by "the use of every imaginative resource at
the writer's command," Malamud fails to make the novel
"more than the merely realistic."[4] Neither the baseball nor all
its mythic associations are important for Malamud. Baseball
has given him only an occasion to represent larger human
issues and probe the "drama of moral issues."[5] The Arthurian
legend and Jungian mythic psychology are used to interpret
the ritual that makes baseball into a symbol of "man's psychological and moral situation."[6] Malamud's primary concern,
therefore, is to probe "the comi-tragic paradoxes of modern
existence," as reflected in the "progressive corruption of a
basically honest professional athlete."[7] Roy Hobbs' career marks
the typical Malamudian protagonist's trial that transforms man
into a *mensch*. Compassion is the driving force behind such an
act of transformation in all Malamudian protagonists.

    The Natural, Malamud reveals, is inspired by the question
"Why does a talented man sell out ?"[8] which suggests a moral
problem. The novel not only confronts the question but also
serves as a painter to the answer in Roy's moral ineptitude
that talent and integrity need not go together. Roy Hobbs, like
his Jewish counterparts in the other novels, is a *schlemiel*
destined to fail—a victim of fate and circumstances as well as a
prisoner of his own prejudices and illusions. Roy's frenzied
pursuit of money, fame and sex, his refusal to learn from
suffering or experience, his inability to come out of the shell of
egotism—all lead to his moral disintegration. Baseball or
human relations call for a code of conduct based on felt
responsibility for others. Roy violates the code and hence his
failure both in human relations and baseball. Suffering ultimately makes him realise the value of love and compassion—
"the God-given fire of decency and determination, that enables
him to overcome everything arrayed against him."[9] Compassion

dawns on Roy very late and when he is at the lowest ebb of moral degradation. The true love of Iris Lemon compels Roy to decide to win the game he had intended to throw by being a "sell-out." Although the decision is too late to be of any avail, it gives him the moral courage to refuse the money given him by the corruptors. He could also now realise his "tragic flaw" and be ready to face its consequences in further suffering. Roy like Frank Alpine or Seymour Levin proves that "Life consists of achieving good not apart from evil but *in spite of it*.[10] The novel indicates better "the nature of forces against which his (Malamud's) later heroes must struggle" and "the ritual gestures by which they must preserve themselves."[11] Thematically, thus, the novel fits into the pattern of Malamud's later work notwithstanding its apparent dissimilarity. Roy Hobbs becomes "an archetype for all Malamud's small heroes, who like their larger Greek and Shakespearean counterparts— fall victim to a tragic flaw aggravated by misfortune."[12]

Although the thematic concerns of *The Natural* are appreciated, the technical aspect of the novel has caused critical dissent. Granville Hicks is puzzled about "what to make of the book as a whole."[13] For Richard Rupp, the novel "celebrates man's immortal moment in flux of time; but it does so badly."[14] Ihab Hassan finds in the novel fusion of "the snappy slang of sport and gloomy language of the soul" while it probes into the meaning of personal integrity. He, however, believes that the fusion fails "to make itself comprehensible."[15] Edward Fitzgerald in the *Saturday Review* says that Malamud's distortion of characters "merely creates an air of unreality."[16] Norman Podhoretz finds fault with Malamud for his use of worn-out mythic conventions without "life and grace" much to the detriment of simple realities and concludes that *The Natural* remains "a loose mixture of cliches (both of the high and the low-brow variety) with the authentic."[17]

In spite of the many parallels imposed upon the action, the novel appears meaningful as it squarely confronts the moral and psychological problem of man in a society which lures one to fall a prey to its corruption by many temptations. One cannot agree with David Stevenson's statement that Roy "never really comes into proper focus either as myth or as man,"[18] since Malamud's evident focus is on man. Myth also plays a subservient part to unfold the human in Roy with its strange combination of evil and good. Sandy Cohen fails to appreciate the functional aspect of the myth as he remarks that "If the protagonists of *The Natural* were to remove their masks we could discover that there is nothing behind them."[19] The strange sense of fatality in the novel does not distort its character, plot and style as Marcus Klein feels.[20] Roy's own lapses are too evident to draw any such conclusion. Minor lapses of technique in *The Natural* could be ignored as in the novel "the modern instance and the remembered myth are equally felt, equally realized and equally appropriate to our predicament. It is this which gives to his (Malamud's) work special authority and special richness."[21]

The Natural is divided into two parts—the smaller one "Pre-Game" and the longer "Better-Up!" The first part presents the misfortunes and inherent weaknesses of Roy which are more or less expanded in the second part. Sidney Richman finds in this first part "the mythic formula of Initiation, Separation, and Return."[22] Roy begins his career as a new champion by outpitching the reigning king, the Whammer at the beginning of the novel. But at the end he is outpitched by a young boy fresh from the country, Herman Youngberry. The fertility cycle is thus renewed. Viewed in this context, history becomes myth. The interest of the novel, however, centres on the character of Roy Hobbs and his growth in self-knowledge.

II

The Natural focusses on the growth of Roy Hobbs from his "selfish infantilism of spirit" to moral forbearance. The movement from egotism to compassion is suggested symbolically in the opening of the novel. Roy looks at the window-pane of the train with a lit match but sees his own image reflected in it as the train passes through a dark tunnel. His own self acts as a hindrance to extend his vision to others or to see through the mirror. But "as the train yanked its long tail out of the thundering tunnel, the kneeling reflection dissolved and he felt a splurge of freedom at the view of the moon-hazed Western hills." (9) His restricted vision becomes broader and free as the image of the self dissolves.

The Natural begins with Roy Hobbs' journey to Chicago to make his career in Baseball to which he wants "to hang on forever." (10) Sam Simpson, a one-time baseball catcher, is the father figure and initiates Roy into baseball career. Roy's immaturity and childishness are evident in his excessive dependence on Sam even for little things such as giving a tip to the porter. Without Sam he would feel "shaky-kneeled" and derelict. Sam is compassionate to Roy. Although Sam expects to get "a few grand" as a reward from Mulligan for introducing Roy, he is ready to go back as a regular scout for the sake of Roy. Sam reserves a berth for Roy while he himself sleeps in the ordinary compartment:

> You take the bed, Kiddo, You're the one that has to show what you have got on the ball when we pull into the city. It don't matter where I sleep. (12)

Sam introduces Roy to Walter Wambold (the Whammer), the leading hitter of the American League on the train and draws the latter into an encounter with his bet that Roy can strike him out with three pitched balls.

In the encounter between Roy and Walter which is described in mock-heroic style, Roy wins and makes his debut in the baseball career. The role of Sam Simpson ends as Roy's ball hits him fatally. Before his death. Sam gives Roy his wallet and exhorts tenderly:

> Go on, Kiddo, you got to. See Clarence Mulligan tomorrow and say I sent you—they are expecting you. Give them everything you have got on the ball—that'll make me happy. (36)

Sam Simpson here exemplifies the spirit of compassion that one's happiness lies in the happiness of others. With the death of Sam, Roy is fated to pursue his quest alone. Roy fails in his quest because of his inability to learn the message of compassion that Sam's life embodies.

Roy's weaknesses from the very beginning of the novel are his egotistic overambition and pursuit of sex. He feels he is

"due for something very big" and that some day he would
"break every record in the book for throwing and hitting." (31)
He thinks his bat, Wonderboy, is made for himself. Defeating
the Whammer, he assumes the postures of a hero. His response
to Harriet Bird, "the silver-eyed mermaid," from the beginning
has been sensual. Except baseball and sex, he is unable to
understand or think of any other thing in life. This is evident
in his conversation with Harriet Bird who plays the role of
"the destructive mother" (Memo Paris takes up the role later)
and subjects him to a test as it were. To her question "What
will you hope to accomplish, Roy ?" Roy says:

> Sometimes when I walk down the street, I bet people will
> say there goes Roy Hobbs, the best there ever was in the
> game. (32)

Harriet is not satisfied with this answer. Her repeated question
"Is that all ?" could only elicit a further shabby answer from
him: "You mean the bucks ? I'll get them too." She again asks
him whether there is not "something ever and above earthly
things—some more glorious meaning to one's life and activities." (32) Roy could only rack his brain. She tries to hint
in vain at the necessity of deriving one's values from the
human.

> "Maybe I've not made myself clear, but surely you can see
> (I was saying this to Walter just before the train stopped)
> that yourself alone—alone in the sense that we are all
> terribly alone no matter what people say—I mean by that
> perhaps if you understood that our values must derive
> from—oh, I really suppose—" She dropped her hand
> futilely. 'Please forgive me. I sometimes confuse myself
> with the little I know." (32)

Harriet struggles to bring home the inescapable link that ties
human beings. Roy thought that she was telling him something
about "LIFE" which to him could only be "the fun and
satisfaction you get out of playing the best way that you know
how." (33) He forgets his father who has taught him how to
throw the ball and Sam Simpson who is responsible for his
entrance into the baseball career. Roy is a self-confessed

failure in Harriet's test. "The worst of it was he still didn't know what she'd been driving at." (33)

The glorious dreams of Roy of becoming a splendid pitcher are dashed by Harriet. Roy goes to her apartment on invitation and finds her naked with a pistol in her hands. When Harriet asks him with bitter sweetness, "Roy, will you be the best there ever was in the game," he still believes "that's right." (39) His hopes for a career get marred for fifteen years with the silver bullet she triggered into his gut. He becomes "the stricken hero" around whom Harriet strangely dances naked "making muted noises of triumph and despair." (39) Max Mercy's casual but prophetic guess at the news of a woman killing a foot-ball player and an Olympic runner that "she may be heading for a baseball player for the third victim" (18) is proved true.

Roy always flees from his humiliating and guilty past. He tries to suppress it from Max Mercy, the merciless sports columnist, and feels "ashamed to be recognised, to have his past revealed like an egg spattered "on the train going nowhere" or "defeat in sight of his goal." (148) He interprets the past in terms of fate and does not bother about his accountability. The "natural" or the naked innocence in Roy is marred by his egotism and ignorance.

Roy's fantasy of killing a boy in an accident reveals the symbolic death of the "natural" in Roy. Roy sees a boy coming out of the woods followed by his dog. He is "unable to tell if the kid was an illusion thrown forth by the trees or someone really alive." (116) Roy cries to Memo to slow down "in case he wanted to cross the road." But Memo does not stop the car. Roy feels they had hit somebody. He says he had even heard somebody groan. But Memo does not believe it and says: "That was yourself." (116) They do not find the boy but meet with an accident. Roy seems to whisper to the boy: "watch out when you cross the road, kid." (121) But he could not save the boy who in his imagination "lay broken-boned and bleeding in a puddle of light, with no one to care for him or whisper a benediction upon his lost youth." (121) The boy's predicament is in fact that of Roy himself when he was shot

down by Harriet in the beginning.   It also appears to be a
foreboding of Roy's tragic fate   at the end. Roy like the
imaginary boy fails to "watch out" at the crucial cross-roads
and turning points of life. [He does not, for example, care for
the advice of Pop Fisher who asks him "to watch out and not
get too tied up with her (Memo)." (120,] Roy's recollection of
himself as a boy very much corresponds to the imaginary boy—
a boy with a dog and a stick.

> Sometimes he wished he had no ambitions—often wondered
> where they had come from in his life, because he remem-
> bered how satisfied he had been as a youngster, and that
> with the little he had had—a dog, a stick, an aloneness he
> loved (which did not bleed him like his later loneliness),
> and he wished he could have lived longer in his boyhood.
> This was an old thought with him. (111)

Under the   impact of selfish and tricky woman Memo, Roy
destroys "the natural" within him.

The second part of the novel "Batter-up!" describes Roy's
fresh attempt at seeking a new life in baseball. Roy successfully
joins the National League's last place New York Knights as an
outfielder   at   the age of thirty-two. Despite the shattering
experience with Harriet, there appears little change in Roy.
Roy is still over-confident and egotistic. He is sure of leaving
his mark in baseball and declaims: "To hell with my old age.
I'll be in this game a long time." (61) He believes that "I am
the type that will die a natural death." (118) All these remarks
however prove ironical at the end when he is almost forced out
of the game.

Roy's overambition in baseball and greed in sex go hand in
hand. His attitude to Memo Paris is completely sensual:

> Always in   the act of love she lived in his mind, the only
> way he knew her, because she would not otherwise suffer his
> approach. *He* was to blame, she had wept one bitter mid-
> night, so she hated his putrid guts. (74)

Roy's initial career in baseball, however, appears glorious and
fantastic. Roy with   his   heroic play rejuvenates the dry
team at the very first chance:

> Wonderboy flashed in the sun. It caught the sphere where
> it was biggest. A noise like a twenty-one gun salute cracked
> the sky. There was a straining, ripping sound and a few
> drops of rain spattered to the ground. (76)

Roy has already become a rival to Bump. Bump's failure and
death ensure Roy a secure place in the team. Roy soon becomes popular with his many short term records inviting "tons
of newspaper comment" on his performance. The crowd
cheers him for himself without any link with Bump. His
success, however, matches his moral degradation in his
ignorance of his debt to Sam Simpson and Bump Bailey who
are vicariously responsible for his career. Ironically enough,
Roy is indirectly responsible for their death.

Roy is always averse to companionship—an essential tenet
of compassion. He does not like to be compared with Bump
Bailey and wants an independent recognition. His teammates
discuss whether Roy is for the team or for himself. Olson says
he is for the team, but Cal Baker insists:

> Those big guys are always for themselves. They are not for
> the little guy. If he was for us why don't he come around
> more ? Why does he hang out so much by himself. (87)

Even when his fans celebrate "Roy Hobbs Day" and shower
him with many presents including a car, Roy forgets to thank
them for their favour. Instead he vainly reaffirms his desire "to
be the greatest there ever was in the game."

Roy's pursuit of Memo (Bump's girl) also betrays his
selfish need to quench his lust. He makes a wrong choice in
opting for Memo, the selfish, money-minded temptress. Memo
who was averse to Roy first comes to like him probably for all
the money and presents he received. Her association brings ill-
luck to Roy and her desertion too causes a "slump" in his
career. In her absence Roy suffers from hitlessness just when
the knights were heading for the pennant. At this juncture Roy
gets an occasion to reclaim himself. Mike Barney begs Roy to
hit a homer so that his son Pete, a fan of Roy now hospitalized,
would be saved. Roy recognizes that his act would save the boy

and also provide "a break through the alienating ego and a rescue by surrogate of the child within" and vows to succeed.[23] But Pop would not allow him to play with Wonderboy while Roy is equally stubborn and would not change his bat. For sometime Roy is in a conflict between his sentimental and selfish attachment to Wonderboy and the impulse to help the anguished father. The latter prevails as Roy decides to "give up" his bat for the sake of the boy. Strangely enough, Pop now allows him to play with his own bat. Roy sees the black lady (Iris Lemon) standing in the audience and hits the ball with glorious success.

> Roy circles the bases like a Mississippi steamboat, lights lit, flags fluttering, whistle banging, coming round the bend. The knights poured out of their dugout to pound his back, and hundreds of their rooters hopped about in the field. He stood on the home base, lifting his cap to the lady's empty seat. (139)

Roy thus saves the boy and for the first time recognizes the value of compassion which lies in "giving up" something of one's own for others.

Iris Lemon who has been a source of inspiration to Roy at the crucial time exemplifies the spirit of compassion. A victim of rape, an unwed mother in her early teens, she has suffered all through her youth for the sake of her daughter much against the will of her parents. The child has meant everything to her and made her happy. When Roy in his first meeting with her acknowledges his gratitude to her for standing in the gallery as a support, Iris says:

> I felt that if you knew people believed in you, you'd regain your power. That's why I stood up in the grand stand. I hadn't meant to before I came. It happened naturally. Of course I was embarrassed but *I don't think you can do anything* for anyone without giving up something of your own. What I gave up was my privacy among all those people. (45-46; Italics mine)

Unlike Memo, Iris plays the role of healthy mother. She instils new courage in Roy and says that she hates to see a hero fail for "without heroes we're all plain people and don't know how far we can go." (145) It never occurred to Roy that the hero could be an "impersonal symbol" of all men as Iris suggests.

The piece of conversation between Roy and Iris acts as the key to understanding Malamud's philosophy of redemptive suffering. When Roy confesses his past and is gloomy about his fate, Iris consoles him and teaches the value of suffering and experience which Roy fails to understand.

> 'What beats me,' he said with a trembling voice, 'is why did it always have to happen to me ? What did I do to deserve it ?'
> 'Being stopped before you started ?'
> He nodded.
> 'Perhaps it was because you were a good person ?'
> 'How's that ? '
> 'Experience makes good people better.'
> She was staring at the lake.
> 'How does it do that ?'
> 'Through their suffering.'
> 'I had enough of that,' he said in disgust.
> 'We have two lives, Roy, the life we learn with and the life we live with after that. Suffering is what brings us toward happiness.
> 'I had it up to here.' He ran a finger across his windpipe.
> 'Had what ?'
> 'What I suffered—and I don't want any more.'
> 'It teaches us to want the right things.'
> 'All it taught me is to stay away from it. I am sick of all I have suffered.'
> She shrank away a little. (148-149)

The conversation makes evident the reluctance of Roy to learn anything out of his experience or suffering. Suffering is of no value and can bring no awareness for the better in a man who refuses to learn anything from life. Naturally Roy cannot be better. While swimming with Iris, Roy goes down deep into the waters to touch the bottom. Iris is frightened at the act,

> A sense of abandonment gripped her. She remembered
> standing up in the crowd that night, and said to herself
> that she had really stood up because he was a man
> whose life she wanted to share . . . a man who had
> suffered. (151)

Finding Roy in the same boat of suffering with her, Iris wanted
to share his life and suffering. When Roy comes out of the
waters, she readily surrenders to him.

Although Roy thinks that Iris is "a nice enough gir.," he
does not want to be involved with her—"Who would be
interested in a grand mother ?" (154) He thus ignores the true
love of Iris and pursues Memo, a false lover. He postpones
reading the letter of Iris till the end and when he finally reads
he crumples it and throws out. He quickly changes his mind to
Memo who tempts him but does not yield. He yearns for her
and for a child by her who would carry the name of Roy Hobbs
"into generations his old man would never know." But the
irony is that Roy's child grows in Iris and not in Memo.

Roy's insatiable gluttony in the party arranged by Memo
reveals the "self-destructive nature of his self-preoccupation."[24]
Preoccupied with the thoughts of having Memo that night, he
gobbles down so much food that he is hospitalized with a shooting pain in the stomach His attempt to possess Memo at the
last moment ends in failure. The fate of "silver bullet" in the
life of Roy recurs in a different way. The doctor advises him
to bid goodbye to baseball. It is inconceivable for Roy that he
should quit the game forever after having broken hundreds of
records in a short time.

In an ambiguous scene of dream or fantasy, Roy searches
for Sam Simpson and confesses to him.

> I swear I didn't do it, Sam.
> Didn't do what ?
> Didn't do nothin'.
> Who said you did ?
> Roy wouldn't answer, shut tight as a clam. (184)

Equally puzzling is Sam's advice to Roy not to do 'it.' Sam
could not comply with Roy's request to accompany him to

home since "it's snowin' baseballs." (184) Tony Tanner interprets these lines as Roy's wish "to retrace his steps to get back
to time before time.[25] But what is done cannot be undone. The
scene also seems to hint at the guilty-conscience of Roy who
fails to discharge his obligations to live up to the expectations
of Sam, his mentor.

Roy's final moral collapse is brought about by Memo and
Judge Goodwill Banner, the owner of the team. In one of
her visits to Roy at hospital, Memo traps Roy with her false
tears over her "dependent life." Roy gallantly offers to help
her by marrying. But Memo says she cannot afford to live a
poor life with anyone. She betrays her money-mindedness:

> ... I am the type who has to have somebody who can
> support her in a decent way. I am sick of living like a slave.
> I got to have a house of my own, a maid to help me with
> the hard work, a decent car to shop with and a fur coat for
> winter time when it's cold. I don't want to have to worry
> every time a can of beans jumps a nickel. (187)

Roy is at once busy with the thoughts of acquiring money.
Detecting the vulnerable moment of Roy, Memo whispers to
him the tempting message of Judge Goodwill Banner. Roy
would get fifteen thousand dollars if he dropped the pennant-
winning game with the pirates. The Judge wants the team to be
made the laughing-stock of organized baseball, and Pop
Fisher destroy himself in humiliation. For sometime Roy is in
conflict. "He couldn't betray his own team and manager. That
was bad." (195) But when the Judge hints at losing Memo to
Gus Sands, Roy settles the deed of his "sell-out" for thirtyfive
thousand dollars for dropping the game and forty-five for the
contract. The consideration that the bribe would fetch him
Memo as wife outweighs Roy's sense of guilt and betrayal.
Roy's initiation into the redeeming moment, however, is
brought forth by Iris Lemon. His misdirected shot in the game
hits Iris Lemon standing among the audience. She falls uncon-
scious and Roy rushes to her leaving his bat. He repents;

What have I done, he thought, and why did I do it ? And he thought of all the wrong things he had done in his life and tried to undo them but who could ? (210)

Iris implores Roy to win the game for the child of Roy she bears. Roy is deeply moved by her love.

'Darling,' whispered Iris, 'win for our boy.'
He stared at her. 'What boy ?'
'I am pregnant.' There were tears in her eyes.
Her belly was slender . . . then the impact hit him.
'Holy Jesus.'
Iris smiled with quivering lips. (210)

Iris's request—'Win for us, you were meant to' makes Roy realise the necessity of doing a thing for others. He kisses her bloody mouth and is overcome with compassion for her. He resolves to win the game for the love of Iris breaking the illegal agreement with the Judge. But it is too late. Roy's thunderous crash of the ball splits his bat "Wonderboy" lengthwise as if to mark Roy's moral disintegration. Roy takes another bat and wants to destroy his opponent Vogelman and save the game, "the most important thing he ever had to do in his life." (213) But it is too much to expect as he had already wasted his hits by making them fouls. "Roy felt himself slowly dying." (214) He has to yield himself to the young player, Herman Youngberry, "Roy's mythical son."

The ritual of burying the broken bat "Wonderboy" marks the end of Roy's career. Unable to stand the sight of broken bat, he ties the pieces with his shoelaces before the burial. It is as though Roy were piecing together his disintegrated self.

Roy is now a changed man. He not only rejects the money offered by the Judge for the corrupt compact but also gives a stiff resistance to the evil conspirators—the Judge, Gus Sands and Memo. He has seen Memo in her true colours—"You act all right, Memo, but only like a whore." (221) He overcomes his conspirators in the fight. Roy has now grown from the state of enormous self-love to that of "an overwhelming self-hatred,"

Going down the tower stairs he fought his overwhelming
self-hatred. In each stinking wave of it he remembered some
disgusting happening of his life. (222)

He has opened his eyes to the fact that "I never did learn
anything out of my past life." He knows the price of it too.
". . . now I have to suffer again." (222) Suffering has brought
the courage and confidence to endure further suffering. Roy has
already fallen into oblivion with his defeat. Nobody recognizes
him on the street except a woman who comments "He could a
been a king." The words float in the air ironically. Roy's
suppressed past and the corrupt deal with the Judge have also
been exposed in the newspaper by Max Mercy under the title —
"Suspicion of Hobbs' Sell-out-Max Mercy." There is also a
statement by the baseball commissioner that if the alleged
report is true, Roy "will be excluded from the game and all his
records for ever destroyed." (223) Roy wanted to tell the newspaper boy that it was not true. But he could not. He is conscious of his share in the guilt. He has not given the game all
he has got under the evil influence of the Judge and Memo and
hence he has to quit.[26] The novel ends on a sense of loss
with Roy's deep remorse and bitter tears. Yet a vague sense of
hope informs the end with Iris Lemon probably waiting for the
changed Roy.

The last act of compassion for Iris enables Roy to revoke
his illegal agreement. The act redeems Roy from abysmal
perdition of inauthentic capitulation to the nefarious agreement.

In Malamud's next novel *The Assistant*, the intense suffering of a compassionate Jew opens up the possibilities of
redemption to his gentile assistant.

NOTES

1. Earl R. Wasserman, "The Natural: World Ceres,"
   Bernard Malamud and the Critics, ed. Leslie Field and
   Joyce Field (New York: New York Univ. Press, 1970) 47.
2. Peter L. Hays, "Malamud's Yiddish-Accented Medieval
   Stories," *The Fiction of Bernard Malamud*, ed. Richard
   Astro and Jackson J. Benson (Corvallis: Oregon State
   Univ. Press, 1977) 87-96.

3. Wasserman 47.

4. Report of Malamud's address at Princeton University, published in *Esquire* 60. July 1963: 6.

5. Granville Hicks, "His Hopes on the Human Heart," *Saturday Review* 12 October 1963: 31.

6. Wasserman 47.

7. Ben Siegel, "Victims in Motion: Bernard Malamud's Sad and Bitter Clowns," *Recent American Fiction: Some Critical Views*, ed. Joseph J. Waldmeir (Boston: Houghton Mifflin Company, 1963) 204.

8. Quoted in Marcus Klein, "Bernard Malamud: The Sadness of Goodness," *After Alienation: American Novels in Midcentury* (New York: Books for Libraries Press, 1970) 256.

9. Charles Alva Hoyt, "Bernard Malamud and the New Romanticism," *Contemporary American Novelists*, ed. Harry T. Moore (Carbondale: Southern Illinois Univ. Press, 1964) 79.

10. Rollo May, *Power and Innocence* (New York: W.W. Norton 1972) 260.

11. Sidney Richman, *Bernard Malamud* (New York: Twayne, 1968) 41.

12. Ben Siegel 204.

13. Granville Hicks, "Generations of the Fifties; Malamud, Gold, and Updike," *The Creative Present*, ed. Nona Balakian and Charles Simmons (New York: Doubleday, 1963) 219.

14. Richard H. Rupp, "Bernard Malamud: A Party of One," *Celebration in Post-war American Fiction* (Florida: Univ. of Miami Press, 1970) 167.

15. Ihab Hassan, *Radical Innocence* (New York: Harper and Row, 1966) 162.

16. Edward J. Fitzgerald, Review of *The Natural*, *Saturday Review* 35.36 6 Sept. 1952: 32.

17. Normon Podhoretz, "Achilles in Left Field," *Commentary* March 1953: 321-26.

18. David L. Stevenson, "The Strange Destiny of S. Levin," *New York Times Book Review* 8 Oct. 1961: 1.

19. Sandy Cohen, *Bernard Malamud and the Trial by Love* (Amsterdam: Rodopi N.V., 1974) 30.

20. Marcus Klein 260.

21. Leslie A. Fiedler, "Malamud: The Commonplace as abused," *Not in Thunder* (London: Eyre and Spottis-woode, 1963) 105.

22. Richman 30.

23. Richman 36.

24. Tony Tanner, *City of Words: American Fiction 1950-1970* (London: Jonathan Cape, 1971) 325.

25. Tanner 326.

26. Pop Fisher had warned Roy at the beginning of his career: "You're starting way late . . . but if you want to get along the best way, behave and give the game all you have got, and when you can't do that, quit." (56)

3

"I SUFFER FOR YOU": *THE ASSISTANT*

"What do you suffer for, Morris ?" Frank said.
"I suffer for you," Morris said calmly.

The Assistant* is a poignant portrayal of the travails of a Jewish grocer smothered by the frustrating effects of Depression and anti-Semitism. The Depression here becomes a "manifestation of Jewish, human, agony."[1] The novel marks a departure from *The Natural* with its accent on the author's resolve "to do a more serious, deeper, perhaps realistic piece of work."[2] Although the novel is not cast to be a social critique, it probes the psyche of individual fated to be lost in the vortex of life. The novel concerns itself with the mysterious "hidden strength" of man that makes him endure colossal suffering with his uncompromising sense of values. The "hidden strength" of both Morris Bober and Frank Alpine lies in their compassion. *The Assistant* offers an added dimension with its

---

*Bernard Malamud, *The Assistant* (Harmondsworth: Penguin Books, 1975). All subsequent references in parantheses refer to this edition.

autobiographical element as Malamud heavily draws on his "father's life as a grocer, though not necessarily my father."[3] The abject penury and the unflinching moral fervour of Malamud's parentage shapes Morris Bober. In his interview with Daniel Stern, Malamud recalls:

> My father was a grocer; my mother, who helped him, after a long illness, died young. I had a younger brother who lived a hard and lonely life and died in his fifties. My mother and father were gentle, honest, kindly people, and who they were and their affection for me to some degree made up for the cultural deprivation I felt as a child. They weren't educated but their values were stable. Though my father always managed to make a living they were comparatively poor, especially in the Depression, and yet I never heard a word in praise of the buck. . . .[4]

The predicament of Malamud's father suits that of Morris who also lives and dies penniless in his store without swerving an inch from his moral rectitude.

Malamud does not want *The Assistant* to be called a simple moral allegory, since "the spirit is more than moral and by the same token there's more than morality in a good man."[5] He is explicitly concerned with man's "struggle for moral excellence, the wish to be good."[6] This striving for morality is not ritualistic as it becomes "more than moral." Morris Bober does not observe any ritual of Jews and yet catches the spirit of Torah in being a man of "good heart." Jewishness means to him "to do what is right, to be honest, to be good . . . to other people." (112-13) The novel is not merely "a brilliant exploitation of pathos"[7] as Barry Ulanov comments but in fact it presents the epitome of Malamud's philosophy of compassion. The key to compassion is interpersonal responsibility, the I-Thou relationship. Peter Hays remarks that Malamud has exemplified here "Buber's precept of the I-Thou relationship, what denying it causes, and what allowing it to exist achieves."[8] The novel might seem defeatist in materialistic terms but "the final effect is one of moral beauty."[9] Malamud seeks moral beauty in compassion which is at times of little value in materialistic terms as shown in the case of Morris Bober. It however enables both Morris Bober and Frank Alpine to get fulfilment.

William Goyen believes that the novel is "about simple people struggling to make their lives better in a world of bad luck."[10] He finds the interest of the novel in "the clarity and concreteness of his style, the warm humanity over his people, the tender wit that keeps them firm and compassionable."[11] Ben Siegel comments that the novel is "a probing and disturbing study of modern man's social and spiritual confusion."[12] Morris Bober with his back-aching exercise in the dingy store lives honestly for the sake of others and exemplifies the selfless spirit of compassion. Frank Alpine, the gentile who robs Morris first and later joins his store as assistant to atone for his guilt, gradually fights his evil and becomes a *mentsch* like Morris Bober. He becomes a prop to the family of Morris after his death. His selfless compassion at the end transcends his sensual love for Helen Bober. Frank represents "the qualified effort of human transcendence"[13] in his gradual transformation from hoodlum to saint, as compassion paves the way for "the painful emergence of selflessness from selfishness."[14] The novel grapples with the values that emerge from existential crisis. Sidney Richman draws parallels to it in Dostoevsky's *Crime and Punishment*.[15]

The critics of the novel have commented on the aspects of suffering and love with sporadic references to compassion which is central to the novel. Francis finds in compassion the link between Malamud's Jewish and Christian characters.[16] Norman Leer's analysis of the characters' search for "a commitment to other individuals" and Hays' study of "the I-Thou relationship" in the novel could be taken as indirect hints at compassion.[17] Walter Allen finds "the theme of purgation through the acceptance of the burden of others' suffering" central to *The Assistant*.[18] Philip Rahv traces the novel's affinity to Dostoevskian idea of universal brotherhood and mutual responsibility in Morris' proposition: "I suffer for you."[19] In these few critiques compassion has been felt as a force shaping *The Assistant*. Yet a detailed study of this aspect will help a fuller appreciation of the novel.

II

Compassion takes the form of interpersonal responsibility in Morris Bober and Frank Alpine. Morris Bober, a poor grocer with his burial before-death-like existence in the store, is a characteristic Malamudian *schlemiel*. Morris is almost entombed in the store for twenty-two years of his life. With his moral honesty and goodness he is anachronistic in a world of wilful guiles. He continues his wretched life in the store to provide for his family without much success.

Ihab Hassan views both Morris Bober and Frank Alpine as typical of *eiron*, "collector of injustices."[20] Morris regrets that he has failed to support the education of his daughter Helen and come to depend on her job instead. The drudgery of dreary routine has made him "weightless, unmanned, the victim in motion of whatever blew at his back: wind, worries, debts, Karp, holdupniks, ruin. He did not go; he was pushed. He had the will of a victim, no will to speak of." (183) His plan to sell the store for a better employment remains a dream all his life. When he finally settles the transaction with Julius Karp, Morris dies and Karp is hospitalised with heart attack. In spite of his poverty, bad luck and travails, Morris Bober does not lose faith in humanity. His attitude to life characterises compassion even at the cost of self-effacement. At the beginning of the novel, he is seen getting up early to give a three cent roll to the Polishesh, his regular customer. He cannot bear to see the tears of the tiny daughter of the "drunk woman" and readily obliges to give her credit though he is on the verge of starvation himself.

Morris has his share of bad luck as a Jew during pogroms. He had witnessed pogroms in Russia, but did not flee to America as suggested by his father before his conscription into the Czar's army lest his father should be punished for his act. Despite his immigration to America, bad luck continues to haunt him in the shape of poor business. Morris' suffering provokes Frank to comment on Jews:

> That's what they live for, Frank thought, to suffer. And the one that has got the biggest pain in the gut and can

hold on to it the longest without running to the toilet is the
best Jew. No wonder they got on his nerves. (81)

In his unrelieved suffering, only sleep was Morris' "one true
refreshment."

Morris suffers chiefly on account of his honesty and moral
integrity. While Karps, another family of Jews, have made
their fortune by establishing a liquor store, Morris would not
appreciate the line of business they have chosen:

> The grocer, on the other hand, had never altered his for-
> tune, unless degrees of poverty meant alteration, for luck
> and he were, if not natural enemies, not good friends. He
> laboured long hours, *was the soul of honesty—he could not
> escape his honesty, it was bedrock. (19; Italics mine)

Morris is against guiles and tricks. When Frank advises him a
few tricks to earn profits, Morris asks him: "Why should I
steal from my customers ? Do they steal from me ?" (78) He
says: "When a man is honest he don't worry when he sleeps.
This is more important than to steal a nickel." (78) It has
become a legend that one day he ran barefoot in winter without hat or coat to give back to a poor Italian lady a nickel
that she had forgotten on the counter. The very idea of cheating
would cause an explosion in him. Yet he has trusted cheats.
In his innocence he was cheated first by his partner, Charlie
Sobeloff who cashed Morris' ignorance and faith in humanity,
and later by his assistant Frank Alpine. Frank however repays
his debt to Morris by opting to be a provider to Morris' family
after his death, while Charlie does not care to help Morris
even when he applies for it.

Morris' innocence is evident even in his final bid to sell the
store to Podolsky, a refugee. Despite Karp's worldly-wise
warning not to tell Podolsky anything about business, Morris
speaks out:

> Overwhelmed by pity for the poor refugee, at what he had
> in all probability lived through, a man who had sweated
> blood to save a few brutal dollars, Morris, unable to stand

the planned dishonesty, came from behind the counter, and, taking Podolsky by the coat lapels, told him earnestly that the store was run-down but that a boy with his health and strength, with modern methods and a little cash, could build it up in a reasonable time and make a decent living out of it. (180-81)

Morris has, of course, lost the buyer of the store.

Morris' inability to plan evil could be seen in his desperate and inept attempt to burn the store for insurance money. The professional fire-maker who descends on the store one day suddenly gives him the idea that he could set the store on fire with his celluloid. Though Morris hates the "monkey business," he is tempted to try fire the next day with the celluloid collar he had once worn. When the flames blaze out, Morris realises the gravity of the situation and tries to put out the fire in vain. He fails as he is always fated to and burns his own fingers. But for the timely appearance of Frank, the fire could have proved fatal to the grocer. Later when Karp's store burns, Morris is very much anguished at the sight because he had earlier in his low spirits wished the same on Karp. He could not brook even the stray thought:

> With a frozen hand the grocer clawed at a live pain in his breast. He felt an overwhelming hatred of himself. He had wished it on Karp—just this. His anguish was terrible. (193)

Victim of a holdup, Morris gets hit on the head. It seems "the end fitted the day. It was his luck, others had better."(28) Morris has to lay in bed for a whole week. Even before his recovery he tries to go to the store punctually at 6 a.m. as usual. Ida's request to sleep for an hour more fails on him, for he thinks more of the Polishesh, a regular customer than himself. The three cent roll to Polishesh means more to him than another hour of sleep. Business is not something purely commercial and mercenary. For him, it is an obligation to fellowmen.

Morris finds kinship with the ill-fated Frank Alpine. With Frank "one wrong thing leads to another and it ends in a

trap." (36)   Morris' tender heart readily accommodates Frank.
He has to pay the price of his innocence. One day he finds
Frank guilty of stealing at the store. Frank confesses that he
did steal "on account of I was hungry." (49) When Frank
groans that "Nobody has any responsibility to take care of me
but myself," Morris is moved and takes him to his house and
feeds him to his content. Despite Ida's protest, Morris permits
Frank to stay in the cellar that night. He says: "He's a poor
boy. I feel sorry for him." (51) Frank looks after the store
during Morris' illness. Morris is grateful to Frank for improving
the business and gives him greater concessions.

   Malamud's philosophy of suffering and compassion is
exemplified in Morris Bober. Frank enquires Morris what a
Jew means. Morris says a Jew is a man of "good heart" and
one who follows the Jewish Laws, the *Torah*. But he is not
concerned with the ritual of the *Torah*; he is interested in the
spirit of the law. Morris does not go to synagogue, does not
eat kosher, and keeps the shop open on Jewish holidays. Yet
he considers himself a true Jew. He says:

> This is not important to me if I taste big or I don't. To
> some Jews is this important but not to me. Nobody will
> tell me that I am not Jewish because I put in my mouth
> once in a while, when my tongue is dry, a piece ham. But
> they will tell me, and I will believe them, if I forget the
> Law. *This means to do what is right, to be honest, to be*
> *good. This means to other people. Our life is hard enough.*
> *Why should we hurt somebody else ?* For everybody should
> be the best, not only for you or me. We ain't animals. This
> is why we need the Law. This is what a Jew believes.
> (112-13; Italics mine)

Jewishness lies in an ethical life of goodness and fellow-feeling.
When Frank asks why Jews like to suffer, Morris retorts: "They
suffer because they are Jews." (113) His stress is on suffering for the Law—"if a Jew don't suffer for the Law, he will
suffer for nothing." When Frank asks, "What do you suffer
for, Morris ?" Morris answers pointblank: " I suffer for you."
Frank is taken aback by the answer and asks in dismay: "What

do you mean ?" Morris says: "I mean you suffer for me." (113)
These perceptive remarks of Morris bring out that Malamud
"transcends all sectarian understanding of suffering, seeing it
as the fate of the whole mankind, which can only be mitigated
when all men assume responsibility for each other."[21]
Jewishness lies in suffering for one another, i.e. interpersonal
responsibility, an essential tenet of compassion. It is in this
context that suffering becomes meaningful. By the same token,
Morris' suffering is meaningful in the light of his commitment
to the family and compassion to fellowmen. In emphasising
one's suffering for others, Morris speaks of the essence of every
religion though suffering has a special stamp of Jewish tradition.
As Frank says: "other religions have those ideas too."

Morris takes a sympathetic view of Frank's pilferage as a
recompense for "slave wages for a workmen's services" (116)
and raises his wages to double. But Ida's warning about
Frank's possible designs on Helen prompts Morris to dismiss
Frank from the store. After the dismissal, Morris searches his
soul time and again "if he had done right in ordering Frank
to go." (151) He loves Frank even after his confession about
the holdup:

> Morris was too unhappy to speak. Though he pitied the
> clerk, he did not want a confessed criminal around. Even
> if he had reformed, what good would it do to keep him
> here—another mouth to feed, another pair of eyes to the
> death watch ? (177)

But his indigent circumstances force Morris to take a sterner
view of Frank and he would not let him stay in the store.

A victim all through his life, Morris dies before the bright
prospect of selling the store is realised. Despite Ida's protest,
Morris shovels the snow on the road that Sunday night so that
the goyim could go to church. This proves fatal; he dies of
pneumonia in the hospital. During the illness, he dreams of
his son Ephraim in rags. Ephraim died young. Morris promises
to give Ephraim "a good start in life" but the boy disappears.
Ephraim is symbolic of the ideal life that Morris craves for
in vain.

Morris' own final assessment of his life is one of discontentment:

> He thought of his life with sadness. For his family he had
> not provided, the poor man's disgrace. Ida was asleep at
> his side. He wanted to awaken her and apologize. He
> thought of Helen. It would be terrible if she became an old
> maid. He moaned a little, thinking of Frank. His mood
> was of regret. I gave away my life for nothing. It was the
> thunderous truth. (200)

In a world where honesty and success go parallel without any
meeting point, Morris' life is bound to fail from the materialistic
view-point. From the spiritual point of view, Morris has given
his life not for "nothing" but for others. The spirit of compassion redeems Morris.

The Rabbi in his funeral speech discerns in Morris the true
embodiment of the spirit of Jewish life—"to want for others
that which he wants also for himself." He concludes:

> He suffered, he endured, but with hope. Who told me
> this ? I know. He asked for himself little—nothing, but he
> wanted for his beloved child a better existence than he had.
> For such reasons he was a Jew. What more does our sweet
> God ask his poor people ? (203)

Helen Bober's assessment of her father is in contrast to that of
the Rabbi. Taking a down-to-earth point of view, she does not
idealize Morris' self-abnegation and honesty although she
concedes his sweet nature and understanding as his strength.
His natural honesty in a world of "natural dishonesty" is
anachronistic. Helen thinks:

> He was no saint; he was in a way weak; his only true
> strength in his sweet nature and his understanding. He
> knew, at least, what was good. (204)

She considers him a "victim" buried in the store without
"courage" needed for success. What she refers to as "courage"
is in fact nothing but compromise with principles. Morris'

uncompromising sense of integrity has made him a "victim." If Morris is not a saint, neither is he a frail human being. His suffering finds meaning in relation to his moral integrity based on compassion.

Marc Ratner observes that Morris Bober, despite his strength, remains "static in sainthood," whereas Frank Alpine, his clerk, gives the novel its narrative movement through his redemption.[22] While Morris evinces exemplary compassion all through his life, Frank Alpine, his gentile assistant, has to struggle much to reach that point. From his initial hatred of Jews, he attains a stage where he becomes one with the Morris family and turns a Jew literally. The novel dramatizes his "successful initiation into a new spiritual life."[23] In portraying the "apprentice" character of Frank, Malamud is concerned with man "in the process of changing his fate, his life." In his interview with William Kennedy in *The National Observer*, he says:

> A man is always changing and the changed part of his is all-important. I refer to the psyche, the spirit, the mind, the emotions.[24]

Frank's evolution from man to *mentsch* is significant.

III

Thinking of Jews and their affinity to suffering, Frank comments:

> Suffering, he (Frank) thought, is like a piece of goods. I bet the Jews could make a suit of clothes out of it. The other funny thing is that there are more of them around than anybody knows about. (204)

Ironically enough, Frank though not a Jew appears to be one of "them around" who has a "talent" for suffering. His sense of guilt regarding Morris Bober coupled with his love for Helen makes him court and accept "Bober fate." He hangs around the store and Bober family even after his dismissal and readily avails himself of the first opportunity to help them. It is again

his love for Helen chastened of its sensual element at the end
that makes him shoulder the entire responsibility of Bober
family after Morris' death. Even when Helen is against him, he
works day and night to fulfil her cherished dream of college
education. Morris' life has taught him compassion which he
exemplifies in his selfless service to the Bober family.

An immigrant from the West in search of better life, Frank
begins his career as a holdupnik, thief and liar. He appears a
man torn in conflict between ambivalent motives and actions,
"a man with two minds" as Ida calls. He thinks of himself as
"a man of stern morality and discipline" and yet acts far from
it. He wavers between guilt and remorse, but unlike Roy
Hobbs of *The Natural* he learns from his experience or suffering
and overcomes his weakness with great struggle. In all his
conflicting motives and actions, Frank is guided by his singular
passion for Helen, at first sensual and in the end selfless.

Frank's guilt in the holdup of Morris Bober haunts him
throughout the novel until he confesses it to Morris and his
daughter. He hovers round the store to atone for his guilt of
share in the holdup. He tries to be an associate to Morris at
the first opportunity trying all sorts of tricks and lies. He soon
gains the sympathy of Morris by telling the sad story of his
days in the orphanage after his mother's death and father's
escape. In his attempt to join Morris' store, Frank is moved
partly by his guilty-conscience and partly by his interest in
Helen Bober whom he had seen earlier. He is ready to work in
the store even without wages, but the proposal is at first turned
down by Morris since "three people would be too much" in
the store.

Frank, however, enters the store unasked when Morris falls
sick and is advised rest. With the improvement of business at
the store, he gains the confidence of Morris' wife. Al Marcus,
a Jew salesman, warns him that "if you stay six months,
you'll stay forever." This warning proves prophetic since
Frank stays in the store throughout his life except for a short
time after his dismissal by Morris. Frank is not led into it; he
lives the grocer's life willingly for Helen and Morris.

In spite of his gratitude to Bober, Frank finds it hard to
give up his habit to steal. He does not account for certain

sales on the register. His conscience pricks him and exhorts
him to be honest. One day he gets back his gun from Ward
Minogue so that no record is left of the holdup. Little does he
realise that honesty lies not in wiping off the record of one's
evil deeds but in staying away from such acts in future. He
rejects Ward's proposal of another holdup, but continues to
steal cash from the store. At times he stoops to justify his
act.

> There were times stealing made him feel good. It felt good
> to have some change in his pocket, and it felt good to
> pluck a buck from under the Jew's nose. He would slip it
> into his pants pocket so deftly that he had to keep himself
> from laughing. (78)

The only saving grace of Frank's stealing is that he marks
down the figure of stolen money with an intention to pay back.

> He might some day plunk down a tenner or so on some
> longshot and then have enough to pay back every lousy
> cent of what he had taken. (78)

Sometimes he is remorseful and feels "as if he had just buried
a friend and was carrying the fresh grave within himself." He
suffers the pangs of guilt and remorse because of his "worri-
some conscience." He wants to confess all his sins to Morris
but cannot for fear of losing Helen. He feels tense and oppressed with these conflicting thoughts. Yet Frank feels a
sudden gentleness descend upon him as

> He felt gentle to the people who came into the store, espe-
> cially the kids, whom he gave penny crackers for nothing.
> He was gentle to Morris, and the Jew was gentle to him.
> And he was filled with a quiet gentleness for Helen and no
> longer climbed the air shaft to spy on her, naked in the
> bathroom. (79)

But such moments of peace are rare. He evokes the suspicion
of Morris who instead of punishing him raises his wages lest
Frank should resort to stealing once again;

Frank's dismissal from the store comes ironically in the wake of his decision to return bit by bit the hundred and forty-odd bucks he had filched from Morris:

From now on he would keep his mind on tomorrow, and tomorrow take up the kind of life that he saw he valued more than how he had been living. He would change and live in a worth-while way. (142)

He starts his pay-back by adding six of his dollars to the store's account and feels "a surge of joy." But when he remembers his appointment with Helen, he manages to take a dollar from a customer without accounting for it in the cash register. Morris catches him red-handed. Frank pleads that he is on the verge of change:

'I confess to it,' Frank said, 'but for God's sake, Morris, I swear I was paying it back to you. Even today I put back six bucks. That's why you got so much in the drawer from the time you went up to snooze until now. Ask the Mrs if we took in more than two bucks while you were upstairs. The rest I put in.' (146)

Despite his pleas, Frank is dismissed by Morris. He could not, however, severe his relationship with the Bober family because of his love for Helen.

Frank has an agonising quest for new life. While Ida takes care that Frank does not meet Helen, Frank is famished for her looks. His mind is solely occupied by the sensual thought of Helen. Frank builds up his relations with Helen regularly visiting her in the evenings at the library. He soon becomes "interesting looking" to her. She shares the ambition of Frank to go to college. She wants "to travel, experience, live" like him. She gives him books like *Anna Karenina*, *Madame Bovary* and *Crime and Punishment*. Frank does not like them but labours hard to read them for the sake of Helen. He dislikes *Crime and Punishment* but finds interest in the series of confessions in it. Frank's presents evoke "a throb of desire" in Helen and yet she returns them to Frank, since she does not like to invite troubles by marrying a clerk in the grocery. She, however, later accepts one of the presents on Frank's assurance: "You don't have to worry that I expect anything for what I give you." (108) Helen's love for Frank conflicts with her craving for a comfortable life and leaves her indecisive. Helen rejects Frank's bold advances saying that he will have to wait "till I am really sure I love you, may be till we're married, if we ever are." (123) Frank regrets his lack of restraint and resolves to be disciplined. He tries to impress upon Helen that he is "a very good guy" in heart, and claims that "Even when I am bad I am good." (126)

Frank always works for the object of his desire and foils it himself with his stupid move. Frank's earlier comment on the irony of his fate is revealing here.

> I work like a mule for what I want, and just when it looks like I am going to get it I make some kind of a stupid move, and everything that is just about mailed down tight blows up in my face. (35)

His guardedly-built relations with Helen go to pieces with his "stupid" move in the seduction attempt. Frank rescues Helen from Ward Minogue's attempt of molestation but forces his own passion on her despite her protest. Helen who is just on the verge of changing to his side is at once distanced by the rash and hasty act of Frank. After the act, she calls Frank "Dog—uncircumcised dog !" although she had earlier considered his non-Jewishness not an obstacle for marriage. The act turns passionate longing of Helen into violent hatred for Frank.

From this point, a spectacular change marks Frank. He realises the stupidity of his actions "that all the while he was acting like he wasn't, he was really a man of stern morality." (157) He smells the stink of "the self he had secretly considered valuable." His penitence increases his debt to the Bober family. When Morris is caught in the gas-filled chamber, Frank readily rushes to him and rescues. He offers to work in the store without a penny till Morris recovers, to discharge his obligation and debt to Morris. When Ida says: "You have no

debt. He has a debt to you that you saved him from the gas,"
Frank is modest in his reply:

> Nick smelled it first. Anyway I feel I have a debt to him
> for all the things he has done for me. . . . That's my nature,
> when I'm thankful, I'm thankful. (162)

He also promises Ida that he would not bother Helen any more.
He decides to convince Morris of his sincerity to stay there and
do anything for Helen. He regrets the wrong he had done to
Helen unintentionally.

> He hadn't intended wrong but he had done it; now he inten-
> ded right. He would do anything she wanted, and if she
> wanted nothing he would do something, what he should do;
> and he would do it all on his own will, nobody pushing him
> but himself. *He would do it with discipline and with love.*
> (164; Italics mine)

He apologises to Helen and says "nothing can kill the love I
feel for you." But Helen brushes him aside saying love is "a
dirty word" in his mouth.

Frank continues to suffer in the store only for the sake of
Helen. With the opening of the new store by the Norwegians,
the business of the store has shrunk. To cover up the shortage
of sales and earnings, Frank adds his money to the store's
account gradually. He works day and night in the store, cuts
the expenditure, and improves the bid to attract the customers.
He spies on the Norwegians to learn the secrets of trade. Ida
could not understand why he works so hard and stays there in
the store. When asked, he wanted to say "For love" but
having no nerve to tell it, says "For Morris." (157) Morris'
earlier exhortation "I suffer for you" and "you suffer for me"
becomes the essence of Frank's practice. He takes up the night
assignment of counterman at a Coffee Pot to help the Bobers
live on. He works literally for twentyfour hours like a penitent
saint. He at last makes his long over-due confession to Morris
about his role in the holdup.

> 'Morris,' Frank said, at agonising last, 'I have something
> important I want to tell you. I tried to tell you before only

I couldn't work my nerve up. Morris, don't blame me now
for what I once did, because I am now a changed man, but
I was one of the guys that held you up that night. I swear
to God I didn't want to once I got in here, but I couldn't
get out of it. . . . Even now I feel sick about what I am
saying, but I'am telling it to you so you will know how
much I suffered on account of what I did, and that I am
very sorry you were hurt on your head—even though not by
me. *The thing you got to understand is I am not the same
person I once was. I might look so to you but if you could
see what's been going on in my heart you would know I have
changed.* You can trust me now, I swear it, and that's why
I am asking you to let me stay and help you. (176; Italics
mine)

Frank experiences "a moment of extraordinary relief" at his
confession but it is accompanied by the stern orders of Morris
to quit the store.

Although Frank quits the store, he has not lost his spiritual
affinity to the Bober family. He hangs around the store and
saves Morris a second time from fire. His fall on the coffin of
Morris is symbolic of his role in the replacement of Morris.
After the death of Morris, Frank works for the Bober family
and upholds the principles of interpersonal responsibility and
compassion for which Morris strove throughout his life.

The uppermost concern now for Frank is to do something
for Helen. He wants to help her get the education she had
always wanted. The sisyphean task he has set himself to, is "a
rocky load" on his head and yet "he *had* to do it, it was his
only hope; he could think of no other. All he asked for himself
was the privilege of giving her something she couldn't give
back." (210) This extraordinary selfless compassion of Frank
even under the most trying circumstances surprises Helen:

Considering the conditions of his existence, she was startled
by his continuing ability to surprise her, make God-knows-
what-next-move. His staying power mystified and frightened
her, because she felt in herself, since the death of Ward
Minogue, a waning of outrage. (211)

Frank succeeds in sending Helen to night college by spending
only for the barest of his necessities.

One day Frank sees Helen kissing Nat and feels jealous. In
a moment of desperation he resorts to doing things against
conscience. He spies on Helen in the bathroom twice and aches
for her company. He takes to cheating the customers in the
store, shortweighing and short-changing. But

> Then one day, for no reason he could give, though the
> reason felt familiar, he stopped climbing up the air shaft to
> peek at Helen, and he was honest in the store. (214)

This marks complete transformation of Frank who has reached
the stage of selfless love and compassion for Helen. He is
purged of the selfish motives or physical yearnings for Helen.
He has transcended the selfish love to selfless compassion.

The change in Helen's attitude to Frank comes when one
night she herself has seen Frank working in a store. Frank is
thin and groggy from overwork, his eyes burning red reflecting
sleepless nights. Helen feels concerned for him "because it was
no mystery who he was working for." She has realised with
gratitude that "He had kept them alive. Because of him she
had enough to go to school at night." (215) She wonders at
the sudden change in Frank:

> It was a strange thing about people—they could look the
> same but be different. He had been one thing, low, dirty,
> but because of something in himself—something she couldn't
> define, a memory perhaps, an ideal he might have forgotten
> and then remembered—he had changed into somebody else,
> no longer what he had been. (215)

The "something" that changed Frank is his spirit of compassion. Helen is impressed by it and thanks him later for "the
help you're giving us." She has agreed at least to think about
Frank's proposal to send her to day college. Her renewed love
for him could be perceived in her remark: "I wanted you to
know I'm still using your Shakespeare." Frank however does
not ask her about his chance with her. He decides to wait

with discipline. He suffers for the Bober family now with a hope.

Frank in a reverie imagines St. Francis turning the wooden rose (carved out by Frank himself earlier) into rose and presenting it to Helen "with love and best wishes of Frank." Helen who had rejected and thrown it in the garbage can, accepts it. This is symbolic of the restoration of love. St. Francis acts as the cause of the union of Frank and Helen.

Frank is cast in the image of St. Francis or as one under his impact. Frank says that as a child he was impressed by the stories of St. Francis of Assissi told by an old priest at the orphanage. He considers him great not just because he had the "nerve to preach to birds" but also for his compassionate humanism. He tells Sam ironically on the evening of the hold-up.

> For instance, he gave everything away that he owned, every cent, all his clothes off his back. He enjoyed to be poor. He said poverty was a queen and he loved her like she was a beautiful woman. (31)

Frank concludes that "He was born good, which is a talent if you have it." (31) Frank accomplishes this talent in the end. Like Francis he gives away everything for the sake of Bober family. When Helen goes to meet Frank at the park, Frank appears to be St. Francis himself.

> Coming up the block, Helen saw a man squatting by one of the benches, feeding the birds. Otherwise, the island was deserted. When the man rose, the pigeons fluttered up with him, a few landing on his arms and shoulders, one perched on his fingers, pecking peanuts from his cupped palm. Another fat bird sat on his hat. (107)

Frank assumes the spirit of St. Francis and Morris Bober completely with his inordinate suffering and compassion. Although Frank is cast in the image of St. Francis, his development reflects the pattern of Jewish history itself—a pattern that Malamud has described as "First the Prophets' 'way of gentleness'; the Sins of the People, Punishment, Exile and Return . . .

the primal problem of man seeking to escape the tragedy of the past."[25]

The circumcision of Frank has prompted the critics to call it "that rarity among modern fiction—the true conversion novel."[26] Having served a Jew and his family all his life, Frank turns a Jew himself:

> One day in April Frank went to the hospital and had himself circumcised. For a couple of days he dragged himself around with a pain between his legs. The pain enraged and inspired him. After Passover he became a Jew. (217)

Although the circumcision marks symbolic conversion to Jewish faith, Frank's conversion need not be viewed in its strict religious sense. Sidney Richman points out that "Frankie's conversion, like Morris' identity, is clearly a humanistic rather than a religious mystery—though the two are not necessarily exclusive."[27] The act of conversion for Frank is "a matter of becoming a new man." Frank's circumcision is a nominal act which rounds off the new way of life he had already taken up after the death of Morris Bober. Frank finds new life in his authentic human relations with the Bober family in which he is guided by selfless compassion. Compassion for him is not mere awareness of others' suffering but intense involvement in their fate.

Richman finds the conclusion of the novel "most puzzling."[28] He remarks: "For all his patterned ascension to sainthood, the final stages of Frankie Alpine's career, unlike Raskolnikov's *are* inconclusive and weak."[29] It is difficult to agree with the opinion of Richman. There is nothing ambiguous about Frank's circumcision as it marks the final phase of conversion which was set into motion quite early with his joining the Bobers in their strain and stress. Without being a Jew, Frank has almost replaced Morris with the assumption of the latter's role, responsibilities and commitments. He has finally vindicated compassion for which Morris suffered all through his life. Viewed in this context Frank's circumcision does not appear ambiguous. It answers Helen's earlier complaint against him—"Dog—uncircumcised dog." Although the novel does not bring about the union or marriage of Frank with Helen, it leaves a sense of hope in that direction with Helen's proclivities once again in Frank's favour. Francis finds Frank's conversion important because "he discovers—not alone, but through another human being—a law of conduct which might give meaning to the burden of suffering, to life. As he accepts faith, he paradoxically eradicates the barriers between theologies."[30] As a Christian-Jew Frank becomes "Everyman, exemplifying the fundamental unity of man's spiritual needs."[31]

In *A New Life* that follows, Malamud brings out Levin's evolution through compassion in the corrupt academic world.

NOTES

1. Jack Ludwig, *Recent American Novelists* (Minneapolis: Univ. of Minnesota Press, 1966) 39.

2. Quoted in Sidney Richman, *Bernard Malamud* (New York: Twayne, 1966) 51.

3. Daniel Stern, "The Art of Fiction LII: Bernard Malamud," *The Paris Review* 16.61 Spring 1975: 53.

4. Stern 43.

5. Stern 53.

6. Walter Allen, *The Modern Novel in Britain and the United States* (New York: E.P. Dutton, 1965) 330.

7. Barry Ulanov, *The Two Worlds of American Art: The Private and the Popular* (New York: Macmillan, 1965) 232.

8. Peter L. Hays, "The Complex Pattern of Redemption," *Bernard Malamud and the Critics,* ed. Leslie A. Field and Joyce W. Field (New York: New York Univ. Press, 1970) 229

9. Walter Allen 33.

10. William Goyen, "A World of Bad Luck," *New York Times Book Review* 28 April 1957: 4.

11. Goyen 4.

12. Ben Siegel, "Victims in Motion: Bernard Malamud's Sad and Bitter Clowns," *Recent American Fiction: Some Critical Views*, ed. Joseph J. Waldmeir (Boston: Houghton Mifflin, 1963) 206.

13. Ihab Hassan, "Bernard Malamud: 1976 Fiction within Fictions," *The Fiction of Bernard Malamud*, ed. Richard Astro and Jackson J. Benson (Corvallis: Oregon State Univ. Press, 1977) 61.

14. Tony Tanner, *City of Words: American Fiction 1950-1970* (London: Jonathan Cape, 1971) 327-28.

15. Richman 55-56.

16. H.E. Francis, "Bernard Malamud's Every Man," *Midstream* 7.1 Winter 1961: 96.

17. Norman Leer, "Three American Novels and Contemporary Society: A Search for Commitment, *"Wisconsin Studies in Contemporary Literature* 3.3 Fall 1962: 67-86 and Peter L. Hays 219-33.

18. Allen 33.

19. Philip Rahv, *Literature and the Sixth Sense* (Boston: Houghton Mifflin, 1969) 284.

20. Ihab Hassan, "The Qualified Encounter: Three Novels by Buechner, Malamud, and Ellison," *Radical Innocence* (New York: Harper and Row, 1966) 161-68.

21. Rahv 284.

22. Marc L. Ratner, "Style and Humanity in Malamud's Fiction," *Massachusetts Review* 5 (1965): 665.

23. Robert Solotaroff, "Bernard Malamud," *American Writers: A Collection of Literary Biographies*, ed. Leonard Unger (New York: Charles Scribner's Sons, 1979) 440.

24. Quoted in W.J. Handy, "The Malamud Hero: A Quest for Existence," *The Fiction of Bernard Malamud* 77.

25. Joseph Wershba, "Not Horror but 'Sadness'," *New York Post* 14 September 1958: M2. Quoted in Richman 56.

26. Rod W. Horton and Herbert W. Edwards, *Backgrounds of American Literary Thought* (Princeton, N.J.: Princeton Prentice-Hall, 1974) 577.
27. Richman 71.
28. Richman 73.
29. *Loc. cit.*
30. Francis 94.
31. Ben Siegel 206.

4

LEVIN'S BURDEN: *A NEW LIFE*

*"To be good, then evil, then good was no moral way
of life, but to be good after being evil was a
possibility of life."*

A New Life* is at once an academic satire and a *bildungsro-
man* depicting Levin's quest for new life. In contrast to the
"mythic placelessness" of his earlier novels, Malamud extends
the social horizon with a more realistic setting, viz. Cascadia
College. Leslie Fiedler remarks that *A New Life* "is about the
Fifties almost as much as it is about the West: the age of Mc-
Carthyism and Cold War."[1] The novel to some degree derives
from Malamud's experience on the faculty of the Oregon State
College which serves as the backdrop of the novel. His yearning
for liberal arts and democracy is evidently the base for the
cause for which the protagonist of the novel also struggles.
Levin, the protagonist, regrets very much like Malamud that

---

* Bernard Malamud, *A New Life* (Harmondsworth: Penguin Books,
1968) All subsequent references to the text with page numbers in
parantheses are to this edition.

the education system at Cascadia miserably fails to teach "how to keep civilization from destroying itself."[2] (103) Prof. Fairchild, Gerald Gilley, C.D. Fabrikant, Leo Duffy and other academic figures of the novel have their counterparts in real life.[3] Malamud, however, does not stretch the analogy too far. He prefers "autobiographical essence to autobiographical history." Even though certain events of his life may creep into the novel, "it is n't necessarily my life history."[4] Malamud further remarks that he is interested in the "simple act of writing a novel out of my experience."[5]

The novel discusses with subtle irony the departmental objectives, politics, consveratism, and the oddities of the so-called academicians of the Cascadia College. It is on this count that critics like John Hollander and Sally Daniels regarded the novel as "the best academic novel."[6] Robert Bowen says: "No other American novel gives as clear a report of normal state university life in the usual administrative procedures of departmental espionage, blackmail, subordination, and assorted shenanigans."[7] But the novel is not merely an academic satire. It probes the development of the soul of Seymour Levin. Levin's career shows us "not man as teacher, but teacher as man."[8] Granville Hicks points out that it is "basically a serious novel, about the difficulties of leading the good life."[9] Page Stegner finds the novel centrally concerned with Levin's "gradual commitment to becoming a man of principles."[10]

Seymour Levin makes a long journey from the East to the West in search of a "new life," his "manifest destiny." He takes up the chosen career of a teacher at Cascadia and wants to seek "order, value, accomplishment, love" in life. For some time he becomes a victim of wrong choices and fails to shed the burden of his past. He seeks physical love in Laverne—a waitress, Avis Fliss—his colleague, Nadalee—a student, and Pauline—his colleague. What begins as an act of adultery with Pauline ends in an irrevocable bond. To begin with, Levin tries to avoid Pauline "out of the fear of getting involved, and the fear of Thanatos."[11] But eventually he evolves to a stage where he takes upon himself the burden of Pauline and her two adopted children at the cost of his career even while he is convinced that she no longer loves him. This evolution of Levin is variously

interpreted as love, *agape, caritas.* Hyman interprets it as "a
classical progress from *eros,* fleshly love to *agape,* the spiritual
love of one of God's creatures for another."[12] Mandel remarks:
"He (Levin) has moved from sex and a waitress, sex and his
colleague Avis, sex and his student Nadalee, sex and Pauline
Gilley to Pauline minus sex, to self-sacrifice for the idea of
love."[13] Jonathan Baumbach says: "Love is sacred in Malamud's universe; if life is holy, love is a holy of holies. At the
end of the novel, Levin achieves a kind of unsought heroism in
sacrificing his career for the *principle* of love, a love in itself dor-
mant, a memory beyond feeling."[14] But it is compassion, more
than love, that prompts Levin to undertake the responsibility of
pregnant Pauline and her adopted children. He discovers in his
act "a way of giving value to other lives through assuring
rights." (222) This is prompted by compassion. If he fails to
give his unstinted love, he succeeds in extending compassion.
Compassion gives him the moral succour to hold the responsibility of Pauline, the ill-treated wife of Gilley, despite the grave
problems such action poses. Levin's act may appear to be one
of disinterested responsibility especially in the final section of
the novel. However, one hardly fails to recognise the fact that
it is prompted by compassionate love for Pauline. In an
interview with Miss Masilomani, Malamud denies the impression
that Levin has ceased to love Pauline at the end of the novel.
He says:

> Levin has not ceased to love her. There can be no responsi-
> bility without some love. The golden hoop rings he gave
> her which she fastened on to her ears are a symbol of love,
> to me symbolic of the wedding ring.[15]

Levin's love for Pauline is chastened by compassion. After his
ambitions and dreams, Levin wakes up to the realisation of the
bitter fact that love goes not with freedom but with entanglement and commitment. He gives up "the Greek drama of
freedom for the Jewish acceptance of responsibility and moral
entanglement."[16] As Grebstein points out, for Levin "sex
becomes love, and love becomes commitment."[17] Levin finds
his new life in a new relationship."[18] His sense of interpersonal

responsibility and moral obligation gives him the courage to shoulder the responsibility of Pauline and when Gilley wonders as to why he was ready to take Pauline with her children at the expense of his promising career, Levin snubs with the retort "Because I can, you son of a bitch." The courage with compassion makes Levin's defeat a triumph.

Anthony Burgess and Edgar Stanley Hyman point out that Levin becomes a saint not through the denial of the flesh as does Frank in *The Assistant*, but "through the assertion of its rights."[19] But in fact both Frank and Levin indulge in flesh in the beginning and reach ultimately a stage where physical love ceases to be important.

Critics in general are sceptical about Malamud's success in use of academic background to portray man fulfilling his personality. Sidney Richman concedes diversity and vigour to the novel, and yet comments: "The weaknesses of *A New Life* . . . stem almost consistently from the author's attempts to find a form that can unite the "two books": the academic world and the intensities of the underground world that appear in *The Assistant*. On the whole, he has not succeeded."[20] Comparing the novel with John Barth's *Giles Goat-Boy*, Olderman finds the setting of university in Malamud's novel not as organic of the over all impact as in Barth. He complains that the university "never becomes more than a setting" and "His hero, S. Levin, could as well have learned his existential lessons against the backdrop of a countinghouse or a sea-going tuna boat."[21] David Stevenson and Sanford Pinsker also fault the novel on its "mixed intentions."[22] Hymn finds absurd the section of the plot which deals with the politics of Departmental elections and Levin meeting espionage with counter-espionage.[23] Baumbach too finds "the satire occasionally pointed, but even at its best it is second-rate Malamud."[24] Grebstein comments that the satire collapses "under the weight of too much academic detail and too much debate."[25] Richard Astro remarks that the college novel is not a sufficient vehicle to support Malamud's tale of human suffering and regeneration."[26] He finds the cumbersome details of the academic life detracting "what is otherwise a serious novel in affirmation of the human spirit."[27]

Although Malamud provides an inside picture of the
academic life and the politics that seized it, Levin appears completely an outsider. Levin is diminished as a character in those
scenes set in Cascadia English department.[28] The portraits of
faculty people are merely stereotypes. The novel appears as
though it is two books and not one. The character of Levin
and his relations are not properly integrated into the academic
life portrayed. This is the reason why *A New Life* is not as
compact as *The Assistant*. The crooked politics of Department
serves as a contrast to bring out the honesty of Levin who
desperately fights against them. Through Levin, Malamud also
vindicates his passion for liberalism and literature as against
conservatism and mechanical language skills. The interest of
the novel in the main lies in Levin's evolution from selfish love
to selfless compassion.

II

Seymour Levin is a typical Malamudian *schlemiel* who
combines in himself the traits of a *schlimazel*. A victim of his
own wrong choices, Levin considers his life "a sad hash of
beginnings." He saw "in the strewn garbage of his life, errors,
mishaps, ignorance, experience from which he had learned
nothing." (228) Like Roy Hobbs he makes one mistake after
another, but ultimately upholds his moral obligations. He
bungles everything he touches. He teaches his first class in
great confusion with his fly open. He is a flop in his affairs
with Laverne and Avis Fliss. His affair with Nadalee is full of
travails. He settles with Pauline, his colleague's wife and
erstwhile lover of Leo Duffy.

Like Roy Hobbs or Frank Alpine, Levin has also a
humiliating past and tries to get over it. In the very opening of
the novel, he is described as "formerly a drunkard." Circumstances compel Levin to become a drunkard. His father died a
thief in prison and mother went crazy after husband's death
and committed suicide. His misplaced love for embittered
woman deepens his sense of frustration. For some time he tries
to drown his miseries in drinking. He says: "I drank, I stank."
He even contemplates suicide. But he had a sudden awakening

to the values of life. He later says to Pauline, "I came to believe what I had often wanted to, that life is holy. I then became a man of principle." (176) With his wisdom of books, he arrives at the conclusion that "the source of freedom is the human spirit." Transformed Levin begins his quest for new life. He is rejected by about fifty colleges including the University of Gettysburgh before his selection at Cascadia college. Grabbing the opportunity, he travels thousands of miles from the East to Marathon, Cascadia of the West to take up his chosen career of teaching.

Levin believes that a new place will inspire change in life. For his purposeless past, he blames none but himself. Asked by Pauline Gilley about the purpose of his journey, he says that he wants to make better use of things and to stand by "an old ideal or two." He does not, however, specify the ideals, but at the end of the novel we learn that he opts for compassion.

Contrary to the hopes of Levin, Cascadia is not a liberal arts college but mostly a science and technical college. It had liberal arts once but lost after First World War and never regained. It prefers composition to literature. The departmental objective as stated by Prof. Fairchild, Head of the Department, is "to satisfy the needs of the professional schools on the campus with respect to written communication." (39) Gilley's statement to Levin at his reception, "One of the first things you'll notice about the West is its democracy," appears ironical since Cascadia never encourages liberal arts or literature. Levin only makes a feeble plea to Gilley and Prof. Fairchild that "Democracy owes its existence to the liberal arts." (38) Even his hopes of teaching literature are belied as Gilley makes clear that he cannot teach literature till he obtained Ph. D. the " 'union card' to stay in College teaching." Interestingly enough, the reason Gilley gives for preferring composition to literature is "You can just see those kids improving from one paper to the next. It isn't easy to notice much of a development of literary taste in a year." (23) Levin is irked by the irrelevance of "teaching people how to write who don't know what to write." (103) He is scared by the persisting nightmare that he may be asked to quit Cascadia:

> He dreamed he had caught an enormous salmon by the
> tail and was hanging on for dear life but the furious fish,
> threshing and bleeding water, broke free: "Levin, go home."
> He woke in a sweat. (26)

This is symbolic of Levin's struggle for his ideals in a world
rocked by corruption and hypocrisy. With his high ideals, he is
merely a fish out of water at Cascadia.

Gilley's suggestion that "if you're our type, it's a good
place to stay" forewarns Levin of his impending troubles. In
fact Gilley's long lecture on the nature of requirement at
Cascadia is a veiled threat.

> What we don't want around are troublemakers. If someone
> is dissatisfied, if he doesn't like what we do, if he doesn't
> respect other people's intimate rights and peace of mind, the
> sooner he goes on his way the better. If he likes it here and
> wants to stay on, at the rate we're growing I'm sure we can
> keep him. We don't offer the best of salaries but we do
> advance people in not too long a time, and once you
> became an assistant professor you're on permanent tenure.
> If you're the type I think you are, Sy—and so, incidentally,
> does Pauline—you can be sure of a worthwhile career here.
> On the other hand, if you don't like the climate, let's say,
> and want to go elsewhere, the experience you get here will
> make it that much easier for you. That's up to you and all
> right with us. (37)

The above passage makes it clear how much "democracy"
prevails in the English Department of Cascadia College. Levin,
who is not of the 'type' Gilley describes, cannot obviously hope
for "a worthwhile career" at Cascadia. Further as if to embrace
failure, he treads the path of Leo Duffy who was asked to quit
without notice for his radically liberal views. He even loves
Gilley's wife Pauline who had earlier loved Leo.

A man with deep sense of alienation, Levin yearns for his
"lost youth" and company. He envies the married people of
the faculty, "the years of loneliness they had escaped." He is
famished for love and wants to marry in vain. His affair with

Laverne betrays only his animal passion contrary to all his resolutions to be principled. He stoops to have an affair with her at a barn as per the latter's suggestion.

In front of cows, he thought. Now I belong to the ages. (75)

Levin feels an irresistible lust for her physical beauty and "considered falling in love with her but gave up the idea." (75) When Laverne shivers with unbearable cold, Levin compassionately gives her his trousers to wear as Sadek wickedly stole the clothes. He is afraid that he might lose his job if the episode is dejected:

> ... Levin's astronomy was the astronomy of fear, in particular, of losing his job. If he could get rid of the girl and her horse blanket he might make it, with or without pants sneak into town and quickly be home. (77)

Reaching Laverne's home safely after much fear and tension, Levin feels for her "a certain tenderness for having for a minute lain under him" and proposes another meeting with her. But Laverne turns it down with scorn.

After his abortive affair with Laverne, Levin's sense of isolation deepens. He feels he has no place in the society as a bachelor and longs for company, love, marriage and children.

> Levin wanted friendship and got friendliness; he wanted steak and they offered spam. Each day his past weighed more. He was, after all, thirsty, and time moved on relentless roller skates. When for God's sake, came love, marriage, children? (111)

Levin's affair with his colleague Avis Fliss is the result of his quest for company. He goes to her one night in the office and after short talk they decide to make love in the office itself. But when Levin learns that Avis has a sick breast to be operated upon, he recedes from the act out of compassion.

> Poor dame, he thought. She has little, why should I make it less? (119)

He suggests they can have an affair "when we have a better place, when you feel better" since "I don't want to hurt you."

A failure in love, Levin feels he has not yet begun to *live*. He buys a second hand car "to escape occasionally from town and loneliness." When his student advises him not to be afraid of accidents and death since all have to die some time or other, Levin says:

> "Better later," Levin muttered. "I have not yet begun to live." (120)

The conflict between character and lust is discernible in Levin's affair with Nadalee Hammerstad, his student. Nadalee is a flippant girl who provokes Levin's frenzy of love by her seemingly unmindful acts of romance. Her frivolity makes Levin long for her. He forgets Prof. Fairchild's warning, "We expect you strictly to refrain from dating students, no matter what the provocation." (47) He is, however, torn between will and lust.

> How escape the ferocious lust that inflamed and tormented his thoughts as it corroded his will? Why must Levin's unlived life put him always in peril? (123)

Levin cannot break the "sacred trust" between the student and the instructor. He tries various means of self-control in vain. He is quite conscious of his evil thoughts representing his "basest self." He cannot betray her. He thinks:

> I must live by responsibility, an invention of mine in me. The girl trusts me. I can't betray her. If I want sex I must be prepared to love, and love may mean marriage. (I live by my nature, not Casanova's). If I'm not prepared to marry her I'd better stay away. (124)

Levin decides not to be a philanderer with Nadalee. If he were to love, he should accept her as life-partner. But ultimately he resolves to give her up to prove the strength of character over lust.

> He would, in denial, reveal the depth of his strongest, truest strength. (124)

When he invites Nadalee for a walk, she makes it explicit that she wants to be treated by Levin as a woman and not as a little innocent girl. Levin falls a prey to her enticing words. Lust prevails over will power. They decide to meet alone in the little motel on the coast owned by Nadalee's aunt.

When Levin starts for the motel he plans to ask her only to be friends with him. His journey by car, however, is full of troubles and reminds us of Yakov's journey to Kieve in *The Fixer*. At last his "purgatorial journey" ends. At the motel, Nadalee greets him naked before Levin tries to explain anything. As he is against sex without love, he feels guilty though Nadalee is not very serious about it.

Levin's integrity is evident in his firm denial to raise Nadalee to B grade from C just because he had an affair with her. Nadalee accuses him of punishing her "because you did something you shouldn't have." Levin explains:

> I will also admit I considered raising you to a B anyway, because, as I just said, I feel a lot of gratitude to you. But the truth of it is that what happened to us, as you must understand, has no connexion with your grade and I can't give it any. I thought it wouldn't be fair to mark you on one standard and everyone else on another. Do you see what I mean, Nadalee ? (140)

Levin does not agree to be dishonest because they were once close to each other. But when he verifies her paper later, he finds an error in totalling and he gives Nadalee B grade. The detected error saves him from the mess. The entire affair with Nadalee only increases Levin's sense of isolation and leaves him in self-disgust.

> He lay in silence, solitude, and darkness. More than once he experienced crawling self-hatred. It left him frightened because he thought he had outdistanced it by three thousand miles. The future as new life was no longer predictable. That caused the floor to move under his bed. (145)

Having failed in his attempt to establish meaningful relationship with any of the girls he had met, Levin remains in the constant grip of fear of failure. Change of place does not seem to inspire in him any change as desired. He also does not fare well in his profession. As the number of failures are more in his batch, many of the students of his group opt for a change to another instructor. Gerald Gilley in fact encourages and effects such transfers without consulting Levin. Levin realises that Gilley is his enemy.

Gilley's wife Pauline is responsible for Levin's job at Cascadia College. Out of the applications discarded by Gilley, Pauline picks up Levin's probably out of her fancy for his beard and recommends it for the job. She along with her husband receives Levin at the station. She gives him her hospitality at home. She nurses him when he falls sick for a short while. But Levin remains passive to her. He is, however, attracted to her at the cocktail party of the Bullocks. He calls her a lovely woman. Pauline shares the anguish of Levin for a new life.

> I too am conscious of the misuses of my life, how quickly it goes and how little I do. I want more from myself than I get, probably than I've got. Are we misfits, Mr Levin ? (165)

Levin's unexpected meeting with Pauline in the forest converts his sympathy to love. He responds to Pauline's "hungry tenderness" addressed to him. In the deep woods they make love. For Levin it is the most satisfying affair.

> He was throughout conscious of the marvel of it—in the open forest, nothing less, what triumph ! (174)

Both Pauline and Levin feel no regrets for the act on either part. Levin says he still respects her, "mother of two " He reveals his troublesome past—his transformation from a drunkard to a man of principle. Pauline assures Levin that she would not interfere with his new plans for himself.

Levin tries to satisfy himself with the consolation that Pauline herself does not want any serious tie with him. There is no commitment. Yet he has his own fears.

> To be involved with a married woman—danger by defi-
> nition, whose behaviour he had no way of predicting was
> no joke. Who could guess what grade *she* would not want
> changed; or what she might whisper to her lawfully-wedded
> spouse in a moment of tenderness, or hurl at him in hatred.
> If she threw Levin up to Gilley, farewell Levin. He feared
> his fate in her hand. (178)

He fears that the slightest revelation of the act under the tree
would be the worst disaster for him. He feels that "Love goes
with freedom in my book" and wants to keep romance apart
from convenience. He consoles himself that his adultery is only
a means of bringing Pauline closer to Gilley.

> If his affair with Pauline inspired Gilley to respond to her,
> and she to love him for responding, so much the freer
> Levin's conscience. It wasn't easy to be helpful while
> enjoying the fruits of another man's wife. (182-83)

Yet Levin feels he is in love with Pauline and the fact hurts
him all the more: "How to live loveless or not live ?" (190) He
could not destroy her place in his mind without maiming himself. What begins as adultery moves beyond sex. Both Pauline
and Levin confess their love to each other.

> 'I love you, Lev. That's my name for you. Sy is too much
> like sigh, Lev is closer to love. I love you, I'm sorry, you
> deserve better.'
> 'I deserve you.'
> 'I should never have let you that day in the woods. But I
> love the kind of man you are, the kind I have to love.'
> 'I love you willingly, with all my heart.' (191)

Levin, however, is not free from his sense of guilt. The question
of morality crops up for him when "a man interfered with
another's 'rights'." (192) He, however, consoles himself that
Gilley himself is not guiltless. He doubts whether Gilley
deserves Pauline's fidelity when he has not used his "rights"
well, "at the very least to keep her from sexual hunger."

Levin at last decides to tell the truth to Gilley but Pauline
asks him to wait till summer. Pauline's problem is that she
cannot unlove anyone she ever loved. Levin feels: "Now we
have truly come to adultery." (216) He had also earlier fearful
visions of trial for adultery, "the scarlet letter."

> Levin had sulphurous visions of himself as Arthur Dimmes-
> dale Levin, locked in stocks on a platform in the town
> square, a red A stapled on his chest, as President Labhart
> stood over him, preaching a hell-fire sermon denouncing
> communist adulterers, the climax of which was the public
> firing of Levin out of the college. (212)

Pauline's indecisive nature puzzles Levin. Without Pauline, he
is a "pathetic fallacy" of his own. He regrets that Pauline is
not the type who gives "all" for love. In a serious mood, Levin
discusses his affair with Pauline as a moral issue. Morality for
Levin is synonymous with compassion.

> Levin felt that the main source of conscious morality was
> love of life, anybody's life. Morality was a way of giving
> value to other lives through assuring human rights. As
> you valued men's lives yours received value. (222)

He feels that "we must protect the human, the good, the innocent." He thinks that the strongest morality does not brook
temptation. He decides to give up Pauline at least now for the
sake of morality. He sees in it the possibility of life.

> To be good, then evil, then good was no moral way of life,
> but to be good after being evil was a possibility of life.
> (223)

Levin, however, receives a set-back in his affair with Pauline
when Avis Fliss informs him that Pauline and Leo Duffy were
once lovers. Avis also tells him that Gilley took a picture of
Pauline and Leo naked on the beach. Levin hates Gilley for
the "betrayal perhaps worse than hers of him." (242) He is
also sorry that Pauline has kept the secret from him. He feels
at once the "victim of a lying life." He suspects that Pauline
must have loved him only to repeat Duffy.

Just when Levin tries to avoid Pauline, she decides to divorce Gilley and go with Levin. She confesses her failure to live with her husband despite her best efforts.

> He gives me little, I give him less. I try but fail with him, we fail together. I don't want to any more. I want a better life. I want it with you. (286)

She seeks "better life" with Levin. Levin is almost petrified at the unexpected decision of Pauline. His lurking suspicion incapacitates him to respond to her love. When asked about her affair with Duffy, Pauline frankly confesses her guilt. She informs him that Duffy committed suicide long back.

Although Levin's response to Pauline is now full of compassionate understanding, he is unable to experience the depth of his earlier love for her:

> In her mind she had parted from Gilley and was alone in his house, possibly frightened at all that lay ahead to be done. *He felt for her a blunted compassion, not enough to give relief but at least a response.* (290; Italics mine)

Levin has no regrets for the love he bore for Pauline "from forest to last frustration." He has recognised their mutual love and the need to live with it.

> I loved her; we loved. She loves me still, I have never been so loved. That was the premise, and the premise you chose was the one you must live with; if you chose the wrong one you were done to begin with, your whole life in jail. (291)

Levin cannot escape the love of Pauline for the sake of freedom. Even without feeling he would hold on to her out of compassion.

> No matter what he had suffered or renounced, to what degree misused or failed feeling, if Pauline loving him loves; Levin with no known cause not to will love her. He would without or despite feeling. *He would hold on when he wanted terribly to let go.* Love had led them, he would now lead

love. Having reasoned thus he cursed reason. (292; Italics mine)

Levin's love for Pauline is new cleansed of its sensuality. When Gilley comes to know of the affair, he accuses Levin of betrayal.

> You goddamn two-faced, two-assed, tin-saint hypocrite, preaching reform all the while you were committing adultery with my wife ! (295)

Levin resents the dastardly act of Gilley in taking the picture of his wife naked and showing it in public. Gilley warns Levin that he would be miserable if he married Pauline because of her discontented nature. He further proposes that he would forgive Levin if he left the place. Levin rejects the proposal.

Levin's affair with Pauline disadvantages the election he contests for Departmental Chairmanship. Gilley stoops to use it in his wily propaganda against Levin and succeeds. Levin loses the election to Gilley and also the hope of restoring liberal arts. As he rejects Gilley's offer to let him stay on on the condition that he would not meet Pauline again, he is fired out of his job like Leo Duffy "in the public interest, for good and sufficient cause of a moral nature." Levin feels shattered.

Levin's compassion for Pauline prompts him to agree to her request and persuade Gilley to let the adopted children be with her although it means a good deal of burden to him in the context. Gilley tries to exploit the predicament of Levin by asking him to give up college teaching altogether as a condition to let the children live with Pauline. Yet for the sake of Pauline, he agrees to Gilley's inhuman terms much to the surprise of the latter. Gilley could not understand why Levin invites so many problems at the cost of his career.

> An older woman than youself and not dependable, plus two adopted kids, no choice of yours, no job or promise of one, and other assorted headaches. Why take that load on you self ? (310)

Levin angrily retorts:

Because I can, you son of a bitch. (310)

Levin's assertion reveals the strength of his compassionate understanding.

Levin accepts Pauline with compassion when she tells him that she has been two-months pregnant by him. Levin does not allow Pauline to think of abortion in any case. He is decisive about the child and says: "I want the child." (314) As he drives Pauline and the two adopted children in his old Hudson, he even thinks of buying a seven-passenger car. As Tony Tanner points out "Levin has given up dreams for reality and has paradoxically found his freedom by willingly taking on the load of family commitments."[29] Having gone through "the Malamudian fire of passion and frustration, sacrifice and insight," Levin finds true freedom in "liberation from the prison of self."[30] He gives Pauline the gold hoop earrings which he had bought and kept for her. Levin's act is symbolic of his true love for her.

The final impression of Levin as he leaves the country is one of sad failure. He grumbles: "I failed this place." But although Levin failed to continue at Cascadia, he has not been completely a failure. He has been responsible for kicking out the boring text book *the Elements* after thirty years. His suggestion of "The Great Books Programme" for dissemination of great literature to one and all including the students of technology is accepted by the Dean. If Levin has not succeeded in transforming the college into a liberal arts college, he has been the driving force behind the flexible attitude of the Department towards humanities and literature. Perhaps this small achievement makes him differ from Leo Duffy, his predecessor.

The novel concludes with Gilley taking a snap of Levin and Pauline as they drove along by car and waving it aloft saying "Got your picture !" (316) Malamud interpreted it as a sign that Gilley will perhaps have been affected enough by Levin's and Pauline's commitments to learn something significant from the experience.[31] One tends to agree with Ruth Mandel that "the whole weight of Gilley's characterization in *A New Life* prevents the reader from arriving at Mr. Malamud's intention in the last line."[32] Gilley takes a diabolic pleasure as usual in snapping his wife with others. The last act confirms Gilley's unscrupulous character. Despite his weaknesses and errors, Levin stands in contrast to Gilley's inhumanity.

Levin, however, learns certain laws of politics from his experience at Cascadia—First, weak leaders favour weak leaders, the mirror principle in politics; second, one becomes his victim's victim; third, stand for something and somebody around will feed the persecuted. Levin's "Laws" apply to his own life. Gilley becomes the victim of Levin's love for Pauline, his wife. But ultimately Levin becomes Gilley's victim, i.e. "victim's victim." Levin stands for a good cause of education, but everyone including Gilley feels persecuted.

Levin's defeat appears quite natural in the corrupt Cascadia College. The "new life" he seeks with Pauline has compassion for its motivating force and it humanises his response to life.

Malamud meditates on the historic trial of Mendel Beiliss to shape his next novel, *The Fixer* and to bring home the truth that suffering not only chastens but becomes an agent of compassion in the evolution of man.

NOTES

1. Leslie Fiedler, "The many names of S. Levin: An Essay in Genre Criticism," *The Fiction of Bernard Malamud,* ed. Richard Astro and Jackson J. Benson (Corvallis: Oregon State Univ. Press, 1977) 150.

2. Malamud also says: "The purpose of the writer is to keep civilization from destroying itself." Quoted in Ihab Hassan, "The Hopes of Man," *New York Times Book Review* 13 Oct. 1963: 5.

3. Richard Astro, "In the Heart of the Valley: Bernard Malamud's *A New Life*," *Bernard Malamud*: *A Collection of Critical Essays*, ed. Field and Field (Englewood Cliffs, N.J.: Prentice-Hall, 1975) 143-55.

4. Daniel Stern, "Art of Fiction LII: Bernard Malamud," *The Paris Review* 16.61 Spring 1975: 57.

5. Leslie and Joyce Field, "An Interview with Bernard Malamud," *Bernard Malamud: A Collection of Critical Essays* 10.

6. John Hollander, "To find the Westward path," *Partisan Review* 29.1 Winter 1962: 138 and Sally Daniels, "Recent Fiction: Fights and Evasions," *The Minnesota Review* 2.4 Summer 1962: 553.

7. Robert O. Bowen, "The View from Beneath," *National Review* 2 December 1961: 384.

8. Louis D. Rubin, Jr., "Six Novels and S. Levin," *Sewanee Review* 70.3 (1962): 512.

9. Granville Hicks, "Hard Road to the Good Life," *Saturday Review* 44.40.7 Oct. 1961: 20.

10. Page Stegner, "Stone, Berry, Oates—and other Grist from the Mill," *Southern Review* 5.1 Winter 1969: 282.

11. Sandy Cohen, *Bernard Malamud and the Trial by Love* (Amsterdam: Rodopi N.V., 1974) 69.

12. Stanley Edgar Hyman, "A New Life for a Good Man," *Standards: A Chronicle of Books for Our Time* (New York: Horizon Press, 1966) 34.

13. Ruth B. Mandel, "Ironic Affirmation", *Bernard Malamud and the Critics*, ed. Field and Field (New York: New York Univ. Press, 1970) 263.

14. Jonathan Baumbach, *The Landscape of Nightmare: Studies in the Contemporary American Novel* (New York: New York Univ. Press, 1965) 105.

15. E.H. Leelavathi Masilomani, "Bernard Malamud: An Interview," *Indian Journal of American Studies* 9.2 July 1979: 35.

16. Field and Field, "Malamud, Mercy, and Menschlechkeit," *Bernard Malamud: A Collection of Critical Essays* 2.

17. Sheldon Norman Grebstein, "Bernard Malamud and the Jewish Movement," *Contemporary American Jewish Literature: Critical Essays*, ed. Irving Malin (Bloomington, London: Indiana Univ. Press, 1973) 193.

18. W.J. Handy, "The Malamud Hero: A Quest for Existence," *The Fiction of Bernard Malamud* 73.

19. Anthony Burgess, *The Novel Now: A Guide to Contemporary Fiction* (New York: W.W. Norton and Company, 1967) 197; and A.E. Hyman 33.

20. Sidney Richman, *Bernard Malamud* (New York: Twayne, 1966) 94.

21. Raymond M. Olderman, *Beyond the Wasteland: A Study of the American Novel in the Nineteen Sixties* (New Haven and London: Yale Univ. Press, 1976) 92.

22. David L. Stevenson, "The Strange Destiny of S. Levin," *The New York Times Book Review* 8 Oct. 1961: 28; and Sanford Pinsker, "Bernard Malamud's Ironic Heroes." *Bernard Malamud: A Collection of Critical Essays* 59.

23. Hyman 37.

24. Baumbach 104.

25. Grebstein 193.

26. Richard Astro, "In the Heart of the Valley," 150.

27. Astro 15-053.

28. Astro 152.

29. Tony Tanner, "A New Life," *City of Words: American Fiction 1950-1970* (London: Jonathan Cape, 1971) 332.

30. Theodore Solotaroff, "The Old Life and the New," *Bernard Malamud and the Critics* 244.

31. Quoted in Ruth B. Mandel 270.

32. *Loc. cit.*

5

GRACE UNDER PRESSURE: *THE FIXER*

*"Suffering I can gladly live without, I hate the taste
of it, but if I must suffer let it be for something."*

The Fixer*[1] is a probing study of suffering of a Jew at the
hands of anti-Semites. It delves into the human psyche and
evokes pathos most poignantly. It also stands unique in the
fictional world of Malamud for its imaginative treatment of
history. It is based on an actual historical incident of Jewish
persecution—the trial of Mendel Beiliss (1913) in Kiev for the
false accusation of "ritual murder" of a Christian child. The
Beiliss case has given Malamud as Alter suggests "a way of
approaching the European Holocaust on a scale that is imagi-
nable, susceptible, of fictional representation. For the Beiliss
case transparently holds within it the core of the cultural
sickness around which the Nazi madness grew."[1]

---

*Bernard Malamud, *The Fixer* (Harmondsworth, Middlesex: Penguin
Books, 1979). All subsequent references with page numbers in parantheses
are to this edition.

The accusation of "ritual murder" or what is termed "Blood Accusation" has not been uncommon in the history of the Jews. It could be traced back to the superstitious belief of the Medieval Period that the Jews kill a Christian male child on Passover and use his blood as a spray over their Passover *matzos* (the unleavened bread Jews eat during this holiday). Maurice Samuel, in his book *Blood Accusation*, explains:

> The Blood Accusation, as it is called, the accusation that the Jewish religion calls for the periodic ritualistic consumption of the blood of a Christian, was born in the Middle Ages at about the time of the First Crusade; ... The nineteenth century was particularly rich in such episodes, the most famous among them being those of Damascus (1860), Sarotov, Russia (1857), and Tissa-Eszlar, Hungary (1882). In the twentieth century, before the Beiliss case, there occurred, among others, the case of Blondes, the Jewish barber of Volna.[2]

Max I. Dimont exposes the baselessness of the charge:

> The fact that human sacrifice was something the Jews had fought against since the days of Abraham, while the Druids in England and Germany still practised it in the First century A.D., or the fact that Jews never eat the blood of animals, which is prohibited in the Old Testament, while Christians did and still do, even to this day, never crossed the medieval Christian mind.[3]

The accusation speaks of yet another of many injustices that the Jews suffered in the history. Malamud explores the fictional concerns of the history of Mendel Beiliss in *The Fixer* to depict human misery and injustice. He appears to accept the Sartrean view that the motivating force in the anti-Semite's bias is not the hatred of the Jew but a basic fear "of himself, of his instincts, of his responsibilities, of solitariness, of change, and of the world."[4] He "distils history into a parable of terror and absurdity resisted, superhumanly, to the last" and "restores to all men not merely justice or dignity but a place, a meaning, in the universe."[5]

In transforming fact into fiction, Malamud, however, does not limit himself to mere "factual reportage." He seeks the "imaginative fact." In his interview with Haskel Frankel, he explains:

> The Fixer is not factual reportage. As a writer I seek the imaginative fact. You can't make a thing more real than it is but you can make it seem more real through the imaginative fact.[6]

Malamud takes liberties with certain facts and turns history into a myth, *an endless story* in order to "disinvent history."[7] Yakov Bok, the fictional counterpart of Mendel Beiliss, becomes a "potential Vanzetti" for Malamud.[8] The suffering of Dreyfus and in fact every Jew in the Holocaust characterises the suffering of Yakov. Malamud could "relate feelingfully to the situation of the fate of the Jews in Hitler's Germany."[9]

Human predicament is viewed as a metaphor of prison. Commenting on the recurrent "prison motif" in his works pointed out by several critics, Malamud says:

> Perhaps I use it as a metaphor for the dilemma of all men; necessity whose bars we look through and try not to see. Social injustice, apathy, ignorance, guilt, obsession—the somewhat blind or blinded self, in other words. A man has to construct, invent his freedom. Imagination helps. A truly great man or woman extends it for others in the process of creating his/her own.[10]

Malamud's interest in "how some men grow as men in prison" has prompted him to turn to the Beiliss case abandoning his original desire to write a novel based on Sacco-Vanzetti and Dreyfus."[11] In *The Fixer* the central metaphor of Malamud coalesces with the action of the novel in its depiction of Yakov's travails in prison, and hence the poignancy of the tale.

The Fixer is in contrast as it were to Maurice Samuel's *Blood Accusations: The Strange Case of Beiliss* in the treatment of the subject. While Samuel gives a dispassionate account of Mendel Beiliss' trial based on authentic research, Malamud's

approach is imaginative and liberal. He is interested in the
psychological and moral development of the fixer and hence
never touches the aspect of the trial of Beiliss. Malamud's
concern has been to unfold the mind of Yakov Bok as he
suffers and endures. He explores the super-human endurance
of Yakov's suffering and grapples with "the Jewish problem
and the indomitability of the human spirit."[12] The change
brought about by suffering in Yakov's attitude to life is the
mainstay of the novel. Malamud remarks: "When I leave him
(Yakov), he is at the next step to commitment. The reason is
that he has suffered injustice. *What has happened to Yakov and
how he changes is the story.* But what happens to Yakov after
I leave him, I don't know."[13] (Italics mine) Malamud leaves
the novel open-ended and does not discuss the possibility of
Yakov's conviction or acquittal though Yakov's historical
counterpart Mendel Beiliss was acquitted in the trial. More
than historical fidelity, he is concerned about how a man is
dragged into history and politics despite his alienation. Hence
The Fixer becomes not "a Jewish story primarily but a political story, ultimately about all men."[14] It is "a statement of
every Jew's—everyman's—vulnerability to history."[15]

The *Fixer* invites comparison to Kafka's *The Trial*. Both
the novels highlight "the existential value of waiting."[16] While
The Fixer draws its strength from the fact that it provides a
hope of trial for Yakov and hints at his exoneration from the
cooked up charges, Joseph K of *The Trial* does not know why
he is arrested. He is executed even before the trial.

Yakov Bok, the protagonist of *The Fixer*, is an agnostic
and free-thinker. He feels the poverty-ridden *shtetl* and his
community for Kiev in search of a new life of material pros-
perity. Out of necessity he conceals his Jewish identity and
works in a district forbidden for the Jews. He comes to pay a
heavy price for this concealment. He has rescued out of compassion a member of Black Hundreds Organization and subse-
quently a Hasid. But the acts of compassion throw him into
a sea of troubles as his enemies distort the contexts to suit their
selfish designs. Yakov is suspected and arrested when one of
the Christian boys who chased the old Hasid is found dead,

His concealment of Jewish faith confirms the suspicion of the prosecuting officers. Yakov pleads his innocence in vain. The authorities cook up false charges and fabricate evidence against him to implicate him further in the case only to give vent to their sadistic anti-Semitism and to accuse the entire race of Jews as such of "ritual murder." They keep Yakov in prison for nearly three years without indictment or trial. They torture him inhumanly and bully him in all possible ways to extort the desired confession. Bibikov, the Investigating Magistrate, tries to rescue him. But he is jailed and forced to commit suicide. Kogin, the guard has a hidden sympathy for the suffering of Yakov. He is shot dead. *The Fixer* dramatises Yakov's expanding perception of reality through suffering in the gruesome backdrop of anti-Semitism. Yakov who wails helplessly at the start grows stubborn at the end. He endures suffering and spurns the prosecution's tempting offer of freedom. He proves that "human dignity can be maintained even at the most minimal levels of existence and among the most brutal examples of mankind."[17] Yakov who thinks earlier that "I am not a political person. . . . The world's full of it but it's not for me. Politics is not in my nature" (45) comes to the bitter realisation that there is no unpolitical man, especially an unpolitical Jew in the world. He who left his community now affirms to stand by it and for it. He decides "if I must suffer let it be for something." He makes a covenant with himself that he will protect the Jews "to the extent . . . he can." We find in him "the shift from egotistical self-concern to a sense of involvement with others."[18] He had left his wife Raisl earlier but now he attains such "radical innocence" devoid of hatred that he readily agrees to own the illegitimate child of Raisl on her request. The evolution in Yakov from isolation and escapism to commitment and compassion is wrought by his inordinate suffering. He attains the necessary "grace under pressure." Though Yakov thinks that "What suffering has taught me is the uselessness of suffering," Edwin Eigner points out that "suffering has taught him (Yakov) to "fear less," and to love Raisl whom he had hated, and to hate the Tsar, whose "loyal subject" he had been."[19]

Malamud's "metaphysic" of suffering in *The Fixer* con-
forms to Daniel Day Williams' "empirical" and "phenomeno-
logical" approach to suffering. Williams points to three aspects
of suffering as identification, communication and healing. He
remarks:

> Suffering does not remain a constant in the metaphysical
> situation. It points forward. It can be transmuted through
> being brought into a community of interpretation with a
> prospective dimension, that is with a hope for creativity
> beyond the present.[20]

Suffering leads to self-knowledge and communication with
others and thus becomes a power "to contribute to the fulfillment of life."[21] This is exactly what happens to Yakov in *The
Fixer*. Yakov suffers because he is "being acted upon."[22] He
is tortured for no fault of his. But suffering plays a significant
part in Yakov's self-knowledge which in turn becomes "the
entry into a significant community of selves."[23] As Williams
comments: "To know myself and to know another it is required that I allow suffering to have its part in defining who we
are."[24] The "shared suffering" becomes "a means of communication," in Yakov's case a vicarious communication with the
entire race of Jews as such. Yakov's resolve to suffer and live
and protect the Jews, his people "to the extent that he can"
is the new consciousness wrought on him by suffering. Suffering is objectified and thus becomes a healing power not only
"through love" as Williams suggests, but also through compassion as seen in Yakov.

Joseph Featherstone recognises Bok's evolution to compassion. He says: "In Bok you recognize the archetypal Malamud
hero, the ironic victim who grows in compassion as he
suffers."[25] Ben Siegel comments that Yakov's suffering has
"toughened his character and will, stripped him of arrogance
and false pride, and increased his compassion and charity,
thereby, enabling him, as Shmuel has admonished, "to fix his
heart."[26] Friedman writes on Yakov's suffering:

> First for only himself, then for Shmuel, and now for Raisl
> as well—Yakov, for all his initial alienation and continuing

agnosticism, has at last earned the right to suffer for others, and he begins to recognize that he is responsible for all his people, that long-suffering nation without a country, alienated by birth and history, whose trials and traditions Yakov had mocked by his rejection.[27]

Comparing Yakov Bok with Yasha Mazur of Isaac Bashevis Singer's *The Magician of Lublin*, Knopp finds "similarity of moral evolution" as both the heroes move from skepticism to acceptance of the ways of God and of the life of restraint and responsibility to his fellow man.[28] Yakov in fact accepts the ways of history and not of God and realises his commitment to community. Ruotolo makes an existential study of *The Fixer* while Gerald Hoag interprets the novel from the point of view of suffering as a means of defining self.[29] Tony Tanner analyses the novel as a fable of "man's reaction to the history he finds happening to him."[30] Yet the critical studies on *The Fixer* have not assessed the scope of the theme of compassion and its significance in the novel. *The Fixer* in fact offers a treatise on suffering and at the same time probes the psyche of Yakov, the victim. The wailings of Yakov appear quite natural and human in the context provided. They bring out a picture of pathos in its most evocative terms. The gradual evolution of Yakov highlights the chastening value of suffering.

II

Yakov Bok, a typical *schlemiel* is chosen for suffering. Like all Malamudian protagonists, he had a miserable past. He was born with "opportunity . . . born dead." His mother died ten minutes after his birth and his father was a chance victim of two drunken soldiers who "shot the first three Jews in their path, his father had been the second." (8) Practically a born orphan, he had to "dig with my fingernails for a living." (10) He says: "In my dreams I ate and I ate my dreams." (9) At the age of ten, he was apprenticed in the trade of a "fixer," a handyman. Despite his hard labour, he suffers from abject penury. His marriage with Raisl had been fruitless. Raisl ultimately eloped with some stranger. Yakov was conscripted

to the Russo-Japanese war which ended before he joined.
Because he was an asthmatic, he was discharged from the
services later. He grows at last sick of his life in the *shtetl*
which to him is like a prison, and decides to venture his new
life in Kiev. He thinks his knowledge of a decent Russian and
love of spinoza would fetch him a living there.

Yakov is hasty and overambitious. He dreams of "good
fortune, accomplishment, affluence." These dreams keep him
restless. Yakov tells his father-in-law:

> Those that can't sleep and keep me awake for company,
> I've told you what wants: a full stomach now and then. A
> job that pays troubles, not noodles. Even some education if
> I can get it, and I don't mean workmen studying Torah after
> hours. I've had my share of that. What I want to know is
> what's going on in the world. (15)

Yakov also exhibits an unusual haste in trying to wipe out his
identity as a Jew. He cuts his beard to give the semblance of a
goy and scorns the Jewish God. He wants to run away from his
community and God for the sake of his selfish benefits. He
could not understand the worldly wisdom of Shmuel, his father-
in-law.

> 'What's in the world,' Shmuel said, 'is in the shtetl—people,
> their trials, worries, circumstances. But here at least God is
> with us'.
> 'He's with us till the Cossacks come galloping, then he's
> elsewhere. He's in the outhouse, that's where he is.' (14)

Yakov fails to see that troubles haunt the Jew wherever he goes.

Yakov and Shmuel present a contrast in their inclinations
and character. Shmuel is a portrait of compassion. Yakov lacks
compassion. Yakov at first takes a harsh view of Raisl's
elopement and conveniently ignores his lack of responsibility.
He fails to understand the spirit of charity and compassion that
Shmuel talks about.

> 'Charity you can give even when you haven't got. I don't
> mean money. I meant for my daughter.'
> 'Your daughter deserves nothing.' (11)

When Yakov curses Raisl, Shmuel is very much agitated. He feels hurt by Raisl's act, yet does not wish her bad. But Yakov has no feeling for her. His lack of compassion is evident in his refusal to show charity to a shnorrer he confronts in his journey to Kiev, scornfully retorting the shnorrer's "Charity saves from death" with "Death is the last of my worries." Shmuel tries in vain to borrow a kopek from Yakov for the shnorrer.

Yakov's journey to Kiev is smooth and undisturbed as long as Shmuel accompanies him. But once Shmuel departs, Yakov's troubles begin. Frequently the horse stops, the right wheel of carriage breaks and the rear wheel collapses. His failure to force movement from the unwilling horse conveys "the psychological inability to project movement from within himself."[31] Yakov had to sell his horse to the boatman towards the cost of the trip to row him across the river Dnieper. He tastes for the first time the bitterness of anti-Semitism from the boatman who pleads for the annihilation of the entire race of Jews.

I don't mean kill a Zhid now and then with a blow of the fist or kick in the head, but wipe them all out, which we've sometimes tried but never done as it should be done. I say we ought to call our menfolk together, armed with guns, knives, pitchforks, clubs—anything that will kill a Jew—and when the church bells begin to ring we move on the Zhidy quarter, which you can tell by the stink, routing them out wherever they're hiding—in attics, cellars, or ratholes—bashing in their brains, stabbing their herring-filled guts, shooting off their snotty notes, no exception made for young or old, because if you spare any they breed like rats and then the job's to do all over again. (28-29)

The boatman is also certain that the Christians will accomplish the job soon and take their "rightful revenge."

At Kiev, "the Jerusalem of Russia," Yakov lives in constant fear of being recognized as a Jew. The thought of returning to *shtetl* is like death to him. Yakov's compassionate rescue of an over-drunken old man lying in snow helps him to get work.

The old man, however, turns out to be a member of the rabidly anti-Semitic Black Hundreds. Nikolai Maximovitch Lebedev, the oldman, and his crippled daughter Zinaida Nikolaevna are grateful to the fixer. Yakov conceals his identity from them and introduces himself as Yakov Ivanovitch Dologushev from provinces. When he gets work in the flat of Nikolai, he seeks to justify the concealment of his identity in terms of necessity.

> Who could afford to say no to forty roubles—a tremendous sum ? Therefore why worry about returning ? Go, do the job quickly, collect the money, and when you have it in your pocket, leave the place once and for all and forget it. After all it's only a job. I'm not selling my soul. When I'm finished I'll wash up and go. (41)

During his work in the flat, Yakov slightly escapes an affair with Zinaida which could have revealed his identity and opened the pandora's box. The fear of "being unmasked as a hidden Jew" continues to haunt Yakov as he had to work in a brick factory in a district forbidden for the Jews. He tries for the counterfeit papers but could not get them. At factory also, he is not happy. His honest efforts to curb corruption, though praised by Nikolai, are relished by none in the factory.

Yakov's misfortunes begin with his rescue of a Hasid from the boys who chase and injure him. He takes the Hasid home and wipes the blood off his beard with his tattered clothes. The Hasid takes out some matzo pieces, prays and eats. Yakov realises that it is passover. With great difficulty he conceals his deep feeling for it. Yakov gives shelter to the Hasid from the snow that night. He takes care not to be observed by anyone as he sends the Hasid off that morning in a sledge. He could not answer the question of the Hasid—"Why are you hiding here ?"

Yakov is shocked to hear the news of the murder of Zhenia Golov, a twelve year old boy, in a nearby ravine. He had chased Zhenia of the yard with his friend a few days ago. It is reported that that boy was stabbed at many points on his body and bled white "possibly for religious purposes." The Black Hundreds Organization avowedly anti-Semitic with the blessings of the Tsar at once exploits the murder for its campaign against Jews. They call it a "ritual murder." Yakov senses something messy and goes out to the printers for his counterfeit papers but finds the place burnt down. He plans to escape to Amsterdam but even before that he is arrested by the police in the name of His Majesty Nicholas the Second.

Yakov is in a state of "unrelieved distress" as he is carried on the road manacled and jeered by the crowd. Imprisoned in the underground cell in the District Courthouse, he realises and regrets his mistake in concealing his identity.

> He had stupidly pretended to be somebody he wasn't, hoping it would create 'opportunities,' had learned otherwise—the wrong opportunities—and was paying for learning, if they let him go now he had suffered enough. (68)

He blames his "egotism and foolish ambition." His quest for success turns to be an "opportunity to destroy himself." Yakov confesses "stupid deception" of hiding his identity with Bibikov, the Investigating Magistrate for Cases of Extraordinary Importance. He pleads innocence about the murder of the child.

> 'Never ! Never ! he cried hoarsely. 'Why would I kill an innocent child ? How could I have done it ? For years I wanted a child but my luck was bad and my wife couldn't have one. If in no other way at least in my heart I'm a father. And if that's so how could I kill an innocent child ? I couldn't think of such a thing, I'd rather be dead. (69)

Answering the various questions of Bibikov on his personal life and philosophical leanings, Yakov sums up his philosophy as "life could be better than it is." (73)

None sympathises with Yakov's predicament except Bibikov. Everyone gives false report and evidence against Yakov's conduct and character. Nikolai Lebedev, despite the honest service Yakov rendered to him, deposes that Yakov had been dishonest and deceitful. Nikolai's daughter, Zinaida, in her statement blames Yakov of having attempted a sexual assault on her. Yakov pleads his innocence desperately with Bibikov and reports the truth. Bibikov trusts Yakov and recommends slight punishment to Yakov only for his illegal residence. Grubeshov, the Prosecuting Attorney, and Colonel Bodyansky, the head of the secret police in Kiev, do not like Bibikov's decision. They are determined to doom Yakov. Grubeshov gets the baked matzos and blood-stained rags found in Yakov's house. He tries to connect them with the ritual murder of the Christian child.

The false testimony of Proshko, the foreman who nursed grievance against Yakov for preventing his corruption at the brickyard, comes handy to Grubeshov. Proshko blames Yakov of swindling money to help a synagogue in Podol. He asserts that he saw Yakov praying with a Hasid, baking matzos, and chasing Christian boys out of the brickyard for no reason. He insinuates the suspicion that Yakov and the Hasid had done some black magic to burn the stableyard though actually it was he and Richter that brunt it.

Finally Marfa Golov, the mother of the murdered child, identifies Yakov as "the Jew Zhenia told me about, who" had chased "him with a long knife." (107) She tells the officials that her son informed her more than once about his fear of the Jew in the brickyard. She concocts the story as told by her son and his friend Vasya.

I heard from the boys that this one here brought other Jews up in his stable. One was an old man with black satchel that the Lord knows what they did with. Zhenia once told this one to his face that he would tell the foreman if he chased him again. "And if you do that I'll kill you once and for all," said the Jew.... I warned Zhenia more than once not to go back there or he might get kidnapped and killed, and he promised me he wouldn't. I think he didn't for a time, then one night he came home frightened and feverish, and when I cried out, "Zhenia, what ails you, tell me quickly what happened?" he said that the Jew had chased him with a long knife in the dark among the gravestones in the cemetery. I got down on my knees to him. "Zhenia Golov, in the name of the Holy Mother, promise me not to go near that evil Jew again. Don't go in that brickyard." "Yes, dear Mamenka," he said "I will promise." That's what he said, but he went back in there again, anyway.

Boys are boys, your honour, as you already know. God knows what draws them to danger, but if I had kept him under lock and key in this house as I sometimes did when he was a little boy he'd be alive today and not a corpse in his coffin. (114-15)

A jar of jam on the table of Yakov is interpreted as a bottle of blood. Yakov cries: "Jam is not blood. Blood is not jam." (115) Marfa reports how the boy did not return home from school one day and due to her severe illness she could not enquire about it for a week at the end of which she found him dead in the cave. Bibikov could not see the logic of Marfa's argument. He cross-examines her regarding her secret connections with a gang of thieves in receiving stolen goods, about her throwing carbolic acid into the eyes of her lover and her lover beating her son severely once. But Grubeshov objects to Bibikov's enquiry considering it irrelevant to the "significant evidence" they are collecting. Their conversation reveals the prejudices of Grubeshov and the struggle of Bibikov for justice out of compassion for Yakov.

'What is the "significant evidence" you refer to ?'
'The evidence we have been engaged in collecting including the evidence of history.'
'History is not law.'
'We will see about that.' (117)

The speech of Father Anastasy on "ritual murder" at the cave where Yakov is taken to show the disinterred body of Zhenia, is inciting and provoking malice on the Jews. Quoting from scriptures and history, the priest tries to prove the custom of "ritual murder" among the Jews as a re-enactment of the crucifixion of Jesus Christ. He infers the conclusion that Zhenia's murder is also one such.

Here in our Holy city, during the Polovostian raids in the year 1100, the monk Eustratios was abducted from the Pechera Monastery and sold to the Jews of Kherson, who crucified him during Passover. Since they no longer

dare such open crimes they celebrate the occasion by
eating matzos and unleavened cakes at the Seder service.
But even this act conceals a crime because the matzos and
cakes contain the blood of our martyrs, though of course
the tzadikim deny this. Thus through our blood in their
Passover food they again consume the agonised body of the
living Christ. I give you my word, my dear children, that this
is the reason why Zhenia Golov, this innocent child who
wished to enter the priesthood was destroyed ! (122)

Yakov cries in vain that "It's all a fairy tale, every bit of it."

It's all right to theorize with a fact or two but I don't
recognize the truth in what's been said. If you please, your
reverence, everybody knows the Bible forbids us to eat
blood. That's all over the book, in the laws and everything.
I've forgotten most of what I knew about the sacred books,
but I've lived among the pepole and know their customs.
Many an egg my own wife would throw out to the goat if
it had the smallest spot of blood on the yolk. (122)

None cares for his explanation. Yakov hastily counts the
number of wounds on Zhenia's dead body and discovers that it
is not the magic number of Jews at ritual murder as alleged by
the priest. He shouts out the number but nobody pays attention to him.

Yakov feels abandoned and forsaken in the hostile world of
anti-Semitism. He fears death and regrets his fate: "I'm a fixer
but all my life I've broken more than I fix." (104) Despite his
frustration and helplessness, Yakov declines Grubeshov's offer
of freedom on condition that he should confess that the Jewish
nation urged him to commit the murder. He hates to sign the
false document and affirms his innocence. Grubeshov at first
persuades him, then subtly warns him of how "Jews were
executed in the not too distant past," and at last makes an open
threat.

'You can cry to Bibikov from now to doomsday,' he
shouted at the fixer, 'but I'll keep you in prison till the

flesh rots off your bones piece by piece. You will beg me to
let you confess who compelled you to murder that innocent
boy !' (130)

Yakov would rather allow his flesh rot in the prison than confess the crime he did not commit.

The suffering and torture of Yakov in the prison is most
gruesome and inhuman. Malamud narrates the inhuman
suffering with such "a compassionate and anguished imagination" that "the readers could be made to feel for this one
man what we could not possibly for the six million."[32]
Yakov finds it "perilous to be alive" under the worst
conditions of prison. His shifting from one prison to
the other adds only to his miseries. At the Kiev prison, Yakov
is imprisoned in a dark stinking cell. He is given a dress "smell-
ing of human sweat." The food offered is no better. One would
often find dead mice and cockroaches in the soup. Yakov who
fasts earlier, takes the same wretched food with little feeling
later. He is cursed at every stage by the authorities. Once
Yakov was cruelly forced to crawl on his wounded legs bleeding
down the stairs to the infirmary without any assistance. The
surgeon operates on his feet without administering anaesthetic
out of sheer hatred for the Jew.

> 'This is good for you, Bok,' said the surgeon. 'Now you
> know how poor Zhenia felt when you were stabbing him
> and draining his blood, all for the sake of your Jewish
> religion.' (169)

Yakov is condemned to an isolation cell closer to the warden.
He has to sleep in pitch darkness. The worst of Yakov's
sufferings comes from the unnecessary "searches" on his body.
The officials would lay him half-naked with only undershirt on,
touch and inspect every part of his body. The number of
searches on Yakov's body varied between three and six per day.
Added to the torture, Yakov has frequent attacks of asthma in
the bitter cold. Yakov is, however, given firewood to protect
himself from cold since "the higher-ups do not want his dying
on them." But he also suffers from diarrhoea and nausea
consequent on the secret poisoning of food by the officials. It

is only after six days of his fast that Yakov is allowed to take
food from the common pot. Yakov undergoes the mental
torture of indefinite waiting for indictment and trial which
always appear in the offing but never come.

Yakov feels the sting of anti-Semitism even from the co-
prisoners. Knowing his Jewish identity, his fellow-prisoners
Potseikin and Akymitch beat him black and blue. Everyone
jeers at him and looks with suspicion. Fetyukov strikes him on
the head, but later learning of his Jewish origin he pities him in
view of his personal experience with a Jew. Yakov is also cheated by Gronfein who pretends to be a sincere Jew and betrays
him to the Deputy Warden with false accusations. This earns
Yakov solitary confinement, "the greatest desperation the
fixer had known."

Yakov cannot understand why he has had "more than his
share of misery in a less than just world." Feeling at bay, he
spites the jealous God of Jews, blames the goyim for their
hatred of Jews and then curses himself. He seems to realise the
predicament of a Jew in history:

> There was no 'reason,' there was only their plot against a
> Jew, any Jew; he was the accidental choice for the sacrifice.
> He would be tried because the accusation had been made,
> there didn't have to be another reason. Being born a Jew
> meant being vulnerable to history, including its worst
> errors. Accident and history had involved Yakov Bok as he
> had never dreamed he could be involved. The involvement
> was, in a way of speaking, impersonal, but the effect, his
> misery and suffering, were not. The suffering was personal,
> painful, and possibly endless. (141)

Still imprisoned in his self, he wishes he were not the martyr
for all the Jews. He feels "entrapped, abandoned, helpless."
Yakov understands what was going on and yet he could not
still "resign himself to what had happened." He curses
history, anti-Semitism fate and the Jews.

In the desert of Yakov's suffering, Bibikov is an oasis of
compassion. Bibikov makes his lone venture to prove the truth
and defend innocence and law. In his investigation he discovers

that Marfa Golov and her lover had themselves committed the murder. He informs it to Yakov in prison.

My theory is that the murder was committed by Marfa Golov's gang of criminals and house-breakers, in particular her blinded lover, one Stepan Bulkin, who, thus, perhaps, revenged himself on her for the loss of his eyesight. The boy was grossly neglected by his mother. She is a wicked woman, stupid yet cunning, with the morals of a hardened prostitute. Zhenia had apparently threatened, possibly more than once, to expose their criminal activities to the District Police, and it is possible that the lover convinced her the child had to be done away with. Perhaps the incident occurred during a time of general drunkenness. The boy was killed, I am all but certain, in his mother's house, Bulkin taking the leading role in the beastly sacrifice. They obviously tortured the poor child, inflicting a large number of wounds on his body and soaking up the blood as it spurted forth, in order not to leave any telltale stains on the floor—I would imagine they burned the bloody rags—and finally plunging the knife deep into the child's heart. I have not been able to determine whether Marfa witnessed his death or had passed out drunk. (154)

Bibikov says he would pool out evidence and try to rescue Yakov by all means. He is worried about Yakov out of compassion and gives him moral courage.

Keep in mind, Yakov Shepsovitch, that if your life is without value, so is mine. If the law does not protect you, it will not, in the end, protect me. Therefore I dare not fail you, and that is what causes me anxiety—that I must not fail you. (159)

In the world of anti-Semitism and misanthropy, Bibikov is an exception. He is an embodiment of compassion and human values and regards Yakov as his own self. Obviously he is a misfit in an unjust and cruel world. He is arrested and put in a solitary cell next to Yakov. Yakov hears somebody's shouts,

cries, questions and beatings on the prison wall—all indistinguishable—from the cell next to his. Then he finds the dead
body of Bibikov "hung from a leather belt tied to the middle
bar of the open window, a fallen stool nearby." (162) We
learn later from Grubeshov that "He was arrested for pecul-
ting from official funds. While awaiting trial, overwhelmed by
his disgrace, he committed suicide." (204) But it is obvious
that Bibikov was killed for his compassionate attitude to
Yakov. No law could protect him.

Bibikov's death intensifies Yakov's agony and isolation.
Yakov's only hope is lost. He reflects:

> Who would help him now, what could he hope for? Where
> Bibikov had lived in his mind was a hopeless hole. Who
> would now expose the murderess, Marfa Golov, and her
> accomplices, and proclaim his innocence to the newspapers?
> Suppose she left Kiev, fled to another city—or country—
> would they ever lay eyes on her again? How would the
> world ever learn about the injustice that had been
> committed against an innocent man? (166)

His future lies before him as an endless series of questions
unanswered. He wails like a small child in desperation:

> 'Mama—Papa,' he cried out, 'save me! Shmuel, Raisl—
> anybody—save me! Somebody save me!' (166)

He walks madly in the narrow cell. To break "the monotony
of long stretches of time, "Yakov invents distractions. He
recalls Spinoza and how he was prosecuted for his ideas.
Spinoza was free in his thoughts, but Yakov's thoughts "added
nothing to his freedom." (187) Yakov is conscious of his
limitations. "Necessity freed Spinoza and imprisoned Yakov."
(188) The knowledge of Spinoza and his ideals could
not reduce the suffering of Yakov. It helps him "to tackle the
burdens of history, not with applicable precepts, but by the
example of resistant mental activity."[33] At times Yakov
recalls psalms he heard in childhood, and recites them aloud.
He imagines God on his side to fight his enemies but God

comes to him only in "a loud Ha Ha." He does not touch the prayer shawl and the phylacteries left in his cell by the officials to trap him. Even when he wears the prayer shawl, he does it only to protect him from the cold. He is still sick of the Jews, "their history, destiny, blood guilt." He curses: "What was being a Jew but an everlasting curse ?" (206)

Yakov recalls Raisl to pass time, but he has now a softened attitude to Raisl whom he had cursed earlier. He thinks "She had tied herself to the wrong future." After a few days, his thoughts turn inward and he probes his faults and failings instead of simply blaming Raisl. He feels sorry for "his bitterness of his accusations" that made her leave him.

Yakov feels sick of endless waiting in the gloomy cell without indictment or trial. He could not "foresee any future in the future." He is enraged at the anti-Semites instead of passively cursing them all by himself helplessly.

'Bastards !' he shouted through the peephole at the guards, prison officials, Grubeshov, and the Black Hundreds. 'Anti-Semites ! murderers !' (196)

At the courthouse where he is taken for indictment, Yakov resists the threats of Grubeshov despite the knowledge that the latter has gathered more than thirty "reliable" witnesses against him. Grubeshov makes the offer of freedom for confession with cunning solicitude. But Yakov does not yield. He knew "A confession . . . would doom him forever. He was already doomed." (203) He prefers wretched suffering to wrong confession.

The passage of time softens Yakov's attitude towards his religion. He becomes an orthodox Jew for some time. He breaks open the phylactery box left with him long back and reads with interest verses from Exodus and Deuteronomy found in the box. The Deputy Warden is excited at this "new evidence." But soon Yakov turns a Christian in his mind reading the New Testament slipped into his cell by Zhitnyak. He even tries to learn some of the verses by heart. He catches the true spirit of Christianity and wonders "How can anyone love Christ and keep an innocent man suffering in prison,"

Quoting from the Gospel of John, he argues with Kogin, the guard:

> 'In the Old Testament we're not allowed to eat blood. It's forbidden,' said Yakov. 'But what about these words: "Truly, truly, I say to you, unless you eat the flesh of the Son of man and drink His blood, you have no life in you; he who eats My flesh and drinks My blood has eternal life, and I will raise him up on the last day. For My flesh is food indeed, and My blood is drink indeed. He who eats My flesh and drinks My blood, abides in Me, and I in him." ' (210)

He obliges Kogin's request to read out from the New Testament. He is not, however, prepared to forgo his identity now. When the priest enters his cell one day and asks him to embrace the Christian faith for sympathetic reconsideration of his case, Yakov declines through his posture that silently affirms Jewishness.

> Yakov stood in the dim light, motionless at the table, the prayer shawl covering his head, the phylactery for the arm bound to his brow. (213)

Yakov's refusal as traced by Gerald Hoag comes "not so much from hostility as from a need to affirm his innocence and to stand independent of the whole alien system that accuses him. It is a positive act."[34]

Yakov, who was formerly sick of the Jews and their history, now evinces keen interest in them. He reads the tattered pages of the Old Testament thrown into his cell—"gripped by the narrative of the joyous and frenzied Hebrews, doing business, fighting wars, sinning and worshipping." (216) He realises his predicament. He can neither understand God like a religious Jew, nor can he grasp the nature of Spinoza's God.

> So he suffers without either the intellectual idea of God, or the God of the covenant; he had broken the phylactery. Nobody suffers for him and he suffers for no one except himself. (217)

This ambivalent attitude is due to his sense of isolation. Yakov still remains an unbeliever in Jewish God and comments with Shmuel during his secret visit:

> To win a lousy bet with the devil he killed off all the servants and innocent children of Job. For that alone I hate him, not to mention ten thousand pogroms. Ach, why do you make me talk fairy tales ? Job is an invention and so is God. Let's let it go at that. (232)

Yakov writes off God who is cruel and indifferent to human fate. He persists in being a free-thinker despite the pleas made by Shmuel.

Chained and manacled to the wall like an animal all day and allowed to sleep on the bedplank with "his legs locked in the stocks" consequent on Shmuel's secret visit, Yakov finds no meaning in life.[35]

> In chains all that was left of freedom was life, just existence; but to exist without choice was the same as death. (240)

Malamud narrates the drudgery of time in an emphatic prose:

> One day crawled by. Then one day. Then one day. Never three. Nor five or seven. There was no such thing as a week if there was no end to his time in prison. If he were in Siberia serving twenty years at hard labour, a week might mean something. It would be twenty years less a week. But for a man who might be in prison for countless days, there were only first days following one another. The third was the first, the fourth was the first, the seventy-first was the first. The first day was the three thousandth. (239)

Yakov thinks of suicide. Yet he wants others to be involved in his death; so he would provoke the officials to kill him during the "searches" on his body. Suffering has chastened Yakov and he realises in an epiphanic moment that he should live and die for others. In one of his hallucinations, Yakov sees Shmuel dying. He wakes up and cries "Live Shmuel. . . . Live. Let me die for you." (245) Shmuel's vision prompts Yakov to live

meaningfully for the sake of others. He grows mature and
realises that his fate is tied with all the Jews. He questions himself: "how can I die for him (Shmuel) if I take my life ?" Death
may liberate him from the horrible suffering, but that should
not be the cause of the others' death.

> What have I earned if a single Jew dies because I did ?
> Suffering I can gladly live without, I hate the taste of it, but
> *if I must suffer let it be for something. Let it be for Shmuel.*
> (245; Italics mine)

Yakov breaks the shell of self-imprisonment and reaches for
others. He wants to live, suffer and die not for his relief from
pain, but for Shmuel first, and then for all the Jews. He has at
last realised that his suffering is not merely personal but historical and represents all the Jews.

> To the goyim what one Jew is is what they all are. If the fixer
> stands accused of murdering one of their children, so does
> the rest of the tribe. Since the crucifixion the crime of the
> Christ-killer is the crime of all Jews. 'His blood be on us
> and our children.' (245-246)

Although Yakov has not been a religious Jew, he identifies
himself completely with the Jews and their disastrous fate. From
his hatred he wakes up to pity the history of Jews and their
sub-human existence. He makes a new covenant with himself to
be bound with people and to protect them.

> He's half a Jew himself. Yet enough of one to protect them.
> After all, he knows the people; and he believes in their right
> to be Jews and live in the world like men. He is against
> those who are against them. *He will protect them to the
> extent that he can.* This is his covenant with himself. If
> God's not a man he has to be. Therefore he must endure to
> the trial and let them confirm his innocence by their lies.
> He has no future but to hold on, wait it out. (246; Italics
> mine)

In his decision to live, Yakov attains a new maturity and moral strength of compassion. It is motivated more by his compassion for mankind than by his hatred for anti-Semites. We cannot agree with Grebstein's remark: "Hate for his tormentors sustains him much more than love for mankind."[36] The more Yakov suffers, the stronger is his will to live and defy injustice. He is ready to wait endlessly:

> If I live, sooner or later they'll have to bring me to trial. If not Nicholas the Second, then Nicholas the Third will. (253)

He understands that the purpose of freedom is to create freedom for others as Bibikov exhorts in one of Yakov's visions.

Yakov's moral transformation is evident in his attitude to Raisl who meets him in the prison. During the conversation, he blames her for her elopement but cannot bypass his own failings pointed out by Raisl. On introspection, Yakov confesses his drawbacks and blames it all on himself.

> I've thought about our life from beginning to end and I can't blame you for more than I blame myself. If you give little you get less, though of some things I got more than I deserved. Also, it takes me a long time to learn. Some people have to make the same mistake seven times before they know they've made it. That's my type and I'm sorry. I'm also sorry I stopped sleeping with you. I was out to stab myself, so I stabbed you. Who else was so close to me? *Still I've suffered in this prison and I'm not the same man I once was.* What more can I say, Raisl? If I had my life to live over, you'd have less to cry about, so stop crying. (259; Italics mine)

Suffering has changed Yakov. He is sympathetic and compassionate to Raisl. He is even ready to own her bastard child, Chaim, as his son for her sake. He writes in Yiddish on a piece of paper without being observed by the guard:

> I declare myself to be the father of Chaim, the infant son of my wife, Raisl Bok. He was conceived before she left me.

> Please help the mother and child, and for this, amid all my
> troubles, I'll be grateful. Yakov Bok. (262)

His moral steadfastness is evident in his refusal to sign the
papers of confession sent by Grubeshov through Raisl as a last
resort to throw the blame of murder on the Jews. Instead of
signing, he writes on the paper that "Every word is a lie."
Tony Tanner finds here "the key moment" of the book: "He
(Yakov) refuses to betray other people in the interest of personal comfort; and he willingly takes on the role of father to a
child not his own. In the Malamud world this is the heroic
moment."[37] In his visionary confrontation with the Tsar,
Yakov replies to the Tsar's question that he is a father "with
all my heart."

   Yakov also refuses to be pardoned as a criminal on the eve
of the three-hundredth anniversary of the rule of the House of
Romanov. The former Jurist of high repute who brought this
proposal of pardon to Yakov could not understand what
difference would it make whether Yakov was pardoned as a
criminal or innocent. But Yakov insists on a "fair trial, not a
pardon," though it earns him further torture. Yakov doubts,
"would they, after this indictment, or the third, seventh, or
thirteenth *at last* bring him to trial?" or "Would they keep him
in chains for ever?" (267) But this scepticism is not born of
self pity.

   Yakov prefers to break rather than bend before Grubeshov
who bullies him to the his line and warns him of a foreboding
tragedy on all the Jews even if he won the trial.

> A trial will not save you nor your fellow Jews. You would
> be better off confessing, and after a period of time when the
> public has settled down, we could announce your death in
> prison, or something of the sort, and spirit you out of
> Russia. If you insist on the trial, then don't be surprised if
> bearded heads roll in the street. Feathers fly. Cossack
> steel invades the tender flesh of young Jewesses. (269)

Despite the threats and insinuations, Yakov wants to compromise with none on the trial. He has now the necessary moral
courage to meet Grubeshov's threats with a rebuff:

'Mr Grubeshov, bring me to trial. I will wait for the trial, even to my death.'

'And death is what you will get. It's on your head, Bok.'

'On yours,' said Yakov. 'And for what you did to Bibikov.' (270-71)

Yakov gradually grows to understand the fate of a Jew. He thinks that his suffering is due to personal fate, "his various shortcomings and mistakes" and also "force of circumstance" though both of them are indistinguishable for a Jew. He realises that in or out the Jew is haunted by history. It is as though a Jew carried on his back, wherever he went, "a condition of servitude, diminished opportunity, vulnerability." (282) It is not necessary to go to Kiev, Moscow or any other place for such fate. Yakov accepts this bitter reality. His learning will not free him from the prison literally. Still he feels it is better than not knowing. "A man had to learn, it was his nature." (283) Yakov is also conscious of change in him. He feels Bibikov in a vision:

Something in myself has changed. I am not the same man I was. I fear less and hate more. (286)

Yakov's hatred for the Tsarist officials is, of course, motivated by his intense compassion for the wronged Jewish community.

Yakov's confrontation with the Tsar in his reverie on his way to trial unfolds his militancy. His passive suffering changes into a potential rage. The passive and self-pitying Tsar appears nothing but the projection of the fixer's former self.[38] The Tsar pretends to be innocent and neutral.

But I am—I can truthfully say—a kind person and love my people. Though the Jews cause me a great deal of trouble, and we must sometimes suppress them to maintain order, believe me, I wish them well. As for you, if you permit me, I consider you a decent but mistaken man—I insist on honesty—and I must ask you to take note of my obligations and burdens. After all, it isn't as though you yourself are

unaware of what suffering is. Surely it has taught you the
meaning of mercy ? (298)

Yakov refuses to learn the message of mercy from the inhuman
Tsar. He curtly says that suffering has taught him merely the
uselessness of suffering. He indicts the Tsar for his inhumanity
and lack of charity and compassion.

Your poor boy is a haemophiliac. Something missing in the
blood. In you, in spite of certain sentimental feelings, it is
missing somewhere else—the sort of insight, you might call
it, that creates in a man charity, respect for the most
miserable. You say you are kind and prove it with pogroms.
(298-99)

The Tsar evades the responsibility of pogroms, calling them
"a genuine expression of the will of the people." Yakov does
not tolerate the hypocrisy and shoots the Tsar with his revolver
for the injustice he heaped on the innocent people.

This is also for the prison, the poison, the six daily searches.
It's for Bibikov and Kogin and for a lot more that I won't
even mention. (299)

Yakov's anger against the Tsar is a just anger since it came
out of his intense suffering for no fault of his own. Perhaps he
would free the Jews from the atrocities of the Tsar by killing
him. It is a positive act emerging out of compassion for his
fellow-beings. Waking from the vision Yakov thinks, "What
the Tsar deserves is a bullet in the gut. Better him than us."
(299) He is clear in his mind about one's role in politics and
history.

One thing I've learned, he thought, there's no such thing
as an unpolitical man, especially a Jew. You can't be one
without the other, that's clear enough. You can't sit still
and see yourself destroyed. (299)

He thinks that without fight, there is no freedom and recalls
Spinoza's saying "If the state acts in ways that are abhorrent
to human nature it's the lesser evil to destroy it." He becomes

a fiery revolutionary advocating the cause of justice and human values. He shouts: "Death to the anti-Semites ! Long live revolution ! Long live liberty !" (299)

The response of the people in the street to Yakov is varied. Somebody throws a bomb at the carriage injuring the leg of a policeman.

> Some, as the carriage clattered by and they glimpsed the fixer, were openly weeping, wringing their hands. One thinly bearded man clawed his face. One or two waved at Yakov. Some shouted his name. (300)

All is not lost; the fixer has won at least the sympathy of a few and infused heroic spirit in some who shouted his name. Despite his inclinations to be withdrawn, he has become a public figure. The novel ends abruptly at this point. It does not tend to narrate the long-awaited trial of the fixer.

The actual exoneration of Mendel Beiliss in the trial is of little consequence to Malamud, for he is chiefly concerned with the process of transformation of the fixer under the stress of suffering. The social fact is less weighty than the individual attitude. Tony Tanner remarks:

> The trial is not a matter of sentence or acquittal but the imprisoned years which preceded it, during which a man has the chance to derive some meaning from what he is caught up in. It is in the prison not in the courtroom, that a man must win his freedom and earn a new life. And what the judges will finally say is less important than man's developing attitude as he moves towards his last reckoning.[39]

Malamud wanted to write "a gutsy, triumphant book, not a book about defeat and sorrow."[40] He finds the triumph of the fixer in his attainment of compassion as "grace under pressure." The fixer's existence acquires meaning for his positive act of responding to history with a feeling or responsibility towards the Jews.

It is interesting to note that change in technique of narration hints at a change in the development of the fixer. The sixth

chapter of Part Six turns to first person narrative in the present
tense as Yakov recalls Raisl. It marks the dawn of sympathy in
Yakov for Raisl. Yakov who cursed her earlier thinks of her
with sympathy realising that "she had tied herself to the wrong
future." (193) The second chapter of Part Eight is written in
the "historic present" to dramatise the fixer's stubborn will to
live and resist injustice for the sake of his community. His
decision to protect the Jews "to the extent that he can" signals
the crucial transformation of Yakov. Malamud employs Monig
Wittig's technique of using the second person "you" in the
present tense in the first paragraph of chapter 7 of Part Six to
dramatise the thoughts of Yakov for freedom in an impersonal
way.

The Fixer employs with conscious artistic purpose the
language and technique of narration to define the theme of
compassion with mythic undertones. Malamud could refer to
the novel with justice as "the best book I ever wrote."[41]

The next novel *Pictures of Fidelman* narrates an American
Jew's futile experiments with art and sex in Italy and his final
espousal of life and its values.

NOTES

1. Robert Alter, "Malamud as a Jewish writer," *Commentary* 42.33 September 1966: 74.

2. Quoted in Maurice Friedberg, "History and Imagination
   —Two views of the Beiliss Case," *Midstream* 12.9
   November 1966: 74.

3. Max I. Dimont, *Jews, God and History* (New York:
   Signet Books, 1964) 234.

4. Jean-Paul Sartre, *Anti-Semite and Jew*, trans. A.J.
   Becker (New York: Schocken Books, 1968) 52-53.

5. Ihab Hassan, "Bernard Malamud," *The Contemporary
   Novelists* (London: St. James Press, 1976) 877.

6. Haskel Frankel, "Interview with Bernard Malamud,"
   Saturday Review 10 Sept. 1966: 39.

7. Frankel 39.

8. Daniel Stern, "The Art of Fiction LII: Bernard Malamud," *The Paris Review* 16.61 Spring 1975: 54.

9. Field and Field, "An Interview with Bernard Malamud,"
   Bernard Malamud: A Collection of Critical Essays
   (Englewood Cliffs, N.J.: Prentice-Hall, 1975) 10.

10. Daniel Stern 54.

11. Field and Field, "An Interview with Bernard
    Malamud," 10.

12. Stephen Farber, "The Fixer," *Hudson Review* 22.1
    Spring 1969: 135.

13. Frankel 39.

14. George P. Elliott, "Yakov's Ordeal," *The New York
    Times Book Review* 4 Sept. 1966: 26.

15. Joseph Featherstone, "Bernard Malamud," *Atlantic*
    219.3 March 1967: 97.

16. Amiya Dev, "The Victims in Malamud: A Note on
    The Fixer," *Asian Response to American Literature*
    (Delhi: Vikas, 1972) 300.

17. Jeffrey Helterman, "Bernard Malamud," *Dictionary
    of Literary Biography* (Detroit, Michigan: A Bruccoli
    Clark Book, 1978) 2: 300.

18. Tony Tanner, *City of Words: American Fiction 1950-
    1970* (London: Jonathan Cape, 1971) 337.

19. Edwin M. Eigner, "The Loathly Ladies," *Bernard
    Malamud and the Critics*, ed. Field and Field (New
    York: New York Univ. Press, 1970) 105.

20. Daniel Day Williams, "Suffering and Being in Empirical
    Theology," *The Future of Empirical Theology*, ed.
    Bernard E. Meland (Chicago and London: The Univ.
    of Chicago Press, 1969) 193.

21. Williams 179.

22. Williams 181.

23. Williams 183.

24. *Loc. cit.*

25. Joseph Featherstone 97.

26. Ben Siegel, "Through a Glass Darkly: Bernard
    Malamud's painful views of the Self," *The Fiction of*

Bernard Malamud, Astro et al (Corvallis: Oregon State Univ. Press, 1977) 136.

27. Alan Warren Friedman, "The Hero as Schnook," *Bernard Malamud and the Critics* 301.

28. Josephine Zadovsky Knopp, *The Trial of Judaism in Contemporary Jewish Writing* (Chicago: Univ. of Illinois Press, 1975) 115.

29. Lucid P. Ruotolo, "Yakov Bok," *Six Existential Heroes: The Politics of Faith* (Cambrigde, Mass.: Harvard Univ. Press, 1973) and Gerald Hoag, "Malamud's Trial: *The Fixer* and the Critics," *Western Humanities Review* 24.1 Winter 1970: 9.

30. Tanner 334.

31. Ruotolo 125.

32. Granville Hicks, "One man to stand for Six Million," *Saturday Review* 10 Sept. 1966: 37.

33. Tanner 336.

34. Hoag 7.

35. Malamud explains that the idea of Yakov in chains came to him from Dreyfus: "There were rumors that Dreyfus would escape through the aid of Jewish forces. To prevent that, they actually built a wall around his cell and placed a guard in the cell of Dreyfus. From that came the idea of Yakov in chains, something that didn't happen to Mendel Beiliss." See Haskel Frankel 39.

36. Sheldon Norman Grebstein, "Bernard Malamud and the Jewish Movement." *Contemporary American Jewish Literature: Critical Essays,* ed. Irving Malin (Bloomington, London: Indiana Univ. Press, 1973) 183.

37. Tanner 337.

38. Ruotolo 139.

39. Tanner 338.

40. Saul Maloff's Interview with Malamud, "Schlemiel Triumphant," *Newsweek* 68.11, 12 Sept. 1966: 110.

41. Maloff 109.

6

ART IS NOT LIFE: *PICTURES OF FIDELMAN*

"Then you are responsible. Because you are a man. Because you are a Jew, aren't you ?"

*Pictures of Fidelman,** cast in the mould of picaresque novel, makes a departure from the author's earlier novels both in its technique and tenor. It is a burlesque of an American-Jew's adventures with painting and sex in Italy. Fidelman's various roles as researcher, painter, pilferer, forger and pimp become farcical. The various facets or pictures of Fidelman are exhibited in the six related stories which have been done into a novel. Five of these six stories had earlier appeared in various journals and Malamud's collections of stories.[1] Malamud got the idea of writing the novel soon after he wrote his first story on Fidelman. He explains: "Right after I wrote 'The Last Mohican,' in Rome in 1957, I worked out an outline

---

*Bernard Malamud, *Pictures of Fidelman: An Exhibition* (Harmondsworth: Penguin Books, 1980). All subsequent references with page numbers in parantheses are to this edition.

of other Fidelman stories, the whole to develop one theme in
the form of a picaresque novel "[2]   The movement of plot
becomes occasionally jerky affecting the thematic coherence of
the novel.

Critical opinion is sharply divided about the technical
experiment of Malamud in this novel. Jeffrey Helterman considers *Pictures of Fidelman* "not precisely a novel, but rather
a series of vignettes built around a single character—a Jewish
American art student, who later becomes a struggling artist
and finally a successful artisan, named Arthur Fidelman."[3]
Howard M. Harper, Jr., however, finds in it "the unity,
coherence, and dimensions of a novel—and a very fine one."[4]
He describes it as an "organic whole, a rich and coherent view
of art and life, and of the relation between them."[5] While
Charles Stetler calls it a triumph from all literary considerations,[6]
Pete Axthelm is convinced that it is "hardly a major triumph."[7]
Walter Sullivan dismisses it as "a bad novel which is charac-
terized by passages of good prose that inevitably flounder in a
morass of vulgarity."[8] It is, however, true that the novel lacks
the tight organic structure of *The Fixer* or *The Assistant*. The
six chapters refract various shades of Fidelman's life and jump
from one episode to the other sometimes leaving the threads
of continuity. Malamud himself conceived it as "a loose novel,
a novel of episodes, like a picaresque piece."[9] Despite the
looseness of structure, the novel gains interest for its depiction
of complexity of a rich and varied life.

The novel mainly deals with the question of relation of art
to life. The answers that emerge in the novel are, as Sheldon
Norman Grebstein points out, "anti-formalistic."[10]   Art is
rooted in life and presupposes an awareness of but not an
escape from the responsibilities of life. The terms art and life
are not antithetical for Malamud. In an interview Malamud
comments on the theme of the novel as follows:

> It isn't life versus art necessarily; it's life *and* art. On
> Fidelman's tombstone read: 'I kept my finger in art.' The
> point is I don't have large thoughts of life versus art; I try
> to deepen any given situation.[11]

Malamud describes Arthur Fidelman as an "artist-manque, the man who wants to find himself in art."[12]   The crux of the problem for Fidelman springs from his relation between art and life. Consequently he fails in his egotistic adventures of painting and sex. He occasionally realises the responsibilities of life guided by the symbolic figures like Susskind and Beppo. "Fidelman's ups and downs," as Guy Davenport remarks, "are variously hilarious and pathetic, for Mr. Malamud is interested in the wear and tear on his soul rather than the trials of his ineptitude."[13] Malamud is concerned with the moral growth of Fidelman and this gives the novel thematic unity with his fiction. Fidelman learns "less how to paint than how to live."[14] During his travel through various Italian cities and in pursuit of different occupations, Fidelman comes to know of his own inadequacies and failures. Regarding the problem of choice referred to by Yeats in the epigraph of the novel that "The intellect of man is forced to choose/Perfection of the life, or of the work," Fidelman makes a greedy demand asking for "Both" and sets out on his travel to Italy. He achieves neither because of his egotism. Fidelman's refusal to give up his suit for Susskind and to return the money to the frustrated visitor of his underground exhibition of holes and his act of stealing his own painting—all betray his self-love and egotism. He has, however, brief moments of transcendence when he offers Susskind his suit even after losing his chapter on Giotto and when he visits his dying sister leaving his cave of art. Jeffrey Helterman remarks: "In his Italian journey, the hero has changed from a dabbler (one who fiddles around) to a man of faith (fidel) in love and life."[15] Fidelman is disillusioned with his pursuit of art and returns to life. Although his decision to leave Beppo, his homosexual companion and also the city of Venice is coupled with a sense of responsibility for Beppo's wife, Margherita, the meaning of love remains elusive for Fidelman as he has not had the deep sense of compassion felt in the portrayal of Frank Alpine or Yakov. The theme of compassion has been very feebly treated in the momentary revelations at the end of the stories "Last Mohican," "A Pimp's Revenge," and "Portraits of the Artist." But the theme is not realised integrally. There is neither evolution nor consistency in the life of Fidelman. The novel however deserves interpretation in the larger perspective of Malamud's concern with compassion. "Last Mohican" alone to some extent has received critical attention in this context by critics like D.R. Mesher, Sam Bluefarb and Sidney Richman.

II

Pictures of Fidelman opens for the reader a gallery of pictures of Fidelman's life. The first chapter "Last Mohican" introduces Fidelman, "a self-confessed failure as a painter," coming to Italy from America to finish his study of Giotto. He carries with him the opening chapter in his new pigskin leather brief-case. His mind is full of the thoughts of history. He wants to lead a "tightly organized life," devouring himself on books, paintings and museums. He is poor but ambitious, and with the financial help of his sister, he arrives at Italy where he happens to meet Shimon Susskind, "a person of about his own height, oddly dressed in brown knickerbockers." Susskind is a schnorrer or a *luftmentsch* who lives by wit and eating "air." He is a wanderer from Israel always "running." He represents the true Jew of the past, "stateless" and does not even want to go back to Israel, his home country.

The confrontation between Fidelman and Susskind is interesting because Susskind plays the role of doppelganger of Fidelman. It follows the technique of "the story of the double" as Susskind finally helps Fidelman in self-recognition.[16] Susskind represents that part of Fidelman which represents his heritage and conscience.[17] Fidelman's refusal to part with his extra suit to the poor Susskind reveals his selfish interests and lack of compassion. He tries to evade Susskind and be free from any obligation to him as a fellow-Jew and human being. It is like a flight from one's own conscience. Fidelman lives in his own world of history, sees "flights of angels—gold, blue, white—intermingled in the sky," (17) and forgets the human aspect of it. Susskind, however, haunts him ceaselessly. Goldman remarks: "He follows the pedantic art critic through Rome like the shadow of a history Fidelman has forgotten in pursuit of a history he hardly understands."[18] Susskind renews his request for the suit at the hotel. Fidelman pleads his inability.

> 'Listen, Susskind,' Fidelman said gently. 'I would gladly give you the suit if I could afford to, but I can't. I have barely enough money to squeeze out a year for myself here. I've already told you I am indebted to my sister. (18)

Susskind refuses all the alternatives suggested by Fidelman. Fidelman grows sick of the refugee's alibis. He does not know why he should be responsible for Susskind. He bluntly questions him, "Am I responsible for you then, Susskind?" (19) Susskind asks in turn "Who else?"

> 'Lower your voice, please, people are sleeping around here,' said Fidelman, beginning to perspire. 'Why should I be?'
> 'You know what responsibility means?'
> 'I think so.'
> 'Then you are responsible. Because you are a man. Because you are a Jew, aren't you?' (19)

Susskind's claim hints at the interpersonal responsibility of man to man and of a Jew to another. This responsibility could be felt only when one has compassion at heart. Fidelman is not ready to share the suffering of the Jewish victim. He retorts:

> Yes, goddamn it, but I'm not the only one in the whole wide world. Without prejudice, I refuse the obligation. I am a single individual and can't take on everybody's personal burden. I have the weight of my own to contend with. (19)

He is concerned about his own problems and not anybody else's. He tells Susskind:

> To my mind you are irresponsible and I won't be saddled with you. I have the right to choose my own problems and the right to my privacy. (21)

Fidelman does not want to be "saddled" with anyone's fate.
He refuses to come out of the shell of his egotistic world.
Susskind at least expresses his wish to give him something if
he had anything with him.

Fidelman's inadequate human responses could be seen in
his eagerness to get rid of Susskind, and in his acts of with-
holding and giving only under duress.[19] He plans to leave for
Florence a week earlier only to be free from Susskind, "the
pest." But surprisingly enough, he finds his briefcase with the
chapter on Giotto in it stolen from his room. It strikes him
that Susskind must have stolen it out of pique. The roles are
reversed now. It is the turn of Fidelman to pursue Susskind
madly.

Fidelman feels wretched at the loss of the chapter on Giotto
and spends sleepless nights.

> Sometimes he smiled wryly at all this; ridiculous, the chapter
> grieved him for itself only—the precious thing he had
> created then lost—especially when he got to thinking of the
> long diligent labour, how painstakingly he had built each
> idea, how cleverly mastered problems of order, form, how
> impressive the finished product, Giotto reborn ! It broke
> the heart. (28)

He reports the loss to the police but does not mention Susskind
out of fear of the "consequences." Being a methodical scholar,
he fails to proceed in his research without the first chapter.
Nor could he recollect and reconstruct the chapter despite
his hard labour. He feels "a murderous hatred" for Susskind
and curses him.

Fidelman's pursuit of Susskind has also symbolic overtones.
As Goldman points out, what Fidelman pursues is "the real
missing chapter of his own past, of himself."[20] Fidelman has
searched for Susskind in the synagogue and the ghetto. The
beadle in the ghetto advises him to "Look in the ghetto."
Fidelman says, "I Looked." But the beadle asks him to look
again. These words point out that Susskind is part of the
ghetto life. It is also a sort of symbolic exhortation to Fidelman for the realisation of his identity with his people in the

ghetto. Fidelman comes into contact with the miserable ghetto
life in his search for Susskind.

> The ghetto lay behind the synagogue for several crooked
> well-packed blocks, encompassing aristocratic palazzi
> ruined by age and unbearable numbers, their discoloured
> facades strung with lines of withered wet wash, the
> fountains in the piazzas, dirt-laden, dry. And dark stone
> tenements, built partly on centuries-old ghetto walls,
> inclined towards one another across narrow, cobblestoned
> streets. In and among the impoverished houses were the
> whole-sale establishments of wealthy Jews, dark holes ending
> in jewelled interiors, silks and silver of all colours. In the
> mazed streets wandered the present-day poor, Fidelman
> among them, oppressed by history although, he joked to
> himself, it added years to his life. (27)

Fidelman's visits to the Jewish cemetery where Susskind is said
to pray for the dead for fees, also exposes him to the horrible
past of the Jewish life. The tombstones reveal the Jewish
history if not Susskind's whereabouts.

> Many were burial places, he read on the stained stones, of
> those who, for one reason or another, had died in the late
> large war. Among them was an empty place, it said on a
> marble slab lying on the ground, for 'My beloved father/
> Betrayed by the damned Fascists/Murdered at Auschwitz
> by the barbarious Nazis/*O Crimine Orribile.*'
> —But no Susskind. (28)

Fidelman at last meets Susskind selling beads, rosaries and
other prayer things by the side of a Church. At first he hides
himself from Susskind as though he feared confrontation with
his conscience. With controlled trepidation, he meets Susskind.
He asks him about the suitcase and the chapter in it and makes
a tempting offer of fifteen thousand. Susskind hardly seems
to hear the words of Fidelman and leaves him in haste. Later
Fidelman surreptitiously ransacks the house of Susskind but
cannot find his briefcase. He returns in vain only to dream
of ghost-like Susskind emerging out of an empty grave in a
cemetery.

The dreams of Fidelman help self-discovery. The conversation Fidelman had with Susskind in his latest dream subtly throws light on the function of art.

> 'Have you read Tolstoy ?'
> 'Sparingly.'
> 'Why is art ?' asked the shade, drifting off. (31)

Fidelman's inability to answer the question "Why is art ?" reveals his ignorance of the meaning of art and its inextricable relation to life. Susskind acts as a guide to Fidelman's self-recognition. Fidelman also had the vision of Giotto's painting of St. Francis giving his gold cloak to a poor, old knight.

> The fresco therein revealed this saint in fading blue, the sky flowing from his head, handing an old knight in a thin red robe his gold cloak. Nearby stood a humble horse and two stone hills.
> Giotto. San Francesco dona le vesti al cavaliere povero. (32)

This is a moment of self-recognition for Fidelman. Being a Giotto scholar himself, he has not delved into the true spirit of Giotto's life rooted in compassion. Awoke, he runs to Susskind only to find the latter burning some papers. He offers the suit without expecting anything from Susskind.

> 'Here, Susskind,' he said in a trembling voice, offering the bundle, 'I bring you my suit. Wear it in good health.' (32)

Susskind returns the empty briefcase to Fidelman unasked. Fidelman is angry that the chapter is burnt. Susskind considers it a favour since "The words were there but the spirit was missing." (32) It is a blow to Fidelman's *hubris*. He runs after Susskind but fails to catch him. In the middle of his pursuit, he has, however, "a triumphant insight" and seeks to forgive Susskind out of compassion in spite of all the loss.

> 'Susskind, come back,' he shouted, half sobbing. 'The suit is yours. All is forgiven.' (33)

But Susskind continues running. "When last seen, he was still running." Fidelman comes to a dead halt. There is no need to pursue Susskind now. He has realised the burden of his past and conscience and consequently the value of compassion. At the end of the chapter, "Fidelman the Esthete, through understanding if not through love, becomes Fidelman the compassionate."[21] He learns the link between art and life: "One who cannot act charitably, and humanely in life cannot really appreciate, or has not sufficiently understood, great art, which has compassion at its root."[22]

<h2 style="text-align:center">III</h2>

Having realised the futility of his pursuit of art-history, Fidelman returns to painting. His sexual adventures and failures with a neurotic woman, Annamaria Oliovino in the second chapter "Still Life" evoke grotesque humour. Enticed by the advertisement of Oliovino, Fidelman joins her studio for rent. The pittrice, Annamaria, is neither attractive nor beautiful. She is a third-rate painter. Fidelman "ever a sucker for strange beauty and all sorts of experiences," plunges in headlong love with her despite himself. He at once agrees to pay the demanded rent and deposit for her sake. He borrows her easel for a thousand lire a month. In his work he often sneaks looks at her work.

Fidelman is servile to Annamaria and patiently does all menial work to win her favour. With little impudence, he carries her garbage down the staircase, sweeps the studio clean every morning, and runs to retrieve a brush or paint tube she dropped—"offering any service, any time, you name it." Spending the hard-saved money of his sister, Fidelman makes many presents to Annamaria. Annamaria accepts Fidelman's small favours "without giving notice," and his presents "without comment." Fidelman bows to all her whims and fancies. He is ready to spend his last lire "to lie on her soft belly." He grows jealous of Augusto Ottogalli, the old man who has obnoxious relations with Annamaria. Stooping to be an eavesdropper and a peeping Tom he finds Augusto passionately clasping Anna's hands in her bed.

Fidelman cares more for Annamaria's sex than for his art. He is glad for any attention she gave his work. To please her,

he experiments with some of the changes Annamaria suggests—
"spontaneous holes, for instance, several studies of 'Lines
Ascending,' and two lyrical abstract expressionistic pieces
based on, interwoven with and ultimately concealing a Star of
David" (40) although his attempts earn him increased scorn of
Annamaria instead of her good will. It is natural that in
Malamud stories, concealment of Jewish identity—in this case
represented by the star of David—leads to failure in love. He
curses his miserable fate.

> Water, water everywhere, spouting, flowing dripping,
> whispering secrets, love love love, but not for him. If
> Rome's so sexy, where's mine ? Fidelman's Romeless Rome.
> It belonged least to those who yearned most for it. (42-43)

Fidelman at last consoles himself painting her without her
permission ironically as "Virgin with Child." He feels a sense
of vicarious possession at this act. This however earns him
Annamaria's favour. She says, "You have seen my soul," and
falls in love with him.

The love-making of Fidelman and Annamaria attains
ridiculous lengths due to frequent disturbances as usual in
Malamud stories. Even after his failure in love, Fidelman does
not stop courting Annamaria. He cringes further to do the
most abominable services to her. Annamaria's invitation to
a party makes Fidelman happy in his depression. When
Annamaria and Balducci enter into a contest of painting a
male nude, Fidelman readily agrees to be a model hoping that
it would arouse her interest. But his hopes are belied.
Annamaria wants to sleep with Balducci and cruelly orders
Fidelman out of her sight.

Annamaria's surrender to Fidelman comes off strangely.
When Fidelman attempts to portray himself in priest's vest-
ments, she falls on his feet and makes a confession of her sins
that have been worming her heart all along.

> 'Forgive me, Father, for I have sinned—'
> Dripping brush in hand, he stared down at her.
> 'Please, I—'
> 'Oh, Father, if you knew what I've done. I've been a
> whore—' (51)

Annamaria's burden of guilt is so heavy that she would not discriminate Fidelman in the priest's garb. Fidelman takes the opportunity to express his willingness to absolve her. Annamaria confesses incest with her uncle, Augusto. Fidelman says he has forgiven her. But Annamaria insists on penance. Fidelman asks her to utter the name of Father and Mary but she is not satisfied.

> 'More' Annamaria wept. 'More, more. Much more.' (51)

Fidelman stoops to exploit the guilty conscience of Annamaria in order to quench his lust. He asks her to undress and indulges in sex nailing her to her cross. The image is a shocking merger of crucifixion and fornication. Walter Sullivan considers it offensive to any properly developed sensibility.[23] The act in no way reveals the genuine love of either of the two. As Barbara F. Lefcowitz rightly remarks:

> ... far from being a genuine encounter between two human beings, or a genuine relationship between self and other, sex becomes a parody of the crucifixion, and Fidelman's 'Love' for Annamaria merely an interchange of neurotic fantasies of a vaguely sado-masochistic nature.[24]

Fidelman, despite his lesson from Susskind, has not grown to the full. Still he fears the figure of Susskind who appears to him vaguely.

> Almost in panic he sketched, in charcoal a coat-tailed 'Figure of a Jew Fleeing' and quickly hid it away. (39)

IV

At Milan, we find further moral degradation of Fidelman. Being penniless he picks his first pocket and runs into the hands of the keepers of a brothel. At the point of gun, he is relieved of his passport and the Texan's vallet by Angelo. Fidelman's attempt to steal cash is foiled by Angelo. Angelo beats him and chains him to the bed for a week. Later he assigns Fidelman the job of cleaning toilets and running errands for the whores.

Fidelman is involved in a bizarre scheme of the Italian criminals to steal a Titian painting from the castello on Isola Bella in Lago Maggiore. Angelo and Scarpio ask him to copy the Titian painting of a nude on the basis of the photographs and the measurements so that they replace the genuine painting with it and make a fortune of four lakh dollars by selling it. The scheme suggests one of Malamud's many examples of the "false appropriation of art for selfish ends."[25] Fidelman is assured his passport and three hundred and fifty dollars for the task. There is no escape for Fidelman from this since the conspirators are cut-throat villains.

Fidelman falls in a dilemma and doubts his talent.

> Am I worthy ? Can I do it ? Do I dare ? He has these and other doubts, feels melancholy, and wastes time. (57)

Despite Angelo's all possible assistance, Fidelman worries about "another painter's ideas and work." The padrone ridicules him.

> The padrone wheezes. 'Tiziano will forgive you. Didn't he steal the figure of the Urbino from Giorgione ? Didn't Rubens steal the Andrian nude from Tiziano ? Art steals and so does everybody. You stole a wallet and tried to steal my lire. What's the difference ? It's the way of the world. We're only human.'
>
> 'It's a sort of desecration.'
> 'Everybody desecrates. We live off the dead and they live off us. Take for instance religion. (58)

This grotesque explanation of the padrone does not satisfy Fidelman. He insists on seeing the original at least once and the padrone reluctantly agrees.

In the castello, Fidelman is moved by the splendid art of "Venus of Urbino." Left alone with the painting, he wonders at the magnificent tones and the harmony of body and spirit in the painting. He makes a sketch of it hastily and shoots several photos of it. He almost falls in love with the picture.

. . . he approaches the picture and kisses the lady's hands, thighs, and breasts, but as he murmurs, 'I love you,' a guard strikes him hard on the head with both fists. (59)

The struggles of Fidelman to copy the painting resembles Harry Levin's (*The Tenants*) travails to finish his unfinished novel. He paints first directly on canvas and scrapes it clean seeing "What a garish mess he has made." (60) It is a distortion of the original. So he makes several drawings on paper of nude figures from art books in vain. He goes back to a study of Greek statuary to compute the mathematical proportions of the ideal nude. All the efforts of Fidelman go waste since he lacks creativity.

> What am I, bewitched, the copyist asks himself, and if so by whom ? It's only a copy job so what's taking so long ? He can't even guess, until he happens to see a naked whore cross the hall to enter a friend's room. Maybe the ideal is cold and I like it hot ? Nature over art ? Inspiration —the live model ? (61)

When Teresa, one of the whores, comes as a model he gets ready to lie down with her instead of painting her. The affair ends with Angelo's discovery and punishment to Fidelman.

Fidelman succeeds in painting the picture at last when he gets an idea of stealing the original himself. In course of painting, he remembers all the women he desired, from Bessie to Annamaria. Ultimately he falls in love with the painting itself.

> Although thus tormented, Fidelman feels himself falling in love with the one he is painting, every inch of her, including the ring on her pinky, bracelet on arm, the flowers she touches with her fingers, and the bright green ear-ring that dangles from her eatable ear. He would have prayed her alive if he weren't certain she would fall in love, not with her famished creator, but surely the first Apollo Belvedere she lays eyes on. Is there, Fidelman asks himself, a world where love endures and is always satisfying ? He answers in the

negative. Still she is his as he paints, so he goes on, plan-
ning never to finish, to be happy in loving her, thus for ever
happy. (o5)

Fidelman desires to steal the picture alone; but Scarpio
accompanies him on the mission. On the verge of stealing the
painting, he changes his mind. He hoodwinks his conspirators
and contrives to steal his own painting instead of the Titian.
Beating Scarpio, he escapes with his painting. Rowing across
the lake towards Alps, Fidelman has a dreadful thought: "Had
he the right painting ?" He unwraps the Venus and is happy
that it is his. His love of his own painting is too intense to
part with it.

In the pitch black, on the lake's choppy waters, he sees she
is indeed his, and by the light of numerous matches adores
his handiwork. (69)

Fidelman's stealing and adoration of his own painting has been
motivated by "self-love as much as anything."[26] Lefcowitz calls
it a "Pseudo-moral act, one which conceals Fidelman's ultimately narcissistic purpose."[27] Though the painting represents
his own "idealized self," Fidelman's attempt to betray the
conspirators in stealing the original attenuates his narcissism.

V

Fidelman goes back to painting. In the fourth chapter, "A
Pimp's Revenge," he appears a "ravaged Florentine" whose
paintings deserve "death for not coming to life." He is now
successful at carving cheap Madonnas rapidly but unable to
finish his would-be master-piece of "Mother and Son" despite
his hard labour at it for five long years. He has high hopes
about his undertaking and thinks that after the completion
of the painting, "I could forgive myself for past errors ?" (87)

It's first and foremost a painting, potentially a first-class
work if I ever get it done. If I could complete it the way I
sometimes see it in my mind's eye. I bet it could be something extraordinary. If a man does only one such painting

in his lifetime, he can call himself a success. I sometimes
think that if I could paint such a picture, much that was
wrong in my life would rearrange itself and add up to more,
if you know what I mean. (87)

He has the model in his photograph as a boy with his mother
sent by Bessie, his sister. With or without model, Fidelman
could not evoke the figure of mother into the painting. It is
because his attachment with the mother was too feeble and
remote to recollect her in flesh and blood. His mother died
when he was about ten. He did not even mourn her death at
that time, nor said *Kaddish*. Lack of authentic experience
naturally fails him in his task.

Fidelman's weakness lies in his inability to correlate life
with art. He has stencilled the best quotations of great painters
on the wall but never understood their spirit.

> Constable: 'Painting is for me another word for
> feeling.'
> Whistler: 'A masterpiece is finished from the beginning.'
> Pollock: 'What is it that escapes me ? The human ?
> That humanity is greater than art ?'
> Nietzsche: 'Art is not an imitation of nature but its
> metaphysical supplement, raised up beside it in order to
> overcome it.'
> Picasso: 'People seize on painting in order to cover up
> their nakedness.' (71)

Fidelman wants to paint to cover up his "nakedness" like
Picasso. Unlike Pollock, he imagines a gulf between art and
life. He asserts: "Art isn't life" and "Without art there's no
life to speak of, at least for me. If I'm not an artist, then I'm
nothing." (88) To Esmeralda's question "My God, Aren't
you a Man ?" Fidelman baffles her with his answer "Not
really, without art." Fidelman takes a topsy-turvy approach
from art to life instead of life to art. In his interview with
Ludovico also, he says: "Art is my means for understandi g
life and trying out certain assumptions I have. I make art, it
makes me." (90) He does not understand Pollock's statement

"humanity is greater than art," while a lay woman like
Esmeralda could make a correct choice—"If I have my choice
I'll take life. If there's not that there's no art." (88) Para-
doxically Fidelman finds life in art.

> I suppose I mean that maybe a painting sort of gives value
> to a human being as he responds to it. You might say it
> enlarges his consciousness. If he feels beauty it makes him
> more than he was, it adds, you might say, to his humanity.
> (91)

He finds morality and truth in his painting while they are
missing in his life.

Fidelman's numerous attempts at painting his masterwork
do not help him finish the mother's face. After incessant labour
he finishes everything except mother's face. During his trials,
his acquaintances in life figure in the picture.

> He had tried it every which way, with Momma alone,
> sitting or standing, with or without him; and with Bessie in
> or out, but never Poppa, that living ghost; and I've made
> her old and young, and sometimes resembling Annamaria
> Oliovino, or Teresa, the chambermaid in Milan; even a little
> like Susskind, when my memory gets mixed up, who was a
> man I met when I first came to Rome. Momma apart and
> him apart, and then trying to bring them together in the
> tightly woven paint so they would be eternally mother and
> son as well as unique forms on canvas. (82)

Painting the true face of mother has become a Herculean task
for him. Fidelman consults a fortune-teller; even this fails to
bring luck.

Fidelman picks on a whore, Esmeralda, thinking she would
relax him for painting. Esmeralda stays with Fidelman in order
to be free from the clutches of her former pimp, Ludovico
Belvedere. Fidelman has no interest in her except for her sex.
Esmeralda's modelling does not help him finish the picture.
Fidelman decides to dispense with "Mother and Son," and
takes up "Brother and Sister." The change also proves futile.
Fidelman takes up odd jobs for his living. When no job earns

him living, he stoops to exploit Esmeralda by acting as a pimp
to her.

The burning of Bessie's old snapshot by Esmeralda snaps
Fidelman's only visible link to "Ma, Bessie, the past." Fidelman now sets to paint the figure of "Prostitute and Procurer."
He successfully portrays himself as a procurer and Esmeralda
as the prostitute. The picture is Fidelman's "most honest piece
of work" since it is in true relation to Fidelman's life and
activities. He feels triumphant and proud of it.

But the feeling of triumph does not last long. Fidelman is
trapped by Ludovico's cunning advice:

> . . . my only criticism is that maybe the painting suffers
> from an excess of darkness. It needs more light. I'd say a
> soupcon of lemon and a little red, not more than a trace.
> But I leave it to you. (101)

Despite Esmeralda's protests, Fidelman attempts to give the
painting lighter shade. It ruins the painting altogether. Ludovico
laughs at him victoriously. Esmeralda in anger tries to stab
Ludovico with a bread knife. But Fidelman does not blame
any one. He blames it on himself and snatches the knife to
thrust it into his own gut.

> When Esmeralda pulled open the curtain and saw the
> mess, moaning, she came at him with the bread knife.
> 'Murderer !'
> F twisted it out of her grasp, and in anguish lifted the
> blade into his gut.
> 'This serves me right.'
> 'A moral act,' Ludovico agreed. (103)

Fidelman forgives Ludovico just as he did Susskind out of
compassion.

VI

Despite his experiences in life, Fidelman lives in his own
ivory tower. He has studied Donatello and church art only to
be sickened by them,

Everybody says you're dead, otherwise why do you never write ? Madonna Adoring the Child, Master Dolorosa. Madonna della Peste. Long White Knights. Lives of the Saints. S. Sebastian, arrow collector, swimming in bloody sewer, pictured transfixed with arrows. S. Denis decapitated. Pictured holding his head. S. Agatha, breasts shorn clean, running enflamed. Painted carrying both bloody breasts in white salver. S. Stephen, crowned with rocks. Shown stoned. S. Lucy tearing out eyes for suitor smitten by same. Portrayed beafing two-eyed omelette on dish. S. Catherine, broken apart on spiked wheel. Pictured married to wheel. S. Laurence, roasted on slow grill. *I am roasted on one side.* Now *turn me over and eat.* Shown cooked but uneaten. S. Bartholomew, flayed alive. Standing with skin draped over skinned arm. S. Fima, eaten by rats. Pictured with happy young rat. S. Simon Zelotes, sawed in half. Shown with bleeding crosscut saw. S. Genet in prison, pictured with boys. S. Fidel Uomo, stuffing his ass with flowers. (104-105)

Withdrawing from the representational art and life, Fidelman digs perfect holes in the ground and passes them off as a novelty in the history of art in Chapter V "Portraits of the Artist."

After attempting first several huge ziggurats that because of the rains tumbled down like Towers of Babel, he began to work labyrinths and mazes dug in the earth and constructed in the form of jewels. Later he refined and simplified this method, building a succession of spontaneously placed holes, each a perfect square, which when seen together constituted a sculpture. These Fidelman exhibited throughout Italy in whatsoever place he came. (105)

Ducharme regards these as the symbolic graves of Fidelman's failure as an artist and man.[28] Fidelman is proud of his originality and "the pleasure in creation is not less than that felt by Michelangelo." (105) Fidelman could however attract only the curious but not the true lovers of Art. Yet like a prig, he thinks "it was his need to create and not be concerned with the commerce of art." When visitors protest against the ludicrous art, they are told that the art is beyond their comprehension. It reveals nothing but Fidelman's deceitful nature.

Fidelman's refusal to return the admission fee to a disappointed poor young man reveals his moral ineptitude and lack of compassion. Disillusioned by the Exhibition, the young man demands his money back so that he could at least buy the bread for his family. He pleads pathetically: "Holes are of no use to me, my life being full of them, so I beg you to return the lire that I may hasten to the baker's shop to buy the bread I was sent for." (108) But Fidelman calls the holes "the elements of a conceptual work of Art" and dismisses the plea on the reason "Because you can't see it doesn't mean it isn't there." (108) In his attempt to earn money by hook or crook Fidelman fails to provide for his fellow-being.

A rigid formalist, Fidelman does not realise the purpose of art in life. He flaunts the emptiness as form and art. As if to mock at these notions it is said that a stranger who visited the exhibition by paying a gold coin one day tossed the core of an apple into one of the art holes and said to Fidelman: "If you will look in the small hole there is now there an apple core. If not for this would be empty the hole. If empty would be there nothing." (110) Vexed with the stubborn argument of Fidelman that "Emptiness is not nothing if it has form," he is also said to have hit Fidelman into the hole and filled it up with earth shouting "So now we got form but we also got content." (111)

Fidelman receives the message of compassion from Susskind who appears as Christ on top of the mountain in his dream.

Tell the truth. Don't cheat. If its easy it don't mean its good. Be kind, specially to those that they got less than you. I want for everybody justice. Must also be charity. If you feel good give charity. If you feel bad give charity. Must also be mercy. Be nice, don't fight. Children, how can we live without mercy? If you have no mercy for me I shall not live. Love, mercy, charity. Its not so easy believe me, (112)

Fidelman pretends regret and throws all his paints and brushes
except one into the Dead Sea. But in this mock sequence of the
Last Supper, Fidelman plays the role of Judas. He betrays
the Christ (Susskind), sells his redeemer for thirty-nine pieces
of silver and runs away to buy paints, brushes and canvas again.
His obsession with the painting is too much to care for anything in life.

The final picture of Fidelman is not any the better. He is
seen laboriously painting the walls of a cave day and night. He
is lost in the varied patterns of the geometric design: "circles
within circles of various hues" and "triangles within triangles
within concentrated circles." (117) He hopes he leaves a mark
in the cave for ages to see. Lost in the painting, he forgets his
obligations to his sick sister, Bessie who lives in the same house
upstairs. Fidelman by intuition feels that she would live till the
completion of his work to witness his achievement. This time
the hundred-watt bulb under which he works in the cave
reminds Fidelman of his responsibility for his dying sister.

> . . . why don't you go at least upstairs and say hello to
> your sister who hasn't seen you in years ? Go before it is too
> late, because she is now dying. (118)

The bulb symbolises Fidelman's conscience. Fidelman does not
care for it and says:

> No, I can't. It's all too complicated, I can't go till I've
> finished the job. The truth is I hate the past. It caught me
> unawares. I'd rather not see her just yet. Maybe next week
> or so. (118)

He cares more for his art than for his dying sister. He wants to
avoid his past which like Susskind haunts him. He is ruthless
in his statement: "It's no fault of mine if people die. There's
nothing I can do about it." (119) Fidelman's refusal to come
out of the cave of art to the house of life betrays his
ignorance and immaturity. His lack of compassion is also
evident in his failure to recognise his obligation to his sister
whose financial help sustained him in Italy. The bulb however
brings down the *hubris* of Fidelman by telling him what
happened to the pride of Greeks. Fidelman is at last convinced,

He goes up to Bessie and says his last hello to her. Bessie dies happily.

> Any way, thanks for coming up to see me, Arthur. It's nice thing to do when a person is so alone. At least I know what you look like and where you are nowadays.
>
> Bessie died and rose to heaven, holding in her heart her brother's hello. (120)

Fidelman's gesture of compassion outweights all his ideas of "still life. Oil on paper," vindicating change in him.

VII

In "Glass Blower of Venice," Fidelman gives up painting and turns a boatman ferrying passengers across the canals of Venice. He comes across a young, attractive Venetian woman who responds coquettishly to his frivolous acts. Fidelman falls in love with her. When the canals go dry, Fidelman, jobless, searches for his lady everywhere. He meets her in a glass trinket shop. The woman Margherita Fassoli, the wife of a glass-blower Beppo, takes Fidelman to her house the next day where they go to bed. Waking from a siesta, Fidelman is horrified to find Beppo's deaf mute mother sitting by the side of the window. He is worried that she might reveal the secret affair to Beppo in writing. The old woman stands as a symbol of Fidelman's guilty-conscience.

Fidelman makes friends with Beppo although he cuckolds him. He visits their house often and the affair becomes "the first long liaison of his life." (130) His interest in Margherita, however, is only sex. It is clear in the conversation he had with Beppo.

> 'I'm ashamed to leech on you.'
> 'What's an extra plate of macaroni ?'
> He thought of Margherita's sex as an extra plate of something. (130)

But the irony is Fidelman turns out to be the homosexual lover of Beppo later.

Beppo, like Susskind, helps Fidelman in self-recognition. He shatters Fidelman's false notions of artistic talent. Fidelman confides to Beppo the failures of his life in art and invites him to see the few paintings he retained with himself. Later he changes his mind and regrets his haste in calling Beppo because he cannot endure the criticism of his art. But Beppo insists on seeing since "if we're friends, we're friends for good or bad, better or worse." (131) Fidelman unfurls his paintings and sculpture, and explains their significance. As feared Beppo makes a scathing criticism of Fidelman's art.

Your work lacks authority and originality. It lacks more than that, but I won't say what now. If you want my advice there's one thing I'd do with this stuff.
'Such as what ?' said the ex-painter, fearing the worst.
'Burn them all.'
'I thought you'd say that, you cruel fairy bastard. (133)

Despite Fidelman's protests, Beppo mercilessly slashes all the treasured paintings of Fidelman with a kitchen knife. Fidelman is angry and wants to stop Beppo's act, but he impulsively lets Beppo slash and burn all his paintings. Beppo suggests to Fidelman not to waste his life doing what he cannot do.

After twenty years if the rooster hasn't crowed she should know she's a hen. Your painting will never pay back part of your life you've given up for it. (134)

Beppo also initiates Fidelman into homosexual love. When distressed Fidelman is in the midst of "violent intercourse" with Margherita, naked Beppo enters the room and lands on Fidelman. In this grotesque act, Beppo teaches Fidelman the meaning of love.

'Think of love,' the glass blower murmured. 'You've run from it all you life.' (135)

Fidelman also responds to Beppo.

Fidelman had never in his life said 'I love you' without reservation to anyone. He said it to Beppo. If that's the

way it works, that's the way it works. Better love than not
love. If you sneeze at life it backs off and instead of fruit
you're holding a bone. If I'm a late bloomer at least I've
bloomed in love. (135)

Fidelman has failed to invent art, so he has decided to invent
life as per the advice of Beppo. It is, however, ironical that
Fidelman should learn the lesson of love from a homosexual.

Fidelman becomes an apprentice to Beppo not only in love
but also in the craft of blowing glass. Beppo and Fidelman
work togther. "Every move they made was in essence sexual."
For the first time in his life Fidelman receives instruction from
another person. When Fidelman tries to bring his half-
knowledge of art into glass-blowing, Beppo warns him of
repeating his "fate."

You're doing the same things you did in your paintings,
that's the lousy hair in the egg. It's easy to see, half a
talent is worse than none. (139)

Fidelman realises that he had no true distinction as an artist.
He has shed his pretensions to art.

Fidelman's decision to leave Venice for America is, of
course, prompted by his gesture of compassion to Margherita.
Margherita begs him to leave her husband free so that she
could have domestic peace.

Listen, Fidelman, we've been friends, let's stay friends.
All I ask is that you leave Beppo and go some place else.
After all, in the eyes of God he's my husband. Now,
because of you he's rarely around and my family is a mess.
The boys are always in trouble, his mother complains all
day, and I'm at the end of my strength. Beppo may be a
homo but he's a good provider and not a bad father when
there are no men friends around to divert him from domestic life. The boys listen to his voice when they hear it. We
have our little pleasures. He knows life and keeps me informed. (139-40)

Fidelman, after a good deal of despair, obliges Margherita. He has evinced compassion in his responsibility for Margherita although it involved no great amount of sacrifice. As Ducharme says "it is an act of higher love that flows out of a broad sense of responsibility for others.[29] Kissing goodbye to Beppo, he leaves for America as a perfect glass blower. The story concludes: "In America he worked as a craftsman in glass and loved men and women." (140)

The ending of the novel provokes doubts about the motives of Fidelman's love for "men and women" which literally is imposssible. It leaves the overtones of homosexuality in the light of Fidelman's earlier relation with Beppo from whom he is said to have learnt paradoxically the meaning of love. Fidelman's relations with women—Annamaria, Esmeralda, and Margherita—have also been quite transient and never extended love beyond sex. Hence it is difficult to agree with Harper's interpretation of Fidelman's love as less "an acceptance of homosexuality than an affirmation of unselfish love for all humanity."[30]

The overall picture of Fidelman through these six stories or chapters is that of a man of inconsistent motives and ludicrous actions. His moral degradation deepens from one chapter to another although there are occasional epiphanies of compassion. In forgiving Susskind and Ludovico despite the harm done by them, in visiting his dying sister Betty leaving his cave of art, in leaving Beppo and the city of Venice for the solace of Beppo's wife Margherita—Fidelman has evinced the redemptive moments of compassion. The momentary acts of compassion bear no relation to his subsequent activities as, for example, compassion attained by Fidelman at the end of the first chapter has no bearing on his sexual pursuit of Annamaria in "Still Life" or in his role as a pilferer and imposter in "Naked Nude." In "A Pimp's Revenge," Fidelman is referred to as "F" to indicate his diminished personality. As Ruth R. Wisse comments, Fidelman appears "a comic strip caricature, a poor stumblebum whose failures remain unmitigated.[31] The novel, in fact a series of stories, has affected the characterization and left the theme of compassion poorly portrayed. The only significant change that marks Fidelman is his abandonment of painting, his much-vaunted pursuit of life. This act of abandonment though unconvincing speaks of the self-effacement of Fidelman, perhaps the only redemptive trait in a life of moral loopholes.

In *The Tenants* that follows, Malamud describes with concern the hostility between the blacks and the Jews. He hopes that the two races will come together and live in harmony.

NOTES

1. Of the six chapters of the novel, five appeared first in journals. "Last Mohican," in *Paris Review* Spring 1958; "Still Life," in *Partisan Review* Winter 1962; "Naked Nude," in *Playboy* August 1963; "A Pimp's Revenge," *Playboy* Feb. 1968; "Pictures of the Artist," in *Atlantic* Dec. 1968; The first three parts were also published in Malamud's short story collections: "Last Mohican," in *The Magic Barrel* (1958); "Still Life," and "Naked Nude," in *Idiots First* (1963).

2. Field and Field, "An Interview with Bernard Malamud," *Bernard Malamud: A Collection of Critical Essays* (Englewood Cliffs, N.J.: Prentice-Hall, 1975) 15-16.

3. Jeffrey Helterman, "Bernard Malamud," *Dictionary of Literary Biography* (Detroit; Michigan: A Bruccoli Clark Book, 1978) 2: 300.

4. Howard M. Harper, Jr., "Trends in Recent American Literature," *Contemporary Literature* 12.2 Spring 1971: 214.

5. Harper 215.

6. Charles Stetler, Review of *Pictures of Fidelman, Studies in Short Fiction* 8.2 Spring 1971: 343.

7. Pete Axthelm, "Holes in the Ground," *Newsweek* 5 May 1969: 112.

8. Walter Sullivan, "Where Have All the Flowers Gone ? Part II: The Novel in the Gnostic Twilight," *Sewanee Review* 78.4 Autumn 1978: 655.

9. Letter of Bernard Malamud to Robert Ducharme, dated 21 April 1970. Robert Ducharme, *Art and Idea in the Novels of Bernard Malamud: Towards The Fixer* (The Hague, Paris: Mouton, 1974) 129.

10. Sheldon Norman Grebstein, "Bernard Malamud and the Jewish Movement," *Contemporary American-Jewish Literature: Critical Essays*, ed. Irving Malin (Bloomington, London: Indiana Univ. Press, 1973) 184.

11. Field and Field, "An Interview with Bernard Malamud," 13.

12. Michiko Kakutani, "Malamud," *International Herald Tribune* 23 July 1980: 14.

13. Guy Davenport, "Elegant Botches," *National Review* 3 June 1969: 549.

14. Ben Siegel, "Through a Glass Darkly: Bernard Malamud's Painful Views of the Self," *The Fiction of Bernard Malamud*, ed. Richard Astro and Jackson J. Benson (Corvallis: Oregon State Univ. Press, 1977) 126.

15. Helterman 301.

16. D.R. Mesher, "Remembrance of Things Unknown: Malamud's 'The Last Mohican," *Studies in Short Fiction* 12.4 Fall 1975: 397.

17. Jackson J. Benson, "Introduction: Bernard Malamud and the Haunting American," *The Fiction of Bernard Malamud* 23.

18. Mark Goldman, "Comic Vision and the theme of Identity," *Bernard Malamud and the Critics*, ed. Field and Field (New York: New York Univ. Press, 1970) 160-61.

19. Ruth R. Wisse, *The Schlemiel as Modern Hero* (Chicago and London: The Univ. of Chicago Press, 1971) 113.

20. Goldman 161.
21. Sam Bluefarb, "Bernard Malamud, The Scope of Caricautre," *English Journal* 53.5. May 1964: 326.
22. Mesher 398.
23. Sullivan 655.
24. Barbara F. Lefcowitz, "The Hybris of Neurosis: Malamud's *Pictures of Fidelman*," *Literature and Psychology* 20.3 (1970) 117.
25. Lefcowitz 117.
26. Ducharme 137.
27. Lefcowitz 117.
28. Ducharme 138.
29. Ducharme 141.
30. Harper, Jr. 215.
31. Wisse 118.

7

HAB RACHMONES: THE TENANTS

*"Some day God will bring together
Ishmael and Israel to live as one people,
It won't be the first miracle."*

The Tenants* probes the agony of creative process as well as the tangled web of strained relations between two ethnic races—the Jews and the blacks. An experimental novel with three endings, The Tenants has frequent shifts in the mode of narration presenting the theme in an "elliptic style blending narrative and dream."[1] Malamud responds to the tension born of the crisis of the times and extends the horizon of his writing to deal with the neglected race of the blacks and their black consciousness. The upsurge of Black Power Movement, the outbreak of virtual civil war in Watts, Newark, Detroit, and Cleveland, the ugly showdown between Jewish teachers

---

*Bernard Malamud, The Tenants (Harmondsworth: Penguin Books, 1976). All subsequent references with page numbers in parantheses are to this edition.

and the black community groups in the New York City School strike in 1968 provide the tense background to the novel. Malamud has explained the factors that caused the novel: "Jews and blacks, the period of the troubles in New York City; the teachers' strike, the rise of black activism, the mix-up of cause and effect. I thought I'd say a word."[2] He has, however, avoided the role of a social realist like Dos Passos and Stein- beck. Steven G. Kellman complains that Malamud makes only a passing reference to the Korean war and Vietnam wars, "an involvement which threatened as much destruction to American society as it entailed on the Asian mankind."[3] Yet Malamud's focus is on the impact of the tense times on the humanity symbolically represented in the mutual hatred, suspicion and guilt of the black and the Jewish writers, Harry Lesser and Willie Spearmint in this novel. He is worried about the lack of compassion in a world of growing nihilistic tendencies. The factual reportage of events is subsidiary. Commenting on the possibility of new relationship between the blacks and the Jews, Malamud says:

It's impossible to predict—it may go one way or another. A good deal depends on the efficacy of American democracy. If that works as it ought—guaranteeing blacks what they deserve as human beings—a larger share of our national wealth, equal opportunity under the law, their rights as men, the relationship of blacks and Jews and other minori- ties are bound to improve.[4]

Malamud's love of mankind includes the ill-treated blacks. He feels, "We, as a society, have to redress the balance."[5] *The Tenants* is thus conceived with great, but almost despairing, love for all men.[6]

Malamud's portrayal of black consciousness has won authenticity on account of his acquaintance with black people and black fiction and history. He reveals:

I lived on the edge of a black neighbourhood in Brooklyn when I was a boy. I played with blacks in the Flatbush Boy's club. I had a friend—Buster; we used to go to his house every so often. I swiped dimes so we could go to the movies together in a couple of Saturday afternoons. After I was married I taught for a year in a black evening high school in Harlem. The short stories drive from that period. I also read black fiction and history.[7]

Delving deep into the psyche of the black and Jew, Malamud has succeeded, as Morris Dickstein remarks, in dramatizing the world of pain and anguish in *The Tenants*.[8] Although the locale in Malamud's novels differs, the basic theme of compassionate commitment to human values continues. He has told Daniel Stern that: "In my book I go along the same path in different worlds." He explains that the basic theme of all his work is derived from "one's sense of values, it's a vision of life, a feeling for people—real qualities in imaginary worlds."[9] In *The Tenants*, Malamud is concerned with the lack of compassion and its bloody consequences. The horror presented in the novel suggests the need of compassion. The novel is not simply a story of black-white relations. For Malamud it is "a sort of prophetic warning against fanaticism," and it argues for "the invention of choices to outwit tragedy."[10] It is not, therefore, "a claustrophobic novel" as Cynthia Ozick remarks.[11] Malamud believes that human values like compassion, love and responsibility alone can outwit the tragedy that has been the lot of the blacks and the Jews in particular, and humanity in general. The ironic tone of the novel, however, betrays Malamud's losing faith in humanity. He has in fact confessed that "My faith in humanity has been bruised to some degree."[12] His ambivalent attitude to the Jew-black relations is suggested in the three endings he gives to the novel.[13] Malamud's bruised faith in humanity is evident in the ambivalent portrayal of the theme of compassion in *The Tenants*.

The Tenants is also regarded as "a wry fable of an artist's labor pains."[14] Like *Pictures of Fidelman*, it deals with the problem of relation of art to life. With two novelists as protagonists, the novel defines the agony of the creative process. Harry Lesser, the Jewish novelist, is a perfect formalist but falls short of ideas and struggles in vain to finish his would-be masterpiece. Willie Spearmint, the Negro novelist, has the

authentic black experience but fails to give it a coherent shape.
The problems of form and theme confound both the writers so
much that they are shut off from the reality of life. Both of
them ultimately give up Irene Bell, their beloved, for their
work. Willie does not appreciate Lesser's criticism of his work
in its right spirit because of his prejudice against the Jews. He
hates Lesser for getting his girl and burns the manuscript of his
novel. As a retaliatory measure, Lesser smashes Willie's typewriter. Ultimately they get ready to kill each other in hatred
and revenge. Levenspiel cries for mercy and *rachmones*. The
word "mercy" is repeated one hundred and fifteen times at the
end of the novel. Jacob Korg points out that mercy "leaves
the pages of the book altogether and hangs in the air, becoming a supplication addressed to the universe in general."[15]
Malamud's recurrent plea for mutual compassion and *rachmones* is thus voiced in the cry of Levenspiel.[16] Kellman
comments on the ending: "Trailing off into a potentially
endless series of *mercys*, the novel halts with a recognition of
the insufficiency of the self."[17] Malamud has asked "for a
sympathetic understanding of the failure of our civilization."[18]

II

The Tenants centres on the creative travails of two writers—
Harry Lesser and Willie Spearmint. Lesser is a Jewish novelist
for whom writing has become an obsession of life. He has
published two novels. His first was a success and the second
was a flop although it was bought by the movies. Now at work
on his third novel, he wants to make it a masterpiece.

> My deepest desire is to make my third my best. I want to
> be thought of as a going concern, not a freak who had
> published a good first novel and shot his wad. (13)

In spite of his laborious revisions for about ten years, the novel
remains incomplete without an end. The prospect of his novel
becoming the envy of the publishers after its completion
remains first a dream. Lesser is seen struggling with the work
throughout the novel. His restlessness is suggested in the very

opening of the novel. "I've got to get up to write, otherwise there's no peace in me." (9)

Malamud ironically juxtaposes the creative process of both Lesser and Willie with the desolate and crumbling tenement in which they work, aloof from life. Lesser almost buries himself in the apartment.

> Only when inside his safe-and-save three rooms Lesser felt himself close off the world and relax. (16)

Lesser's involvement with writing keeps him off from the world.

> He would not think how much of life he made no attempt to use. That was outside and he was in. (16)

The tenement provides an image of death and desolation. Lesser once hears "mournful winds, Aeolus bag" and graveyard music, and suspects funeral parlour on the premises. He thinks each book he writes nudges him "that much closer to death" and not life.

Lesser is less than human in his response to the repeated pleas of his landlord, Irving Levenspiel. As a statutory tenant he refuses to leave the tenement, his "pleasure dome," till the completion of his unfinished novel. Levenspiel wants to construct a modern six storey apartment with the Metropolitan Life loan and make himself "a comfortable life." He has his own domestic problems and craves for the mercy of Lesser.

> Hab rachmones, Lesser, I have my own ambition to realize. I've got fifteen years on you, if not more, and I'm practically naked as the day I was born. Don't be fooled that I own a piece of property. You know already about my sick wife and knocked-up daughter, age sixteen. Also I religiously go one afternoon every week to see my scrazy mother in Jackson Heights. All the time I'm with her she stares at the window. Who she thinks she sees I don't know but it's not me. She used to weigh ninety pounds, a skinny lady, now she's two-twenty and growing fatter. I sit there with tears. We stay together a couple of hours

without words and then I leave. My father was a worry-
wart immigrant with a terrible temper who couldn't do
anything right, not to mention make a living. He wiped his
feet all over my youth, a bastard, thank God he's dead.
What's more, everybody—everybody—wants financial
assistance. . . . Outside of your $72 monthly rent, which
doesn't half pay for the oil I use on you, I have
no income coming in from here. So if you're really a man,
Lesser, a reasonable being, how can you deny me my simple
request ? (19-20)

Levenspiel emerges as a symbolic reminder of life and its values
which Lesser disregards. Lesser betrays a total lack of compassion. He refuses Levenspiel's offer of bribe and involves
him in a prolonged legal battle. He is worried only about his
future as a writer.

'If I don't write this novel exactly as I should—if, God
forbid, I were to force or fake it, then it's a dud after nine
and a half long years of labour and so am I. After that
folly what good can I expect from myself ? What would I
see when I look in the mirror but some deformed fourassed
worm ? And what's my future after that with the last of my
movie money gone ?—redemption in another book I'll may
be finish when I'm forty-six and starving to death ?' (22)

Levenspiel wishes Lesser were "a less egotistical type" to
realize others' predicament. He tries unsuccessfully to break
Lesser's shell of egotism with his sarcastic remarks.

'For Christ's sake, what are you writing, the Holy
Bible ?'
'Who can say ? Who really knows ? But not while you're
making that fucking racket. How can I think if my mind
hurts already from the sound of your voice ? My pen is
dead in its tracks. Why don't you go somewhere and let
me work in peace ?'
'Art my ass, in this world it's heart that counts. Wait,
you'll get yours one of these days, Lesser. Mark my words.'
(22)

Buried in his art, Lesser does not understand the value of heart. When Levenspiel informs about the ill-health of his daughter, Lesser dryly conveys his lip sympathy.

Lesser finds his kin in Willie Spearmint, the black writer who also chooses the same desolate tenement in his search for a private place to do his writing. One day Lesser discovers Willie in his flat seriously typing. His first thought was to devise a means to get rid of him. Willie's response to Lesser is also very sullen. He complains, "Man . . . Can't you see me writing on my book ?" (27) When Lesser apologetically says, "I'm a writer myself," he just stares at him. The gulf between the two writers is suggested in Willie's lack of response to Lesser's out-stretched hand for a shake.

> No handshake though Harry was willing, in fact had stuck out his white paw. There it remained—extended. He was, in embarrassment, tempted to play for comedy: Charlie Chaplin, with his moth-eaten moustache, examining his sensitive mitt to see if it was a hand and not a fish held forth in greeting before he told it to come back home; but in the end Lesser withdrew it, no criticism of anyone intended or implied. (29-30)

Lesser takes it in good spirit and invites Willie to meet him any time for any need. Willie meets Lesser to leave his typewriter with him for a day. Lesser hides Willie from the landlord and buys him the required furniture. Both discuss their writing. Writing has different impacts on the writers. It makes Willie warm to his toes while it does not affect Lesser who freezes even with the heater going. Willie does not like the labour of Lesser. He thinks "Writing down words is like hitting paper with a one ton hammer." (31) While Lesser writes about love, Willie says his work is about "me." Both however cherish writing more than life.

The inadequacy of both the writers, Lesser and Willie, in their response to life and love is evident in their relation to Irene Bell. Having been Willie's lover for two years, she realises: "Outside of his love for black people I don't really think he loves anything but his work. Otherwise I think we'd've been married by now." (93) Willie "pits his black

book against his white bitch" and almost avoids visiting Irene
for the sake of his book. Irene thinks that Willie loves his
black book more than her. When Willie is buried in writing,
Lesser seizes the opportunity to come closer to Irene. But
his passion for the book is more than his passion for Irene. His
loyalties are divided between Irene and the book. He suppresses
his thoughts of marriage, a home for the sake of his book. He
is at times tormented by the thoughts of stealing Willie's girl,
yet grows jealous to see Willie with Irene. He reveals to Willie
his love for Irene and invites troubles for himself. But when
Irene proposes marriage, Lesser hesitates: "That's what we'll
do, . . . As soon as the book is out of the way." (132) In
his mad pursuit of rewriting the burnt novel, Lesser visits Irene
only during weekends just as Willie did earlier. Paradoxically
he prefers writing his book on love to marriage with Irene.
Irene once taunts Lesser: "What do you know about love ?"
(45) Lesser also thinks: "I write about love because I knew
so little about it." (97) Irene recognizes that both Willie and
Lesser are of the same bent of mind in their attitude to love—
"You're both alike." (109) She describes them as "men more
deeply involved in their work than with me." Irene likes them
both, but neither of the two writers comes out of the den of
writing to enter life. She has already left Willie and now she
bids goodbye to Lesser too. She finally leaves a note for
Lesser without her address.

No book is as important as me. (170)

Here as in *Pictures of Fidelman*, Malamud suggests that life
is more important than art. Both the writers in *The Tenants*
fail to recognize the truth.

Lesser is a formalist who is good at craft but ill at ease with
theme. His dilemma is that he is unable to "see or feel except
in language." (85) He often thinks of abandoning his project,
but his love of writing does not let him do so. He writes his
book on love, tentatively entitled *The Promised End*. Ironically
the promised end never comes both for Lesser and the writer
he writes about. Lesser depicts the psychological oppression of
a writer who loves a girl and yet is "stricken by anxiety
because he finds it hard to give love." (146) It reflects his own

predicament. What Lesser's writer does is what Lesser does. Lesser's writer writes a novel in which he creates love seeking vicarious satisfaction through the imagined character.

> What it may come to in the end, despite the writer's doubts, is that he invents this character in his book who will in a sense love for him; and in a sense love him; which is perhaps to say, since words rise and fall in all directions, that Lesser's writer in his book, in creating love as best he can, if he brings it off in imagination will extend self and spirit; and so with good fortune may love his real girl as he would like to love her, and whoever else in a mad world is human. Around this tragic theme the story turns. (146-47)

The problem of Lesser's book and his writer's book is thus invariably linked with Lesser's life. Lesser could neither complete his book nor marry Irene. He is an "occluded self" as his character is. "Thus Lesser writes his book and his book writes Lesser. That's what's taking so long." (147) John Alexander Allen correctly puts it:

> Lesser has been struggling for a decade with a novel about a novelist writing a novel about the same things bothering him, that is, *a writer's deficiencies in compassion and love.*[19] (Italics mine)

While Lesser's writing reveals psychological tensions, Willie's work characterises a revolutionary outburst of black anger. The soul of Willie is in his writings. Willie who was imprisoned for some time by the whites, feels that he will be the "best soul writer," by writing about "the terrible and violent things of my life." (32) It eases his self. The violence shows the depth of Willie's "unspent rage." Unlike Lesser, Willie has ameliouristic aim of the sociological approach to literature. He believes that he can help his people overthrow racism and economic inequality through writing. He wants to "make black more than color or culture, and outrage larger than protest or ideology." (54) Lesser is moved by "the affecting subject" of Willie's work and his attempt to define

himself and his sense of suffering and injustice. But he finds
Willie woefully lacking the craft of writing. Emotion overpowers
technique. While Lesser's craft outweighs his theme, Willie's
powerful theme betrays poor treatment.

The first sign of disharmony between Lesser and Willie
comes out with Lesser's genuine criticism of Willie's manuscript. Although Lesser is surprised by Willie's revelation that
what he considered autobiographical of Willie's work is purely
fictional, he insists that the book could be better in terms of
art.

> There's a flawed quality, what you call blurred, that gives
> the shifting effect that bothers you. (58)

He also points out that black experience cannnot become
literature "Just by writing it down." (60) Willie, who is deeply
prejudiced against whites, fails to accept Lesser's criticism in
right spirit. He considers Lesser unfit to judge the black
experience as he is white.

> This is a *black* book we talking about that you don't
> understand at all. White fiction ain't the same as *black*. It
> *can't* be. (60)

Willie is more a revolutionary moved by the suffering of his
people than a writer. For Willie, all concerns of literature—
theme, technique, art—tantamount to black experience and
nothing else. He retorts to Lesser betraying his egotism.

> Art can kiss my juicy ass. You want to know what's really
> art ? I am art. Willie Spearmint, black man. My form is
> *myself*. (61)

Willie's intense hatred of the whites is evident in his statement
to Lesser.

> The point I am making, Lesser, in case you not with it, is I
> think this is the main way the blacks have to head along—
> to kill whites still those who are alive vomit with pain at the
> thought of what wrongs they have done us, and better not
> try to do any more. (67)

Willie also infers from the rejection of his book by Jewish publishers that "they are *afraid* of what the book says." (75)

Willie, who changes his name to Bill Spear, wants to revise his ideas about writing and form after reading Lesser's novels, but that too only to enrich his black experience in form.

> Lesser, I want to know what you know and *add on to that* what I know *because* I am black. And if that means I have to learn something from whites to do it better as a black man, then I will *for that purpose only*.' (66-67)

Willie struggles with the grammar book given by Lesser and improves his writing a bit. The first chapter of his new novel, *Book of Black* is praised by Lesser as "well formed and written." (83) The subject of the new novel is also the hatred of a black child for the white. The first chapter deals with the retrieval of a lost child to her mother and the child's contempt for his mother's illicit contact with a white for the sake of bread. He makes his hatred clear in his deliberately affected "nigger talk." In his next chapter, Willie narrates in the first four pages mother's vain attempt to kill her son, and her suicide after the son's escape. In the remaining 36 pages, Willie has overworked the stream of consciousness technique to bring about the impact of mother's life and death on her son. Lesser is not happy with Willie's language—"a compound of ashes and glue" in spite of the authentic experience. Willie misunderstands Lesser's experience:

> 'Lesser, you tryin to fuck up my mind and confuse me. I read all about that formalism jazz in the library and it's bullshit. You tryin to kill off my natural writin by pretendin you are interested in the fuckn form of it though the truth of it is you afraid of what I am goin to write in my book, which is that the blacks have to murder you white MF's for cripplin our lives.' He then cried out, 'Oh, what a hypocrite shitass I am to ask a Jew ofay for advise how to express *my* soul work. Just in readin it you spoil what it says. I ought to be hung on a hook till some kind brother cuts off my white balls.' (126-27)

Willie wants to quit writing to help his suffering black brethren, but egotistic concern of being a writer does not let him do
so. Lesser's revelation at this point about his love for Irene
Bell, Willie's girl, adds fuel to fire. Willie loses his poise and
enters into headlong savage fight with him. Willie who at one
time saved Lesser from the attack of Sam and other blacks is
now full of hatred for the Jew.

> 'You trick me, Jewprick, got me writin so deep you
> stole my bitch away.'
> 'Let's stop and talk or we're dead men.'
> 'What's wrong is I forgot to go on hatin you, white-
> shit. Now I hate you till your death. (129)

Outraged Willie also goes to Irene and injures her. He later
steals and burns Lesser's manuscript in revenge. He writes the
charcoal message on the wall.

> REVOLUTION IS THE REAL ART. NONE OF
> THAT FORM SHIT. I AM THE RIGHT FORM.
> He signs it NEVER YOUR FRIEND. And pukes in
> the smoking ashes. (136)

Lesser's agony of reconstructing his burnt novel from the
notes he preserved recalls that of Fidelman. Like Carlyle who
rewrote the whole *French Revolution* and T.E. Lawrence who
reconstructed *The Seven Pillars of Wisdom*, Lesser sets out on
the venture. He consoles himself: "The book is not the writer,
the writer writes the book." (137) A rigid formalist, he thinks:
"Habit and order fill the pages one by one. Inspiration is
habit, order; ideas growing, formulated, formed." (140) In
the process of his work, he encounters all possible problems
peculiar to writers.

> Sometimes the writing goes really badly. It is painful
> when images meant to marry repel each other, when reflec-
> tions, ideas, won't coalesce. When he forgets what he meant
> to write and hasn't written. When he forgets words or
> words forget him. He types wither for either all the time,

> Lesser sometimes feels despair's shovel digging. He writes against cliffs of resistance. Fear, they say, of completing the book ? Once it's done what's there to finish ? Fear of the ultimate confession ? Why ? If I can start another book after this. Confess once more. What's the distant dark mountain in my mind when I write ? It won't fade from inscape, sink, evanesce; or volatilize into light. It won't become diaphanous, radiance, fire, Moses himself climbing down the burning rock, Ten lit Commandments tucked under his arm. The writer wants his pen to turn stone into sunlight, language into fire. It's an extraordinary thing to want by a man his size and shape given all he hasn't got. Lesser lives on his nerve. (140-141)

The "double labour" does not fetch any results. Lesser recalls painfully the original draft, but cannot put it on paper as he had done earlier. He desperately realises the travails of writing the same thing twice. He turns back to the disjunct past and contemplates the futility of life.

> Death of his mother in a street accident when he was a kid. She had gone out for a bottle of Grade A milk and had not come back. Death of his older brother in the war before this war. He had disappeared, 'missing in action,' no sign of him ever. No last word. Still waiting in some Asian jungle for a train ? Useless deaths. Life so fragile, fleeting. One thing about writing a book you keep death in place; idea is to keep on writing. An aged father he hasn't seen in years. (150)

Lesser has the background of a *schlemiel* in the tragic death of his mother and brother. His lack of compassion is seen in his insolent attitude to the aged father.

Willie's unfinished writings discovered by Lesser in the garbage can too betray his fanatic attachment to blackness. One of the stories entitled "Goldberg exits Harlem" depicts killing of a Jew slumlord by three old men and Jamaican woman who taste his flesh. The Jamaican woman says: "He tastes Jew-taste, that don't taste like nothin good." (154) The experimental pages of Willie under the title "Manifested Destiny" strangely convey how the word "black" grows into "BLACK-NESS" engulfing the word "white" which diminishes through "whit," "Whi," "w" to nothingness. This stands as the "objective correlative" of the mind of Willie and his overwhelming black consciousness. Another story is followed by the word "pogrom" twelve times. Willie also writes some poems on Irene expressing his frustration in love.

The second ending of the novel comes off at this stage. It is Lesser's fantasy of "double wedding" of himself and Mary and Willie and Irene.

> Here's this double wedding going on, that's settled in his mind. (156)

The ritual of the unconventional marriages between blacks and whites performed by the risk-taking priest is graphically portrayed. Even in the dream, Lesser confesses to Mary his inability to love.

> Mary, I am short of love in my nature, don't ask me why, but I'll try to give you your due. (161)

The rabbi preaches the value of love and mutual trust to the black and white couple.

> Willie and Irene, to enjoy the pleasures of the body you don't need a college education; but to live together in love is not so easy. Besides love that which preserves marriage is that which preserves life; this is mutual trust, insight into each other, generosity, and also character, so that you will do what is not easy to do when you must do it. What else can I tell you, my children? Either you understand or you don't. (163)

The rabbi also longs for amity between the blacks and the whites.

> Someday God will bring together Ishmael and Israel to live as one people. It won't be the first miracle. (163)

The hope of the rabbi is very much the hope of Bernard Malamud. Lesser says to Irene. "It's something I imagined like an act of love, the end of my book, if I dared." (164)

Contrary to the dream of the rabbi is the bitter reality of strained relations of the blacks and whites. After the fall out, Lesser becomes more and more suspicious of Willie. His "frightened imagination" creates "optical illusions" of dreadful images of Willie. At the same time, he also longs for a silent communication with Willie which is impossible in the context of their estrangement.

> Hey Bill, Lesser thought in the hallway, moved by the sight of a man writing, how's it going ?
>
> You couldn't say that aloud to someone who had deliberately destroyed the almost completed manuscript of your most promising novel, product of ten years' labour. You understood his history and possibly yours, but you could say nothing to him.
>
> Lesser said nothing. (168)

Lesser also imagines Willie listening to him at work. Both Lesser and Willie feel "mutually repelled" when they meet one winter's night on the frigid stairs. They, however, seem to forgive each other. Yet the black is not free from his prejudices against the Jews. Lesser's exhortation for peace fails on Willie. Willie is sore that on account of Lesser he "can't write the way I used to any more." (169) Lesser out of frustration in his work destroys Willie's typewriter and thinks that the writing might go well thereafter, but it does not. He vainly hopes he could write after the exit of Willie from the house. The final ending of the novel shows Lesser and Willie bloodthirsty. One moonless night, they meet near a bush and kill each other.

> They aimed at each other accurate blows. Lesser felt his jagged axe sink through bone and brain as the groaning black's razor-sharp sabre, in a single boiling stabbing slash, cut the white's balls from the rest of him. (173)

The last sentence—"Each, thought the writer, feels the anguish of the other" (173) reveals that it is a fantasy. If may be inferred from the sentence that both of them would feel the anguish of the other at least at the time of their death. Feeling the anguish of the other is one's capacity for compassion. Lesser thus emerges out of the tragic encounter with a new insight. "Here is suggested a sort of limited 'redemption'; it implies a recognition of 'the other' and an insight into his anguish."[20]

The ending of the novel in bloodshed appears melodramatic. But the end may be considered a fantasy as Ben Siegel remarks:

> Tension and violence build to a 'final' scene that seemingly spurts blood. But neither the blood nor the apocalyptic conclusion is real.[21]

Kellman too considers it "a fantasy of violent confrontation between Jew and black."[22] Lindberg-Seyersted points out that the ending is surrealistic. "The novel ends not in real killing, but in an imagined act of violence, which is perhaps meant to have a cathartic result, but, more importantly, which is, intended as a reminder and a warning."[23] Further this is one of the three endings to the novel suggested by the author. All the three endings are fantasies. When asked "Why the three endings?" Malamud replied in an Interview, "Because one wouldn't do."[24] The first ending of the novel comes at page 23 when the black writer does not enter into picture. Lesser, the stubborn tenant, imagines that Levenspiel has set the crumbling tenement on fire. He thinks it is construction in the neighbourhood and continues his work. The fire engulfs the entire building and the flames lash into Lesser's doors. The second ending in wedding at page 164 reveals Malamud's hope that the Jews and blacks might someday live as brothers compassionate to each other without hatred or ill-will. But the possibility of their mutual annihilation is also hinted at the last ending of the novel at pp. 172-73. The mutual killing of Lesser and Willie in the last ending suggests with a prophetic note the horrible consequences of lack of compassion. Since all the three endings of the novel are only fantasies, it may as well be said of the novel that there is no ending to the novel. Malamud like Lesser gropes for the end which is beyond his reach as suggested in the epigraph of the novel.

'I got to make it, I got to find the end. . .' Bessie Smith.

Ben Siegel says that Malamud's "trick" has enabled himself and Lesser to "close" their novels indicating that the time is not ripe for the dream of rabbi's miracle, and concept of "one-people."[25] Cynthia Ozick remarks that the book has no conclusion as it stops in the middle of an incoherency.[26] The end is perhaps in conformity with the incoherent lives and relations around. The open-ended nature of the novel is evident from the fact that Levenspiel's cries of mercy follow the third ending of the novel. The novel closes unmistakably with the message of "Hab rachmones" (Have mercy or compassion) as Levenspiel cries and begs for mercy in vain.

In his last novel *Dubin's Lives*, Malamud writes of the problems of a middle-aged biographer to uphold his commitment to life.

NOTES

1. Ihab Hassan, "Bernard Malamud," *Contemporary Novelists*, ed. James Vinson (London: St. James Press, 1976) 878.

2. Daniel Stern, "The Art of Fiction: LII Bernard Malamud," *The Paris Review* 16.61 Spring 1975: 61.

3. Steven G. Kellman, "Tenants in the House of Fiction," *Studies in the Novel* 8.4 Winter 1976: 459.

4. Field and Field, "An Interview with Bernard Malamud," *Bernard Malamud*: *A Collection of Critical Essays* (Englewood Cliffs, N.J.: Prentice-Hall, 1975) 14.

5. Stern 61.

6. Joseph Catinella, "The Tenants," *Saturday Review* 25 September 1971: 36.

7. Stern 61.

8. Morris Dickstein, "*The Tenants*," New York Times Book Review 3 Oct. 1971: 22.

9. Stern, 62.

10. Israel Shenkar, "For Malamud It's a story," *The New York Times Book Review* 3 October 1971.

11. Cynthia Ozick, "Literary Blacks and Jews," *Bernard Malamud: A Collection of Critical Essays* 97.

12. E. H. Leelavathi Masilamoni, "Bernard Malamud: An Interview," *Indian Journal of American Studies* 9.2 July 1979: 36.

13. Barbara Gitenstein, "Bernard Malamud," *Novelists and Prose Writers*, ed. James Vinson (London: The Macmillan Press, 1979) 794.

14. Catinella 36.

15 Jacob Korg, "Ishmael and Israel," *Commentary* May 1972: 84.

16. John Alexander Allen, "The Promised End: Bernard Malamud's *The Tenants*," *The Hollins Critic* 8.5 December 1971: 4.

17. Kellman 466.

18. Roderick Craib, "*The Tenants*: Bernard Malamud," *Commonweal* 21 Dec. 1974: 311.

19. John Alexander Allen, 4.

20. B. Lindberg-Seyersted, "Reading of Bernard Malamud's *The Tenants*," *Journal of American Studies* 9.1 April 1975: 100.

21. Ben Siegel, "Through a Glass Darkly: Bernard Malamud's Painful Views of the Self," *The Fiction of Bernard Malamud*, ed. Richard Astro and Jackson J. Benson (Corvallis: Oregon State Univ. Press, 1977) 139.

22. Kellman 466.

23. B. Lindberg-Seyersted 100.

24. Stern 61.

25. Ben Siegel 139.

26. Ozick 84.

8

TO KITTY WITH LOVE: *DUBIN'S LIVES*

> *He (Dubin) said he desperately wanted her to.*
> *"Pay attention to your wife," said Maud, rising. "She's*
> *not a happy woman."*

Malamud's recent novel *Dubin's Lives*,* delves into the
psyche of a middle-aged man racked with the problems of sex,
love and infidelity. Malamud has in mind "a man's crises
during a period of three years," and the novel is "about one
human being, not all human beings."[1] Having experimented
with a painter in *Pictures of Fidelman* and novelists in *The
Tenants*, Malamud here provides a creative insight into the
craft of biography. With a larger-than-life atmosphere in
Dubin's Lives, Malamud emulates the complexity of the 19th
century novel in the tradition of Thomas Hardy and George
Eliot.[2] As Richard Gilman points out, the "double-edged"
title of the novel refers at an immediate level to the lives of

---

*Bernard Malamud, *Dubin's Lives* (New York: Avon Books, 1979).
All subsequent references with page numbers in paranthese are to this
edition.

Thoreau, Lincoln, and Mark Twain whose lives Dubin wrote, and "more poetically to the divisions within his own being."[3] Robert Rubenstein remarks that "*Dubin's Lives* opens out to address the limits of love and marriage, of familiarity, of self-fulfillment and fiction themselves by articulating the inconsistencies and emotional contradictions of real people."[4]

Seemingly different in form from Malamud's other novels, *Dubin's Lives* reveals the familiar moral stance of the writer. For Peter S. Prescott, the novel deals with the common question of Malamud: "how shall a man create for himself a new life ?"[5] The answer also remains the same—"One is reborn to life, and to one's life's work, by discovering passion, and by learning how to balance the conflicting demands of passion and commitment."[6] The commitment ultimately gets an upper hand over passion in Malamud's works as in *Dubin's Lives*. Yet one perceives a change in the overall tone of the novel. From the "sad-eyed ironist of human suffering," Malamud turns into "an unself-conscious celebrant of the Self."[7]

Dubin is a peculiar writer who lives the lives of others as he writes them and tries to understand his own self. He loves nature like Thoreau, but Lawrentian motives of sex, love and guilt haunt him. His marriage with Kitty, a widow is a bond of convenience dictated by mutual need. Both Dubin and Kitty live in their own worlds away from the present—Dubin in his lives of the dead, and Kitty in her reminiscences of her former husband and estranged children. Dubin at the age of 56 is attracted by Fanny, a promiscuous girl less than half his age. He is in a conflict between his obligation to his wife and passion for Fanny. His work halts and moves only when he continues his illicit contact with Fanny. He is, however, torn by a sense of guilt towards his wife. Dubin and Kitty drift from each other as Kitty has an affair with Evan Ondyk. Dubin's affair with Fanny ceases when in the end he goes back to his wife with love. The obligation to wife triumphs over the passion for mistress. Theme of compassion is suggested in *Dubin's Lives* in realisation of one's obligations and responsibilities. But the development of the theme is considerably marred by the long descriptions of sexual bouts of Dubin with

Fanny and the mechanically contrived situations of lust. The
inner conflict of Dubin is evident. Yet the end is abrupt as
Dubin returns to Kitty on a sudden. The book does not end,
but "just stops like a car running out of gas; or like a writer
whose weariness with his creatures has become intolerable."[8]
The novel also wants the compactness of narration. The
longest of Malamud's novels is filled with "mechanically turning wheel of seasons, depressions, deaths, and rebirths, the
monotonous cycle of jogging, Lawrence, summer, Fanny,
winter, aging, impotence, spring, jogging, Lawrence, summer,
etc."[9] Richard Locke considers it a failure because of its moral
obtuseness and the series of melodramatic events. He adds that
it is "a sign that the author has grown desperate with his book,
doubts its psychological validity, and feels obliged to pile on
effects to liven things up."[10] Robert Towers thinks that "the
action of the middle section flags rather seriously, becomes
slack and repetitious."[11] He is unhappy with the final section of
the novel which is complicated and "frenetic" with "new plot
twists" inadequately developed.[12] Dean Flower finds it "a very
mixed performance: uneasy in rhythm, tonally jarring, uninven-
tionally funny, boring yet suspenseful, deeply ambivalent."[13]

The characterisation of the novel also has become the butt
of criticism. Gilman faults the novel on imperfectly drawn or
overdrawn characters of Dubin's daughter and son.[14] Saul
Maloff also supports the view.[15] Bell considers that "The novel
is so overloaded with exigesis that no character but Dubin
emerges with any credible human clarity."[16] The minute details
about weather, flowers, trees, clothing, food do not leave us
with any solid idea about Dubin, Kitty and Fanny. Evidently
Dubin's Lives has little of the artistic control of plot and
characterization one is familiar with in Malamud's other novels.
The image of Lawrence hangs too much on Dubin and there is
not enough to account for the conflicting motives of Dubin.
Malamud has tried in vain to achieve too many things in
Dubin's Lives. Despite its "Tolstoyan ripeness and wisdom,"
Dubin's Lives shows that Malamud's "reach exceeds his
grasp."[17] Dubin cast under the shadow of Lawrence and
Thoreau fails to measure up to the crisis of morality. This
explains the weakness of the theme of compassion in *Dubin's*

Lives. Commenting on the novel Malamud has said that "the texture of it, the depth of it, the quality of human experience in it is greater than in my previous books."[18] Yet one has hardly any doubt that *Dubin's Lives* falls short of Malamud's achievement in *The Assistant* and *The Fixer* from the point of view of consistency in moral vision and technique of narration.

II

The novel introduces Dubin at the age of 56 thinking of winter in summer. It reflects Dubin's worry about the growing signs of old age in middle age. He has to his credit a gold medal from President Johnson for his distinction as a biographer. Having written the lives of Thoreau and Mark Twain out of his love of nature, Dubin chooses Lawrence. Although he finds it difficult to write on Lawrence "so intricately involuted, self-contradictory, difficult a man," (18) his discovery of unpublished correspondence of Lawrence kindles in him a hope with a new perspective. The biographer feels, "Everybody's life is mine unlived. One writes lives he can't live. To live forever is a human hunger." (10) He tells Fanny that he has a "souped-up sense of other people's lives so that I don't always mind my business." (23) He considers writting "a mode of being," and says: "If I write I live." (111) But like Lesser or Willie of *The Tenants*, he has buried himself in writing so much that it overrides his responsibility for his wife and children. Kitty at times reproaches him—"I'm married to you, not your book." (169)

Dubin prefers solitude to human company. In fact loneliness is the besetting sin of his whole family. Maud, his daughter by Kitty, and his step-son Gerald live away from the parents and are lonely. Dubin, of course, loves to be alone:

As a rule he enjoyed solitude. Being away from home, or occasionally remaining alone there, awoke moods he rarely experienced when his life was geared with Kitty's. What he felt now was more than a melancholy sense of being alone, or perhaps remembrance of that feeling in the past; this seemed a spontaneous almost soiled awareness, more apparent than ever, of one's essential aloneness: the self's separate closed self-conscious subjectivity. Dubin defined it for all time, as previously defined: death's insistence of its presence in life, history, being. If so, nothing new but why once more at this moment ? (41-42)

Dubin's gloomy family background, unhappy domestic life with Kitty and neurotic children are the causes of his loneliness. As the son of a waiter, Dubin shared his father's "inertia, fear, living fate—out of habit, compassion, impure love." (92) Brother's death by drowning, mother's insanity and father's passivity furthered his loneliness. His life is an unplanned journey on a wrong train. The image recurs in the novel.

Years after Hannah Dubin's death he seemed not to know what to do with himself. If your train's on the wrong track every station you come to is the wrong station. The wrong stops, year after year, were vocation and women he couldn't make it with. It seemed to William Dubin he was not prepared to invest a self in a better self—give up solitude, false dreams, the hold of the past. The train chugged on: the wrong train. (92)

Dubin's marriage with Kitty comes off quite strangely. Working as an assistant editor of *The Nation*, Dubin comes across the matrimonial advertisement put up by Kitty which she later cancelled by another letter. Dubin who has drifted all his life wants to change his life by marrying a goyish widow with a child. Dubin and Kitty like each other before marriage. Dubin rejects his father's racial objection to the marriages with his usual idealism.

. . . How can a man be a Jew if he isn't a man ? How can he be a man if he gives up the woman he wants to marry ? (73)

But the temperamental incompatibility leaves them without peace after the marriage.

Dubin's wife could be overly intense, reserved, impatient under stress, punitive, too often anxious. He could be egoistic, time-bound, impulsive, defensive, too often anxious. Though they were alike in more ways than they had guessed; or grew to be alike; often the unmatched elements of their temperaments and tastes—disjunctions, he called them—caused tension, disagreements, quarrels. Her senses were highly charged conductors. She knew before she knew; he got the message more slowly. (105-06)

Kitty has a phobia of the leakage of gasburners and every night goads Dubin to check them. She always compares Dubin with her former husband Nathanael and finds him inferior. Understandably annoyed Dubin tells her "I want to run my life my own way, not like yours or Nathanael's. I don't want to go on sharing with you to my dying day the benefits of your previous marriage." (140) They argue about "taste, habit, idiosyncrasy." (106) Kitty dislikes Dubin's incessant pursuit of biographies. She is not sure that she is *truly* in love with him. Guilty of her love for Roger Foster, she feels free only after her confession to Dubin. However she opts for Evan Ondyk when Dubin seeks other women. She frankly tells Dubin about her affairs, while Dubin often deceives her to live with Fanny. Dubin is bored of Kitty's "sameness, dissatisfactions, eccentricities" and "her fears, her unforgotten unforgettable past." (269)

Dubin unlike the other Malamud heroes prefers sexual liberation to restraint. His philosophy of life is "to live life to the hilt." He tells Fanny:

If you don't live life to the hilt, or haven't, for whatever reason, you will regret it—especially as you grow older— every day that follows. (36)

Although he dislikes Lawrentian blood theory, he realises it in his passion for Fanny. He seems to approve Lawrence's "I don't believe in the idea of one man for one woman, do you ? I mean, there just isn't one woman and one only that a man can marry." (127) Dubin is ready to have an affair with Betsy Croy who has rescued him from an accident. Quite unscrupulously he had an affair with Flora while her husband Greenfeld suffered from a heart attack elsewhere.

Dubin's affair with Fanny Bick and the consequent conflict forms part of the main action of the novel. Kitty employs Fanny to clean the house. Dubin feels her sexuality keenly and gets worried whether he "had responded to her as his usual self, or as one presently steeped in Lawrence's sexual theories, odd as they were." (24) He finds her "gifted in femininity" and falls for her.

Fanny is more than a match for Dubin. Although she lived for a while in a Buddhist commune, she is known for her promiscuous affairs with married and unmarried men. She shares Dubin's hedonistic concept of "seizing the day":

> To me life is what you do. I want it to enjoy, and not make any kind of moral lesson or fairy tale out of it. (36)

They soon embrace and kiss. Fanny quits the job when Dubin refuses to make love to her in Kitty's absence. Later he feels: "Being married doesn't mean being tied like cats by our tails." (53) He pursues Fanny and persuades her to spend a week with him in Venice.

The Venetian Interlude exposes Dubin as a comic victim subject to frustration and agony instead of anticipated sexual pleasures with Fanny. He feels guilty that a man of his age should flirt with a girl of his daughter's age. Yet he wants to enjoy because "I have it coming to me." (59) He thinks of Kitty and justifies his action as being necessary to protect "marital fidelity."

> 'I love her,' the biographer responded. 'I love her still but differently. Time passes, needs and feelings change. One tries, with others, to recover past pleasures, past privileges. One looks for diversion.' (62)

Fanny objects to the word "diversion" saying "I'm not a hooker." Dubin apologizes. The dilemma of Dubin is clear. He cannot deceive his wife, nor can he give up Fanny.

> Dubin then said 'I'm sure you understand, Fanny—I won't bring this up again—that she mustn't know about us, not

have the remotest suspicion. Her life hasn't been easy. I
wouldn't want to hurt her."
'Would you hurt me, William ?'
He swore no. 'I feel tender to you, Fanny, and hope you
feel something similar for me.' (65)

Dubin is a pathetic *schlemiel*. During the week in Venice
Fanny grows sick with diarrhoea and vomits. Dubin has to
nurse her like "a mother duck."

Dubin's agony is further increased when he finds his daughter Maud moving with a man of his age. After his futile search
for her, he returns to the Hotel in dejection only to find Fanny
in bed with a gondolier. Dubin thinks momentary pain is
better than long heart-break and bids goodbye to her. Back
home with a guilty conscience, Dubin tries to be nice to Kitty
and keeps her in good humour. He approves of her decision
to work part-time with Roger Foster in a library. His work
runs well and he also feels a rush of affection for his wife. But
Fanny's letters disturb his poise of mind. He regrets that "A
thoughtless girl, careless of him, had made a jackass of Dubin,
shamed him as he hadn't ever been." (124) He fails to rid
himself of Fanny's thoughts:

> There were too many reverberations of Fanny, too much
> static in his head, too much guilt. He had reacted as
> though his character had failed him; the true failure was
> one of judgment. (129)

He burns one of the letters which reveals Fanny's affairs with
Arnaldo in Murano and a sixty-two year old singer in Rome.
While Dubin wonders why he is so much drawn to Fanny,
Kitty complains that he is indifferent to her:

> You seem to want nothing *I* have to give. You hide
> your life, whispering what I can't hear. You're not affectio-
> nate. We never really talk to each other. (155)

Caught in a blizzard, Dubin feels abandoned with various
disturbing thoughts.

> What a mad thing to happen. What a fool I am. It
> was the having I wanted more than the girl. Who is she to

me ? She doesn't deserve the feeling I give her. See what I've done to myself. I'm like a broken clock—works, time, mangled. What is life trying to teach me ? (162)

The stormy Nature outside is symbolic of Dubin's mind. Kitty rescues him in time. She hates Dubin's "beastly love of solitude."

Dubin's pursuit of Fanny is in fact "related to his anxiety about his own aging and the whereabouts and safety of his daughter."[19] Away from Fanny, Dubin yearns for the company of his daughter. Maud has "electra complex." She often complained that her father never cared for her as much as he did Gerald. Maud finds in her old lover "father, friend and lover" and thinks that there is something "extraordinary" in their relationship and "that it had been happening since man appeared on earth." (362) When Maud comes home after a long absence, Dubin walks with her at her request and expresses his love for her. Their conversation reveals the deep-seated Freudean complex.

As he was following her along the path through Kitty's Wood Dubin stopped and said, 'Maud, I love you.'
She turned to him. 'I love you.'
'I love you more than anyone.'
'Papa,' Maud said, 'I'm not your wife.'
Dubin said he hadn't asked her to be.
'You neglect Mother. She's lonely.'
'It's a long story,' he said, 'but I'am addressing you. You're my daughter, I need you. Let's stay more closely in touch.'
'You have me.'
They embraced on the path in the white wood. Maud kissed him quickly. (183)

Dubin's resolution to "act the age I've earned" (201) fumbles the moment he meets Fanny. At the touch of her arm, he flings on to her. They make love in the open grass just as Levin does with Pauline in *A New Life*. Dubin thinks "This evens it, . . . for the cruel winter." (221) Dubin's sexual liberation does not bring him any happiness. In the Malamud canon, sexual

liberation "means no less turmoil than restraint."[20] Dubin
loves both Kitty and Fanny and cannot break with anyone.

> 'Do you love her—this minute ?'
> 'Yes.'
> 'Do you love me ?'
> 'Yes.'
> 'Bullshit.' (236)

Fanny could not understand Dubin's ambiguous nature. Dubin
registers at Gansevoort to convince Kitty of his pretext of
research, but spends the time with Fanny. He is also worried
about his growing dishonesty to Kitty. It acquires menacing
proportions in the context of Kitty's innocence. He desires "to
protect his relationship with Fanny, at the same time not hurt
Kitty." (255) He cannot properly conceal his real self from
Kitty. Kitty receives him "almost with compassion, as if he
had come back with a wound and only she knew it." (256)

Dubin seeks fulfilment in love with Fanny and "What he
desired she (Fanny) gave him." (262) It serves as a "break-
water against age, loss of vital energy, the approach of death."
(275) He likes Fanny's passionate feeling for him. But he is
unable to make up his mind to throw his lot with Fanny. She
grows sick of his indecision and decides to leave him. Soon
he comes across Fanny in the farmyard she has bought at
Center Campobello. Fanny informs Dubin that they could just
be friends. Dubin reduces himself to be "a Peeping Tom"
eavesdropping as Roger locks himself with Fanny in her room.
He however wins her back with his feverish pursuit.

Dubin's affair with Fanny is counterpoised with his daughter's relationship with a married man past sixty. He is shocked
to learn that Maud is pregnant and does not opt for abortion.
Maud questions her mother: "You've taught me to value life.
I value life. How can I have an abortion ?" (364) She tells her
mother that she has left the Zen Commune unable to concen-
trate. Then she saw her lover, a black teacher, and got pregnant. She does not care to inform her lover of her pregnancy
or worry about her marriage. She wants to live her life without
Dubin But Dubin tells her that he wants her. Maud retorts—

"Pay attention to you wife, . . . She's not a happy woman."
(363)   At the time of her departure, Dubin tells Maud wryly:

> 'I'd expect to help you,' he offered. 'But things are
> tight with us now. Inflation isn't helping. I'm worried
> about money.' (365)

Maud leaves for New York. Kitty accuses Dubin of having
driven her out of the house.

Dubin gets his due from Kitty. His cold response to Kitty
prompts her to draft to Evan Ondyk whom she often consulted
for therapy. She confesses her guilt but holds Dubin responsible for it.

> 'But what I want to say now is that I've broken it off. I
> don't regret what I've done, but I didn't do it easily. If it
> weren't for you I don't think I would have done it.' (375)

Kitty like Dubin does not want divorce either. Dubin feels the
deception of Frieda to Lawrence. Frieda became a lover of
Middleton Murry after Lawrence's death.

Fanny's sympathy for Kitty marks the turning point of
Dubin's life. One day Fanny tells Dubin that she had met
Kitty at the grocery market. She says that she has "felt sorry
for her. She looks mousy and sort of sad." (385) She sympathises with the predicament of Kitty and suggests that Dubin
could stay three days in a week with her and four with his
wife.

> She could have Thursday to Sunday. I'd like you to be with
> me Monday to Wednesday. There's a nice warm room with
> a desk for you to work in downstairs while you're here. I'd
> like to have that to look forward to. It would be less lonely
> those nights you aren't here. (385)

Dubin doubts Kitty's assent for this arrangement. Fanny
wonders why Dubin stayed married to Kitty.

> 'It wasn't so hard,' he explained. 'I'm a family man.
> We had kids we loved. I had my work to do. Condi-
> tions were good. There are other things.'

> 'But do you love her ?'
> 'I love her life.'
> 'Do you love me ?'
> He said he did. (385-386)

Dubin loves both Kitty and Fanny. Hugging Fanny he whispers "God bless you, dear Fanny." (386) On a sudden he jumps out of the bed, dresses himself and runs up the moonlit road "for his wife with love." (386) This return of Dubin to his wife as a loving husband is prompted by the realisation of his responsibility to Kitty and her children. He remembers that "in loving Fanny he withheld love from his wife and daughter." (296) Fanny's sympathy for Kitty has made Dubin realise his responsibility. He is obliged not only to his wife but also to his children. Gerald is caught in the vicious circle of KGB service and cannot get rid of it with any security. He has informed Dubin of his pathetic condition in a long letter. Dubin and Kitty plan to go to Russia after obtaining the visas and hope to do what they could. They are also anxious about the pregnant Maud lonely away at New York without any communication. Fanny could look after herself independently, but Kitty alone cannot solve all these problems. The last act of Dubin is seemingly impulsive and yet it marks a change in him and resolves his prolonged moral dilemma. At the end of the novel we find a list of the books by Dubin which includes the biography of Anna Freud written in collaboration with Maud. Obviously Dubin was able to protect Maud with his affection. He has a sense of fulfilment as he was able to finish Lawrence's biography besides his <i>The Art of Biography</i>.

Dubin's return with love to Kitty and her children is born of his awareness of commitment to their lot. It is an epiphanic act of grace and compassion. Dubin is changed by the epiphany of Fanny's guileless sympathy for Kitty.

Malamud's last novel <i>God's Grace</i> describes in a primitivistic setting the desperate efforts of lonely Cohn to achieve a sense of community with the animals as well. The emphasis on the need of compassion becomes markedly explicit in the novel.

NOTES

1. Ralph Tyler, "A Talk with the Novelist," *The New York Times Book Review* 18 Feb. 1979: 32.
2. *Loc. cit.*
3. Richard Gilman, *"Dubin's Lives,"* *New Republic* 24 March 1979: 29.
4. Robert Rubenstein, "Search for Self," *The Progressive* 43. June 1979: 58.
5. Peter S. Prescott, "A New Life," *Newsweek* 12 Feb. 1979: 83.
6. *Loc. cit.*
7. Dean Flower, "Picking up the Pieces," *The Hudson Review* 32.2 Summer 1979: 305.
8. Pearl K. Bell, "Heller and Malamud, Then and Now," *Commentary* 67.6 June 1979: 75.
9. Bell 74.
10. Richard Locke, "Malamud's Reach," *Saturday Review* 17 March 1970: 69.
11. Robert Towers, "A Biographical Novel," *The New York Times Book Review* 84.7. 8 Feb. 1979: 30.
12. Towers 30.
13. Flower 305.
14. Gilman 30.
15. Saul Maloff, "Loveliest Breakdown in Contemporary American Fiction: Malamud's Lives," *Commonweal* 106.8. 27 April 1979: 245.
16. Bell 75.
17. Locke 69.
18. Tyler 32.
19. David Levin, "The Lives of Bernard Malamud," *The Virginia Quarterly Review* 56.1 Winter 1980: 165.
20. Mark Schechner, "Jewish Writers," *Harvard Guide to Contemporary American Fiction*, ed. Daniel Hoffman (Cambridge, Mass.: Harvard Univ. Press, 1979) 211.

9

AFTER THE SECOND FLOOD: *GOD'S GRACE*

"If you depreciate lives, the worth of your own diminishes."

Malamud's last novel *God's Grace** is an effort to protect civilization from self-destruction and from the horrible consequences of a nuclear war. Malamud presents through fantasy and fable the tragic intensity of alienation and the desperate yearning for community in the context of total annihilation of life. Greed for arms, cold war situation and spiritual nullity in the world of today seem to lend support to Malamud's prognostication.

Though *God's Grace* differs from other Malamud novels as it employs fantasy as technique, its essential similarity could, however, be traced to his preoccupation with compassion as a means of transformation and redemption. Malamud presents a primitivistic setting in *God's Grace* and conveys the need of

compassion through the symbolic interplay of the Noble Savage
and the ignoble civilized. The desperate efforts of Cohn to
found a community with animals, and to create a new society
based on responsibility and compassionate concern for fellow-
beings reflect Malamud's humanistic fervour and primitivistic
concern. But such efforts of Cohn are bound to fail even in
the Malamudian fantasy since the basic human weaknesses of
lust, sexual jealousy, selfishness and greed overtake the
chimpanzees also, re-enacting as it were the drama of man's
self-destruction. The irony is obvious—how could animals
learn to be humane when men fail to be human ? The only
saving grace in the novel is gorilla George's offer of Kaddish
to Cohn to mourn his death at the end. George emerges
as the Noble Savage. The possibilities of good are not
altogether ruled out despite the formidable fate. *God's Grace*
becomes a telling commentary on the need for compassion
which is the only means to save the world from the impending
doom.

   God's Grace evokes the atmosphere of the *Bible, Robinson
Crusoe* and *The Tempest*.[2] It also draws comparison with Nevil
Chute's *On the Beach* which prognosticates the deadening
effect of atomic radiation in an "electronic paradise."[3] In the
animal world devoid of morality and compassion, Cohn cannot be a successful messiah, nor has he like Prospero magical
powers to set it right. The dialogues between Cohn and God
reveal the irresponsibil'ty of man more than God's inscrutable
wrath. The novel in essence is not an attempt to justify the
ways of God to men but to indict man's irresponsibility to
man, and God comes handy as a symbolic agent to unravel
this truth. The myth of the Flood and Noah's ark recurs with
a difference. The chosen few, this time only a man and a few
animals, are condemned to be free but they hasten to bring
about their own ruin. Cohn's attempt to inspire nobility in the
animals through Jewish religion fails, driving home the point
that religion can be of little use in the absence of intuitive
self-responsibility and fellow-feeling. To call *God's Grace*
Malamud's *A Guide to the Perplexed* as Epstein does is to take
the novel for a religious tract which it is not.[4]

II

In pointing out the lacunae of modern civilization Malamud lends primitivistic setting to *God's Grace*. He symbolically recasts this Hesiodic and Ovidian prophecy by indicting man for destruction in the imaginary war between Djanks and Druskies and the Second Flood of God. He emphasizes that the cause of destruction was man's "self-betrayal" and not God's wrath. "The war was man's: the Flood God's." (17) God roars at Cohn through the bulbous cloud: "Man after failing to use to a sufficient purpose his possibilities, and my good will, has destroyed himself." (12) He complains of destruction by men of everything natural and good.

> They have destroyed my handiwork, the conditions of their survival: the sweet air I gave them to breathe; the fresh water I blessed them with, to drink and bathe in; the fertile green earth. They tore apart my ozone, carbonized my oxygen, acidified my refreshing rain. Now they affront my cosmos. How much shall the Lord endure ?
>
> I made man to be free, but his freedom, badly used, destroyed him. In sum, the evil overwhelmed the good. The Second Flood, this that now subsides on the broken earth, they brought on themselves. They had not lived according to the Covenant. (12-13)

Malamud indicts modern civilization for destroying primitive values. The entire effort of Cohn, the lone survivor, is to realize man's errors and not to repeat them.

Malamud recreates primitive conditions by contriving the escape of Cohn from the nuclear war and the Flood. Calvin Cohn, a paleologist, working under the sea at the time of devastation, survives, as if it were God's *felix culpa*. (Later we come to know that some chimpanzees and baboons also mysteriously escaped destruction.) Malamud intends to stress the dreadful isolation of man through Cohn to underline the value of companionship. Drifting aimlessly on the lone oceanographic vessel Rebekah-Q Cohn realizes that "right words" and "right life" acquire meaning only in relation to other human beings.

On good days Cohn told himself stories, saying the Lord
would let him live if he spoke the right words. Or lived the
right life. But how was that possible without another
human life around ? (17)

He, however, makes a significant decision to "live on" despite
the wrathful God.

On the island Cohn is Adam endowed with awakened conscience. Malamud casts him in the figure of the Noble Savage
who lives the life of a hard primitivist. Cohn has to search for
everything and face the existential crisis like the primaeval man
assuming "a future for better or worse." He consoles himself
that his life in the cave is "better than death." All alone, he
offers *Kaddish* to the dead. The Telephone Directory he has
with him serves as a sort of "Book of the Dead." Cohn's act
of kaddish is not a mere rite but a symbol of his reverence for
life. He feels "The Dead must be acknowledged if one respected
life." (41) Death and destruction have brought him the
value of life. He remains a fructivore and vows "never to ingest
what had once been a living creature." (49)

Malamud gives us another "Noble Savage" in George, the
gorilla. The silent, unoffensive, serviceable gorilla also becomes
a symbol of Jewish endurance and compassion in contrast to
the noisy and naughty Buz. Its "saddened" eyes reflect the
Jewish suffering. Cohn realises that it was this gorilla that
nursed him silently and invisibly when he had fallen ill on the
island because of radiation poisoning. He names it George
after his late wife's father, a dentist who fixed people's tooth
for nothing. George is the only animal to profit by Cohn's
teaching both at home and at the Schooltree he set up later.
He is moved to hear the story of Egyptian persecution of
Israelites. Buz on the contrary appears as an antithesis to
George. Endowed with speech abilities by Dr. Bunder's
operation on its larynx, Buz becomes the product of modern
civilization. It represents as its name indicates the noise and
haste as well as the querrulousness, and finally ingratitude of
modern man in its betrayal of Cohn. It always offends George
and remains deaf to Cohn's lesson of compassion: "If we
expect to go on living we have to be kind to each other." (78)
Against the Jewish image of George, Buz seems to suggest the

"Christian" failure. We see Buz in its very first acquaintance giving a cross to Cohn. In the discussion of various tricky issues of the Bible, Buz takes the stance of a Christian as Cohn advocates the Jewish point of view. Buz shows interest in 'God and Son' rather than 'God and Father' and believes in the resurrection of 'Jesus of Nozoroth.' It belittles Abraham's sacrifice of Isaac as the story of "the Dod who cut his little boy's throat" (70) and expresses its dislike for the violence in the Old Testament. Cohn has to argue a great deal to convince Buz that there is plenty of violence and blood in the New Testament and that Abraham had never cut the boy's throat; in his place he offered a ram as sacrifice. But for Buz it remains just "a pretty simple story." (74) Malamud however does not stretch the analogy too far.

Cohn almost becomes a spokesman of Malamud in his concern for compassionate coexistence. As the tribe of chimpanzees on the island increases, he usurps the role of a teacher by establishing a "Schooltree" to impress on the brutes the need for ethical restraint. He tries to inspire a new awareness in them of the cosmos and of the mankind which had fallen because "men had failed each other in obligations and responsibilities—failed to achieve brotherhood, lost their lovely world, not to mention living lives." (p. 119) He is not however, free from the doubt: "Why hadn't He created man equal to whom He had imagined?" (136) This apparently provokes the wrath of God who fantastically descends on the island as a Pillar of Fire to knock him off his stool saying:

I am the Lord Thy God
who created men
to prefect Himself. (127)

This fantastic encounter is a symbolic manifestation of Cohn's guilty conscience seeking its blame in God for man's imperfection.

For Cohn as for a hard primitivist, animals become exemplars. He responds favourably to Mary's (the female chimpanzee) unnatural passion for him although he refuses to mate with her in the beginning. He does not agree with Buz that he is of a different kind from them and says that there is only one kind on the island—"sentient, intelligent living

beings." Cohn's consummation with Mary marks his complete
identification with the animals like a primitivist. It also results
in the birth of a new species of "humanoid infant, or
chimpanzee-human baby." Cohn hopes that "she may someday be the mother of a newer race of men." (165)

The optimism kindled in Cohn for a new civilization is
soon shattered by the ghastly deeds of Easu and other chimpanzees. Sex and cannibalistic violence become once again the
bone of contention. It recalls the description of the concluding
phase of man's earliest historical stage before the Deluge in
the Christian Chronological primitivism of *Clementia*.[5] Easu
rapes Sara, one of the baboons newly landed on the island. The
other chaimpanzees—Esterhazy, Bromberg, Saul and Luke—
just remain passive spectators. Easu kills the female baboon
later and eats it cannibalistically with others:

> After a solitary meal, relishing every morsel, grunting over
> the ravishing taste of fresh meat, Easu at length distri-
> buted a leg ligament to Saul of Tarsus, a small strip of gut
> to Esterhazy, the bloody windpipe to Luke, who fruitlessly
> blew into it; and Bromberg was permitted to suck Sara's
> eyeballs before Easu began to pry out the brain. (171)

Though Easu and his followers now and Buz later appear to be
ignoble savages, they are in fact portrayed to represent the ignoble civilized who perished in violence. Cohn, the Noble Savage,
is pitted against them with his missionary zeal to humanize the
brutes. His admonition "If you depreciate lives, the worth of
your own diminishes" (174) goes waste. Easu attacks Cohn
when he was exiled by the latter, and continues to kill the
baboons. Cohn is now disillusioned:

> Cohn felt himself a failure.
> I have failed to teach these chaimpanzees a basic truth.
> How can they survive if they do to fellow survivors what
> men did to each other before the Second Flood ? How will
> they evolve into something better than man ? (183)

The apocalypse recurs. Cohn fails to protect his only hope,
Rebakkah (his daughter)—"the future of another civilization."
The apes kill it cruelly. Cohn is heart-broken. He accuses Buz

of ingratitude for betraying his family to the murderous apes. He pulls away the knotted rusty wires which gave Buz speech. Ironically Buz's last words are: "I am not Buz, my name is Gottlob." (194) Things are now completely out of control. The apes at the Schooltree just mock at Cohn's grief. Mary is seen freely cohabiting with Easu and Gottlob (Buz). The apes attack Cohn's cave and drag him up the mountain with a bundle of split wood against his chest to burn him. Cohn becomes a Christ-figure to be martyred. On the way he meets a mysterious beggar who asks for a blessing. Cohn regrets his inability. The sonlike Buz now thrusts the knife into his throat. Cohn has the epiphanic awareness of god's mercy.

> 'Merciful God,' he said, 'I am an old man. The Lord has let me live my life out'. (201)

All the while Cohn had feared God more than he loved Him. He had in fact warned the chimpanzees in one of his seven admonitions that "God is not love, God is God."

The prophet has failed to reform the chimpanzees and ended up as a martyr. But George—the gorilla—who had always silently listened to the teachings of Cohn has imbibed the essence of Jewishness. Wearing a mudstained white yarmulke George reads a long *Kaddish* for Cohn. It is perhaps a consolation for all the ceaseless efforts of Cohn for meaningful existence. As a Malamud hero Cohn's only hope could be "to save a single soul before dying."[6] The conversion of George, however, comes off to fulfil Cohn's task partially despite the latter's failure with the chimpanzees. Malamud does not resort to the extreme forms of cultural primitivism such as cynicism, epicureanism or stoicism. He does not, like the cultural primitivists, believe that "the end of life was personal self-sufficiency (*autarky*), freedom from all claims made by the external world upon the soul of the individual."[7] He prefers bondage with fellow-beings in compassion to freedom. Though Malamud faults modern civilization on its narcissism and violence, his chief concern is for preservation of civilization and human values.

Malamud provides a fitting context for deep reflection on values. It is difficult to agree with Epstein that Malamud is on the decline as a novelist and *God's Grace* "takes on something of the quality of a television situation comedy, with symbolism added."[8] It is true that Malamud does not exert "the same imaginative powers upon the macrocosm as he does upon the microcosm" in the novel.[9] But one should remember that Malamud is not interested so much in the act of atomic destruction of the human race as in the portrayal of its horrendous consequences. That is the reason why Malamud describes the trauma of the Flood and the thermonuclear war quite cryptically in the beginning within a few sentences and launches the proper setting for the subsequent drama with Cohn.

Malamud's focus is on the microcosm of Cohn's trials for a meaningful society with brutes which is in a way the human microcosm imperilled by inhuman strifes.

Malamud's short stories in *The Magic Barrel, Idiots First* and *The Rembrandt's Hat* reveal the contexts of suffering and compassion in varied situations of life.

NOTES

1. Malamud refers to *God's Grace* in the making as "a short novel, a fable in which God is present." See Katha Pollit, "Bernard Malamud (Interview)," *Saturday Review* Feb. 1981: 39.

2. Clive Sinclaire, "The falling-out in Paradise," *Times Literary Supplement* 29 Oct. 1982: 1188.

3. Srinivas Iyengar, "In this year of anxiety: Anno Bombini, 40," *The Hindu* 17 July 1984: 17.

4. Joseph Epstein, "Malamud in Decline," *Commentary* October 1982: 53.

5. George Boas, "Primitivism," *Dictionary of the History of Ideas*, 4 Vols. (New York: Charles Scribner's Sons, 1973) 3: 582.

6. Clive Sinclaire 1188.

7. George Boas 585.

8. Joseph Epstein 53.

9. Clive Sinclaire 1188.

10

IN DEFENSE OF THE HUMAN: *THE MAGIC BARREL, IDIOTS FIRST* AND *REMBRANDT'S HAT*

"There's only one human color and that's the colour of blood."

"Black Is My Favorite Color"

With the publication of three collections of short stories, Malamud has emerged also as a short-story writer of considerable skill. He is often compared with such great Yiddish masters as I. L. Peretz, Mocher Seforim, and Sholom Aleichem not only for his technique of story-telling but also for his "concern for morality and ethics."[1] The compassion which shapes Malamud's moral vision in his novels is evident in many of his short stories as well. Dogged by misfortune and injustice, Malamud's characters strive to seek redemption in compassion. Although Malamud's short stories, like his novels, deal with the same "thorny" subjects—"spiritual growth and decay, the terrors of alienation and salvation," as Richman points out, "there is about many of them an echo of a long-dead voice intoning directly, 'I will tell you now of Dragons.' "[1] They create a lively atmosphere moving as they do from sheer fantasy to stark realism. A deep concern for compassion unifies Malamud's apparently dissimilar stories. To suggest the theme of compassion, Malamud explores the backdrop of inordinate suffering in the *Magic Barrel*, inhuman violence in *Idiots First* and failure of communication in *Rembrandt's Hat*.

II

The Magic Barrel[3] reveals Malamud's love of Jews, of "humanity, compassion, and all the virtues."[4] The citation of the National Book Award Committee reads: "Compassionate and profound in its wry humor, it captures the poetry of human relationship at the point where reality and imagination meet." R. C. Blackman points out that "a tone of resigned and humorous wisdom and an unsentimental central compassion" unify the stories of *The Magic Barrel*.[5] The tragic suffering of Panessas in "The Bill," Lieb in "The Loan" and Roses in "Take Pity" acquire meaning in their compassionate response to the needs of the suffering brethren.

Compassion at the cost of self-effasive suffering is poignantly evoked in stories like "The Bill" and "Take Pity." The predicament of Panessa and Axel in their stories recalls that of Morris in *The Assistant*. Although poor himself, Panessa in "The Bill" readily gives credit to Willy Schlegel, a poor janitor. His compassion is prompted by an unflinching faith in humanity. His concept of "credit" is the recognition of the fact "that people were human beings, and if you were really a human being you gave credit to somebody else and he gave credit to you." (130) His innocence, is, however, exploited by Willy who buys all his needs from the shop only on credit even when he has money. When the credit reaches eighty-dollars and odd, Panessa is forced to ask for payment with a smiling face. But Willy instead of paying the bill stops coming to the grocery. He later feels guilty and dreams of paying off the debt but could not, because of his abject penury. One day he receives a note from Mrs. Panessa requesting him to pay at least ten dollars since her husband is ill. Willy, helpless as he is, tears the letter and hides himself all day in the cellar. The next day in a sudden impulse to help, he pawns his coat for ten dollars and goes to Panessas. But it is too late. Panessa is dead; his coffin greets Willy. Willy feels an incommunicable despair. "He tried to say some sweet thing but his tongue hung in his mouth like dead fruit on a tree, and his heart was a black-painted window." (136) The bill remains unpaid. The story reveals how "in a world ruled by the ineluctable demands of economies and accidents, even the good turn rank."[6]

In contrast to Willy, Rosen in "Take Pity" is keen on helping the starving family of Axels by all possible means. He gives credit to Axel, a Polish refugee because "I didn't want them to Suffer." (80) Out of pity he advises Axel to quit the "dead neighbourhood." Axel does not listen to him and dies of starvation. He suggests to Eva, the wife of Axel, to leave the place for good and seek a job. He offers his two-family house in a different place. But Eva does not heed his advice. She spends the insurance money of her dead husband on the store in vain and starves herself and her two daughters. Despite her steadfast refusal Rosen tries to help her because "what else could I do ? I have a heart and I am Human." (83) Though a sick man, Rosen offers to marry her to be a prop to her family. When Eva is averse to him, he devises a scheme to send her twenty dollars a week through a friend of Axel in Jersey. Eva returns all the post. Rosen takes it as a challenge and stubbornly decides to help her.

> "Here," I said to myself, "is a very strange thing—a person that you can never give her anything.— *But I will give.*" (87)

Rosen commits suicide bequeathing all his property and investments by a will to Eva and to her daughters after Eva's death. As he narrates the story to Davidov, the census-taker, in a mysteriously grotesque atmosphere, Eva appears at the door with outstretched hands for him. Having nothing to give her, Rosen curses her and asks her to go back to her children. The story suffers from an abrupt conclusion and leaves sneaking doubts as to how a man who turned on the gas and put his face in the stove could tell his story to Davidov.

Tommy's compassion for a little girl who has pilfered chocolate bars from his candy store is depicted in "The Prison." Feeling sorry that "She was so young and a thier," he decides to rescue her "before she got trapped and fouled up her life before it got started." (91) He fails to warn her because "the fear in her eyes bothered him." (91) At last he plans to conceal in the chocolate bar the message—"Don't do this any more or you will suffer your whole life." Before his message reached the girl, the girl is caught red-handed by Rosa, Tommy's wife. Tommy not only rescues the girl from Rosa's iron hand but also lies to the mother of the girl saying that he let her take the chocolate. As she is dragged away by the mother, the girl manages "to turn her white face and thrust out at him her red tongue." (94) Obviously the message has not reached her.

In the story "The Mourners" compassion emerges as an epiphany from the bleak atmosphere of inhumanity. Kessler, the poor tenant, is thrown out of "the decrepit tenement flat" by the landlord Gruber and Janitor Ignace. The passers-by are indifferent to him although he freezes almost to death in the snow. The old Italian lady of the top floor, however, is horrified at the sight. She gets him upstairs into his room with the help of her sons and gives him a plate of hot macaroni. This act of compassion moves Kessler to realise his own guilt to his wife and three children whom he had recklessly abandoned long back "without even in some way attempting to provide for them." (28) Torn by grief for his lack of compassion, he engages himself in an act of mourning. His visible suffering moves the angry Grubeshov too. He is stricken by the "unbearable remorse for the way he had treated the old man," and feels that "the mourner was mourning him: it was he who was dead." (28) With a cry of shame, he too becomes a mourner by the side of Kessler.

"The Loan" is a story of miserable people haunted by bad luck. Kobotsky could not cover the grave of his wife with a stone even after five years of her death. He approaches his old friend Lieb for a loan. Lieb whose bakery business has just improved, is ready to give the loan forgiving Kobotsky's earlier evasion of debt, but his wife objects. She is moved by the story of Kobotsky, but instead of giving the loan recounts her own tragic past which overcomes the woe of Kobotsky. As the loaves in the trays burn into "blackened bricks—charred corpses," Kobotsky and Lieb embrace, kiss each other, and part forever.

Love redeems the suffering of Sobel in "The First Seven Years" and the loneliness of Leo Finkle in "The Magic Barrel." Sobel, the lonely concentration camp survivor, works as an assistant to Feld, the shoemaker, for "stingy wages" for five long years only with the hope of marrying his daughter, Miriam. As Feld has other plans for her, Sobel quits the job. Learning Sobel's love for his daughter, Feld asks him to wait for two more years till she is twenty-one. Sobel agrees and continues to pound leather "for his love." (20) He is cast in the mould of Frank Alpine of *The Assistant.*

Leo Finkle's impulsive love for Stella in "The Magic Barrel" does not leave him even when he learns from her father of her sinful life. After a conflict he resolves "to convert her to goodness, himself to God," (187) with compassion. When the rendezvous is arranged, he goes to her in high spirits and "pictured, in her, his own redemption." (188)

Manischevitz's realisation that "there are Jews everywhere" ("Angel Levine")—a faith that transcends the confines of differing skins—reveals the spirit of Malamud's moral vision.

III

Idiots First[7] invests the Malamudian *schlemiels* with "dignity as well as pathos."[8] Malamud's compassion for the suffering protagonists redeems the stories of ensnarement "from being merely oppressive."[9] The title of the book itself reveals the author's "moral concern for the afflicted."[10] While the title story stresses the redemptive value of compassion, stories like "The Death of Me," "The German Refugee," and "The Cost of Living" speak out for compassion in the wake of violence and depression.

"Idiots First" graphically describes the agony of a dying father for his retarded son. To send his idiot son to the safe custody of his uncle at California, Mendel makes a compact with death (personified as Ginzburg) to spare him for one evening, and runs from pillar to post to acquire the thirty-five dollars he fell short of for the train ticket. The inhuman pawn-broker refuses to give more than eight dollars for Mendel's old watch. The so-called philanthropist, Fishbein, rejects Mandel's request reiterating his "fixed policy" never to encourage "un-organized charity." (7) The old rabbi, however, pities Mendel and parts with his fur-lined caftan resisting his wife. Mendel goes to the railway station with sufficient money but it is too late. Ginzburg appears as ticket collector and stops him. His iron law knows no commodity called "pity." Asking "don't you understand what it means human?" (14) frustrated Mendel grabs Ginzburg by the throat. In the scuffle that follows, Ginzburg overpowers Mendel, but seeing in the eyes of Mendel his own awful wrath, relents long enough for Mendel to place the son on board the train and return. The motto "Tsdokeh (Charity) will save from death" governs the story as in most of Malamud's fiction.[11]

The racial prejudices and anti-Semitism in the stories "Black Is My Favorite Color" and "The Jewbird" amplify the idea of brotherhood. "Black Is My Favorite Color" is considered one of the best stories in the collection.[12] Nat Lime, the Jew, beli-eves that "there's only one human color and that's the color of blood." (18) For his love of the blacks, he has to court only their hatred. His predicament reminds us of Harry's (in *The Tenants*) in the hands of the black writer Willie. Despite his repeated requests, Charity Sweetness, the cleaning woman, prefers bathroom to his kitchen for eating bread. He receives a kick in the teeth for his help to a blind old blackman. He regrets, "I give my heart and they kick me in my teeth." (30) In his childhood, he longed for the friendship of Buster Wilson, a black boy who went with him to the movies and accept-ed his candys but ultimately hit him in the teeth saying —"Take your Jew movies and your Jew candy and shove them up your Jew ass."[13] (22) Later as a young man, Nat loved a Negress widow, Ornita Harris. Ornita loves him, but accosted one day by the black thieves as a traitor, leaves him for ever. As a result, Nat remains a bachelor even at the age of forty-four. Despite the set-backs, he believes "black is still my favorite color" but says "you wouldn't know it from my luck except in

short quantities. . . ." (18) The paradox is that nobody bothers
to understand the language of the "heart" of Nat.

"The Jewbird" shows the cruelty and lack of compassion
of anti-Semites. Schwartz, the crow-like talking Jewbird, is the
"victim" figure and "the compound image of opportunist and
saint who tests to the extreme the humanity and the compassion of others ?[14] Harry Cohen hates the bird right from its
arrival for its stinking fish-smell and jewishness. Cohen's son
Maurie and wife Edie, however, like the bird very much.
Maurie plays with the bird and the bird usurps the role of
father taking full responsibility for Maurie's performance in
school. As the hatred grows, Cohen invents dirty tricks of
torture to force the exit of the bird. He brings a cat home
which, being a continuous nightmare to the bird, robs its peace.
One day when he is alone, Cohen flings the bird forcibly out
into the dark night, throwing with it the chances of his redemption. Maurie recovers the dead bird later and asks with grief
"who did it to you, Mr. Schwartz ?" Maurie tells him, "anti-
semeets." (113) The first words of the bird at Cohen's house—
"Gevalt, a pogrom !" (102)—come true.

The saddest of all the stories, "The German Refugee"
depicts Oskar Gassner, a German refugee's feat of death and
sense of alienation against the backdrop of Nazis' capture of
Poland and massacre of Jews. Gassner is tormented by his guilt
of wilful abandonment of his goyish wife at Germany and
failure of any real accomplishment in America where he emi-
grated. He hires Martin Goldberg, the narrator, to teach
English so that he could successfully deliver the first lecture in
the Fall. He goes through an arduous phase of depression in
the process of learning and vows to kill himself if he failed to
deliver the lecture in English. The narrator with his undaunted
faith in Gassner reads on the latter's topic and shows his
notes to him. Gassner is roused to think creatively—"no, it
wasn't love of death they had got from Whitman—that ran
through German poetry—but it was most of all his feeling for
Brudermensch, his humanity." (209) In his attempt to answer
the narrator, Gassner finds himself having written the half of
his lecture. The lecture goes well. He reads some of the lines of
Whitman as though he believed them.

And I know the spirit of God is the brother of my own,
And that all the men ever born are also my brothers, and
    the women my sisters and lovers,
And that the Kelson of creation is love. . . . (211)

This changed attitude of Gassner from death to life does not
last long amidst the oppressed times and his own haunting guilt.
Learning the horrible death of his wife at the hands of Nazis,
Gassner commits suicide. The shocked narrator learns from
the mother-in-law's letter to Gassner that Gassner's wife,
forcibly converted to a Jew by a vengeful rabbi, was trans-
ported by the Nazis to Poland and shot dead along with many
other Jews.

"The Death of Me" narrates the desperate efforts of a
clothier, Marcus, to reconcile his ever-fighting assistants. Josip
Bruzak, the presser and Emilio Vizo, the tailor, live in perpe-
tual hatred of each other, and create a hullabaloo every day
much to the detriment of business. The thick wooden partition
constructed between them does not keep them quiet for long.
They seem to listen to Marcus' entreaties for peace and
message of compassion, but the moment the master is out they
are in for a fight. Saddened and maddened at the eerie violence, Marcus' heart is broken.

The heart-breaking efforts of Sam Tomashevsky in "The
Cost of Living" with his grocery store, a losing concern,
recalls the fate of Morris Bober of *The Assistant*. Sam's bleak
hopes of business are dashed by the new grocery opened in the
neighbourhood. His attempt to get a shoe-store opened there
instead of the grocery fails. All his efforts to renew his store
fetch him nothing. The auction of the store gets Sam not even
a quarter of the sum needed to pay the creditors. He silently
moves away with his wife Sura and would not return to look
at his old store dreading the possibility of its emptiness.

In all these glommy situations, Malamud suggests that
"unless love balances the bleak negativism of the Law . . .
there can be no rebirth, no triumph of the spirit against
egotism and evil."[15]

IV

Commenting on *Rembrandt's Hat*,[16] Jeffrey Helterman has remarked that it "continues his (Malamud's) concern with the growth or collapse of the fine bond of compassion that binds two human beings together."[17] While the theme of compassion appears in the foreground in *The Magic Barrel*, it tends to be implicit and suggestive in *Idiots First* and *Rembrandt's Hat*. The wasteland theme serves as a subtle pointer to the need for compassion in *Rembrandt's Hat*. The characters here fail to communicate with each other and miss the visible sign of compassion. Robert Phillips points out that "The two themes, spiritual isolation and failure of communication pervade all eight stories."[18] Stories like "Talking Horse," "The Letter" and "My Son, the Murderer" graphically depict the chasm of failure of communication in an anxiety-ridden world leading to absurd situations. Malamud seems to suggest here that communication is the minimum sign of interpersonal responsibility and understanding which are the bases of compassion.

"The Letter," shortest of all the stories, speaks symbolically of "our estrangement from the world about us."[19] Teddy, a patient in the mental hospital, waits endlessly at the gate to post his empty letter—"four sheets of cream paper with nothing written on them" (101) to his father Ralph. Ironically enough, Ralph is also in the same hospital as a patient. Both father and son request Newman, who visits the place for his father every Sunday, to post the letter. Newman complains: "There's nothing to mail. There's nothing in the letter. It's a blank." (106) But Ralph asserts: "There's a whole letter in there. Plenty of News." (106) In a way the letter is a sad commentary on the growing isolation between man and man. It also stands as a replica of Newman's guilty conscience. Newman himself feels his Sunday visits to his father "murderous" and wants to take relief for a week if only his father permits. The letter stands as "a potent symbol for the absence of communication between father and son."[20] While the predicament of insane father and son calls for our sympathy, it suggests the absurd deeds of the so-called sane people like Newman who discharge their obligations reluctantly without love.

The communication gap between father and son is complete in "My Son, the Murderer." The father-son conflict appears in a situation reverse to that of Saul Bellow's novella *Seize the Day*. While son craves for the sympathy of his indifferent father in *Seize the Day*, it is the turn of father in Malamud's story to beg of his callous son to refrain from the acts that endanger his life. Living under the same roof, Harry does not talk to his father Leo. He is an isolated type and does not accept any job in his worry about the Vietnam war. "I expect to be drafted any day but it doesn't brother me the way it used to. I won't go. I'll go to Canada or Somewhere I can go." (167-168) The war has made Harry tense. He refuses Leo's suggestion to be relaxed. To understand his son's complexity Leo spies on his son and reads his letter stealthily, but the son warns: "If you do this again, don't be surprised if I kill you." (172) Yet Leo haunts his son. One day finding his son with his feet deep in water, Leo implores him to come out lest he should catch cold. His comment on life is significant:

> Harry, what can I say to you ? All I can say, to you is who says life is easy ? Since when ? It wasn't for me and it isn't for you. It's life, that's the way it is—what more can I say ? But if a person don't want to live what can he do if he's dead ? Nothing. Nothing is nothing, it's better to live. (174)

The passage reveals Malamud's commitment to human values. Having intense reverence for life, Malamud affirms it in spite of all the misery that attends it. Leo's inability to persuade his son not to die shows lack of understanding between them. On his way back home Leo runs after his own hat blown off by the gush of wind. This pursuit of the hat is "as elusive as the bond between himself and his son."[21]

"Man in the Drawer," the longest of the short stories, depicts the anguish of a writer to communicate his ideas to others through publication. Feliks Levitansky is a taxi-cab driver who writes for his drawer since his powerful Russian stories were refused publication on the pretext that they violate "social realism." He cannot write "acceptance" stories much against his conscience. So he requests Howard Horvitz, the American tourist in Russia who also writes, to smuggle his work to

America and get them published there for his "interior liberty."
Though he finds the stories interesting, the timid tourist does
not accept the proposal fearing the mess of Russian espionage.
In his refusal, Harvitz fails in his responsibility as man to
another man. Levitansky makes it clear.

'What exactly is my responsibility to you, Levitansky?'
I tried to contain the exasperation I felt.
'We are members of mankind. If I am drowning you must
assist, to save me.'
'In unknown waters if I can't swim?'
'If not, throw to me rope.' (72)

The conversation between Harvitz and Levitansky is similar to
that of Fidelman and Susskind in *Pictures of Fidelman*.

'. . . Am I responsible for you then, Susskind?'
'Who else?' Susskind loudly replied.
'. . . Why should I be?'
'You know what responsibility means?'
'I think so.'
'Then you are responsible because you are a man. Because
you are a Jew, aren't you?"[22]

Malamud emphasises that the mere fact that one is a member of
mankind is enough to presuppose one's responsibility for other
men. The true spirit of compassion lies in the innate, not imposed, sense of responsibility of man for the fellow-sufferer. As
Harvitz half-heartedly realises this, Levitansky refuses to take
his help. Levitansky's brother-in-law, however, gets the stories
to Harvitz who accepts them reluctantly.

The frustration of Levitansky with the so-called Revolution
in Russia without freedom of expression is narrated in one of
his short stories where the protagonist burns all his stories—the
refused stuff—in the sink. To the enquiry of his nine-year old
son, he says "I am burning my integrity," and "My talent, my
heritage." (95) In the clash between personal integrity and
social authoritarianism, it is the former that scores a spiritual
victory over the letter despite its material failure.

The theme of the title story "Rembrandt's Hat" is "mis-
communication."[23] The art-historian Arkin's innocent compari-

son of the sculptor Rubin's white cap with "Rembrandt's Hat" develops a wedge between them. Rubin not only stops wearing the hat, but also consciously avoids Arkin. Arkin is at a loss to know the cause of Rubin's misunderstanding and hates Rubin for hating him. When his own white-cap presented to him by a student is missing, he suspects Rubin. But the veil of misunderstanding is cleared with his discovery that Rembrandt's hat does not resemble Rubin's. Arkin feels that Rubin's misery is complicated because of his poor accomplishment in sculpture. He immediately apologises to Rubin for the wrong remark. Thereafter they become friends again. Rubin once again wears his "Rembrandt's Hat," "a crown of failure and hope." (141) Malamud suggests here that all misunderstanding can be cleared with proper communication and sympathy.

"The Silver Crown" reveals that true sense of responsibility cannot rest in fake passion. Albert, a high school biology teacher, has done nothing for his father all his life, and now guilt-ridddn he wants to save his dying father at any cost. Having failed with doctors, he goes to the rabbi J. Lifschitz, the faith-healer, despite his disbelief in such cures. Though empirical in mind, he is taken in by the illusion of the "Silver Crown" created by the rabbi in a mirror. Impressed by the vision, Albert pays 986 dollars for a bigger crown for instant cure of his father's disease. But later he realises that it was just a case of hypnosis. Regretting his action, he insists that the rabbi should refund his money. The rabbi begs him to be "merciful to an old man. Think of my poor child. Think of your father who loves you." (29) Albert who has no genuine love for his father, says: "He hates me, the son-of-a-bitch, I hope he croaks." (29) The magical crown is as palpable and unsubstantial "as the son's wish to save his father's life. When the wish falters, the crown dissolves."[24] Elder Gans dies. The fault is not actually that of the duping priest but that of the duped son who has no genuine love for his father. Albert's attempt to save his father is not motivated by felt responsibility. He is far more concerned about the money he has lost than for the life of his father.

"Talking Horse" is "an existential statement on man's search for identity and freedom."[25] Abramowitz (the talking horse) feels that he is man hidden in horse, and yearns for freedom both from the false image and the clutches of the "deaf-mute" master, Goldberg. Goldberg is sullen and does not brook any questions from the horse. The "morse-code" messages he communicates to the horse are only in the shape of a tyrant's threats. The master who ekes out his living on the horse-show does not listen to its appeals for freedom. The horse pleads in vain with audience to help restore its original form. "I wish to be what I really am which is a man." (202) At last finding the gate-doors unlocked one day, the horse gallops out. In the struggle with the master he loses his horse-head into the hands of the master. Like a centaur with a man's head, he runs out free.

In all the stories of *Rembrandt's Hat*, failure of communication causes lack of understanding or vice versa. Such contexts have no room for compassion since understanding has in it "the beginnings of compassion, of pity and of charity."[29] Levenspiel's cry (in *The Tenants*) "Hab rachmones" (Have Mercy) in fact sums up Malamud's philosophy of compassion. Malamud condemns the life-negating factors like absence of communication and affirms a positive view of life. To him "Life is better than Death" and it is compassion that makes life better. This affirmative vision is the unifying force of his novels and short stories.

NOTES

1. Ben Siegel quoted in Irving Malin, *Jew and Americans* (Carbondale: Southern Illinois University Press, 1965) 171.

2. Sidney Richman, *Bernard Malamud* (New York: Twayne, 1966) 99.

3. Bernard Malamud, *The Magic Barrel* (Harmondsworth: Penguin Books, 1958). All subsequent references in Part II with page numbers in parantheses are to this edition.

4. Henry Popkin, "Jewish Stories," *Kenyon Review* 20.4 Autumn 1958: 641.

5. R.C. Blackman, *Christian Science Monitor* 15 May 1958: 11.

6. Richman 107.

7. Bernard Malamud, *Idiots First* (New York: Farrar, Straus, 1964). All subsequent references in Part III with page numbers in parantheses are to this edition.

8. David Boroff, "Losers, But not Lost," *Saturday Review* 12 Oct 1963: 33.

9. Robert Alter, "Out of the Trap," *Midstream* 9.4 December 1963: 88.

10. Alter 88.

11. Everlyn Gross Avery, *Rebels and Victims: The Fiction of Richard Wright and Bernard Malamud* (New York Kennikat Press, 1979) 45.

12. Richman 138.

13. The incident is autobiographical. Malamud as a young boy had a black friend, Buster who fell out with him when Malamud teased him with a remark about watermelon. See Avery 94.

14. Richman 126.

15. Herbert Leibowitz, "Malamud and the Anthropomorphic Business," *New Republic* 21 Dec. 1963: 22-23.

16. Bernard Malamud, *Rembrandt's Hat* (New York: Farrar, Straus, Giroux, 1973). All subsequent references in Part IV with page numbers in parantheses are to this edition.

17. Jeffrey Helterman, "Bernard Malamud," *Dictionary of Literary Biography*, 4 Vols. (Detroit, Michigan: A Bruccoli Clark Book, 1978) 2: 302.

18. Robert Phillips, Review of *Rembrandt's Hat*, *Commonweal* 99 (1973): 245.

19. *Loc. cit.*

20. *Loc. cit.*

21. *Loc. cit.*
22. Bernard Malamud, *Pictures of Fidelman* (Harmondsworth: Penguin, 1980) 19.
23. Phillips 245.
24. Robert Kiely, *"Rembrandt's Hat,"* *New York Times Book Review* 3 June 1973: 7.
25. Phillips 246.
26. Rollo May, *Power and Innocence: A Search for the Sources of Violence* (New York: W. W. Norton, 1972) 258.

11

CONCLUSION

The study in the preceding chapters reveals Malamud's concern with the theme of compassion. Malamud is sensitively alive to the human suffering in the Jewish personae and suggests compassion as the "grace under pressure." His compassionate attitude to life is in conformity with the Jewish tradition and history. Although every religion teaches human values of compassion and love, the Jewish history has imparted special significance to it. Although Malamud does not want to limit himself as a Jewish writer, he acknowledges his debt to the authentic Jewish experience and sensibility. In fact he acclaims that the advent of the World War II and the Holocaust first made him sure that he had something to say as a writer.[1] He values authentic human experience in the act of writing because: "What moves me moves me to art."[2] The impact of Jewishness on Malamud's work has provided him with a compassionate and tragic vision of life. His work reveals a profound reverence for human dignity.

Malamud is at his best in *The Assistant* and *the Fixer* where theme of compassion is evoked most effectively. These two novels are crucial to the understanding of Malamud's philosophy of compassion. The theme of compassion is consistent in the first novels of Malamud, while the subsequent three novels somewhat falteringly suggest it. The last novel *God's Grace* reveals that Malamud has not lost his faith in humanity. To him "Life is better than Death" and compassion makes life better.

NOTES

1. Michiko Kakutani, "Malamud," *International Herald Tribune* 23 July 1980: 14.

2. Bernard Malamud, Speaking of Books: Theme, Content and the 'New Novel'," *New York Times Book Review* 26 March 1967: 2.

BIBLIOGRAPHY

I Primary Sources

A. Novels

Malamud, Bernard. *The Natural*. New York: Harcourt, Brace, 1952.

——. *The Assistant*. New York: Farrar, Straus and Cudahy, 1957.

——. *A New Life*. New York: Farrar, Straus and Cudahy. 1961.

——. *The Fixer*. New York: Farrar, Straus and Giroux, 1966.

——. *Pictures of Fidelman: An Exhibition*. New York: Farrar, Strauss and Giroux, 1969.

——. *The Tenants*. New York: Farrar, Straus and Giroux, 1971.

——. *Dubin's Lives*. New York: Avon Books, 1979.

——. *God's Grace*. Harmondsworth: Penguin Books, 1982.

B. Short Stories

Malamud, Bernard. *The Magic Barrel*. New York. Farrar, Straus and Cudahy, 1958.

——. *Idiots First*. New York: Farrar, Straus, 1963.

——. *Rembrandt's Hat*. New York: Farrar, Straus and Giroux, 1973.

C. Articles and Speeches

Malamud, Bernard. Report of Malamud's address at Princeton University, *Esquire* 60 July 1963: 6.
——. "Speaking of Books: Theme, Content and the 'New Novel'," *New York Times Book Review* 26 March 1967: 2 and 29.
——. "The Writer's Task," *Writing in America*, ed. John Fisher and Robert B. Silvers. New Brunswick, N.J.: Rutgers Univ. Press, 1960: 173.

II. Secondary Sources

A. Books

Astro, Richard and Jackson J. Benson, eds. *The Fiction of Bernard Malamud*. Corvallis: Oregon State Univ. Press, 1977.

Baumbach, Jonathan. *The Landscape of Nightmare: Studies in the Contemporary American Novel*. New York: New York Univ. Press, 1965.

Bewkes, Eugene G., Howard B. Jefferson et al. *The Western Heritage of Faith and Reason*. New York: Harper and Row, 1963.

Bolakian, Nona and Charles Simmons, eds. *The Creative Present: Notes on Contemporary American Fiction*. New York: Doubleday, 1963.

Bryant, Jerry H. *The Open Decision: The Contemporary American Novel and its Intellectual Background*. New York: Free Press, 1970.

Buber, Martin. *Between Man and Man*. New York: Macmillan, 1975.

Burgess, Anthony. *The Novel Now: A Guide to Contemporary Fiction*. New York: Norton, 1967.

Chase, Richard. *The American Novel and its Tradition*. New York: Doubleday, 1957.

Cohen, Sandy. *Bernard Malamud and the Trial by Love*. Amsterdam: Rodopi N.V., 1974.

Dimont, Max I. *Jews, God and History.* New York: Signet Books, 1964.

Ducharme, Robert. *Art and Idea in the Novels of Bernard Malamud*: Towards *The Fixer.* The Hague, Paris: Mouton, 1974.

Fiedler, Leslie A. *Love and Death in the American Novel.* New York: Criterion, 1960.

———. *The Jew in the American Novel.* New York: Herzl Press, 1959.

Field, Leslie A. and Joyce W. Field, eds. *Bernard Malamud*: *A Collection of Critical Essays* (TCV). Englewood Cliffs, N.J.: Prentice-hall, 1975.

———. *Bernard Malamud and the Critics.* New York: New York Univ. Press, 1970.

Finklestein, Sidney. *Existentialism and Alienation in American Literature.* New York: International Publishers, 1965.

Fromm, Erich. *You Shall be as Gods*: *A Radical Interpretation of the Old Testament and Its Tradition.* New York: Holt, Rinehart and Winston, 1967.

Harap, Louis. *The Image of the Jew in American Literature*: *From Early Republic to Mass Immigration.* Philadelphia: The Jewish Publication Society of America, 1974.

Hassan, Ihab. *Radical Innocence*: *Studies in the Contemporary American Novel.* Princeton, N.J.: Princeton Univ. Press, 1961.

Hicks, Granville. *Literary Horizons*: *A Quarter Century of American Fiction.* New York: Univ. Press, 1970.

Knopp, Josephine Zadovsky. *The Trial of Judaism in Contemporary Jewish Writing.* Chicago: Univ. of Illinois Press, 1975.

Kort, Wesley A. *Shriven Selves*: *Religious Problems in Recent American Fiction.* Philadelphia: Fortress Press, 1972.

Kostelanetz, Richard, ed. *On Contemporary Literature.* New York: Avon, 1969.

Lewin, Lois Symons. *The Theme of Suffering in the work of Bernard Malamud and Saul Bellow.* Michigan: Univ. of Microfilms—University of Pittsburgh, Ph.D., 1967.

Lewis, R.W.B. *The Picaresque Saint: Representative Figures in Contemporary Fiction.* Philadelphia and New York: J.B. Lippincott, 1959.

Liptzin, Solomon. *The Jew in American Literature.* New York: Bloch, 1966.

Malin, Irving and Irvin Stark, eds. *Breakthrough: A Treasury of Contemporary American-Jewish Literature:* New York: McGraw-Hill, 1964.

Malin, Irving. *Contemporary American-Jewish Literature: Critical Essays.* Bloomington and London: Indiana Univ. Press, 1973.

——. *Jews and Americans.* Carbondale: Southern Illinois Univ. Press, 1965.

May, Rollo. *Power and Innocence: A Search for the Sources of Violence.* New York.: W.W. Norton, 1972.

Meeter, Glenn. *Bernard Malamud and Philip Roth: A Critical Essay.* Grand Rapids, Mich.: William B. Eerdmans, 1968.

Moore, Harry T., ed. *Contemporary American Novelists.* Carbondale: Southern Illinois Univ. Press, 1964.

Narasimhaiah, C.D., ed. *Asian Response to American Literature.* Delhi: Vikas, 1972.

Olderman, Raymond M. *Beyond the Wasteland: A Study of the American Novel in the Nineteen Sixties.* New Haven: Yale Univ. Press, 1972.

Pinsker, Sanford. *The Schlemiel as Metaphor: Studies in the Yiddish and American Jewish Novel.* Carbondale: Southern Illinois Univ. Press, 1971.

Richman, Sidney. *Bernard Malamud.* New York: Twayne, 1967.

Rubin, Louis D., Jr. *The Curious Death of the Novel: Essays in American Literature.* Baton Rouge: Louisiana State Univ. Press, 1967.

Ruotolo, Lucio P. *Six Existential Heroes: The Politics of Faith.* Cambridge, Mass.: Harvard Univ. Press, 1973.

Rupp, Richard H. *Celebration in Postwar American Fiction, 1945-67.* Coral Gables, Fla.: Univ. of Miami, 1970.

Schulz, Max F. *Radical Sophistication*: *Studies in Contemporary Jewish-American Novelists*. Athens, Ohio: Ohio Univ. Press, 1969.

Sheed, Wilfrid. *The Morning After*: *Selected Essays and Reviews*. New York: Farrar, Straus, and Giroux, 1971.

Sherman, C. Bezalel *The Jew Within American Society*: *A Study in Ethnic Individuality*. Detroit: Wayne State Univ. Press, 1961.

Tanner, Tony. *City of Words*: *American Fiction, 1950-70*. New York: Harper and Row, 1971.

Ulanov, Barry. *The Two Worlds of American Art*: *The Private and the Popular*. New York: Macmillan, 1965.

Umphlett, Wiley Lee. *The Sporting Myth and the American Experience*: *Studies in Contemporary Fiction*. London: Associated Univ. Press, 1975.

Unger, Leonard. *American Writers*: *A Collection of Literary Biographies*, Supplement I, Part 2. New York: Charles Scribner's Sons, 1979.

Waldmeir, Jospeh J. *Recent American Fiction*: *Some Critical Views*. Boston: Houghton Mifflin, 1963.

Weinberg, Helen. *The New Novel in America*: *The Kafkan Mode in Contemporary American Fiction*. Ithaca and London: Cornell Univ. Press, 1970.

Wisse, Ruth R. *The Schlemiel as Modern Hero*. Chicago: Univ. of Chicago Press, 1971.

B. Articles

"A Corrupt Compassion." *The Times* (*London*) *Literary Supplement* 1 April 1960: 205.

Adams, Phoebe. "The Burdens of the Past." *Atlantic* Nov. 1961: 184-85.

Alter, Iska Sheila. "The Good Man's Dilemma: Social Criticism in the Fiction of Bernard Malamud." *DAI* 38: 6128 A.

Alter, Robert. "Malamud as Jewish Writer." *Commentary* 42 (1966): 71-76.

Axthelm, Peter. "Holes in the Ground." *Newsweek* 5 May 1969: 110.

Bailey, Anthony. "Insidious Patience." *Commonweal* 66 (1957): 307-08.

Barsness, John A. "A New Life: The Frontier Myth in Perspective." *Western American Literature* 3.4 Winter 1969: 297-302.

Baumbach, Jonathan. "The Economy of Love: The Novels of Bernard Malamud." *Kenyon Review* 25 (1963): 438-57.

——. "Malamud's Heroes: The Fate of Fixers.'' *Commonweal* 85 (1966): 97-99.

Bell, Pearl K. "Heller and Malamud, Then and Now." *Commentary* 67.6 June 1979: 71-75.

——. "Morality Tale without Mercy." *New Leader* 18 Oct. 1971: 17-18.

Bennington, Nort, Vt. "A Talk with Bernard Malamud." *The New York Times Book Review* 8 Oct. 1961: 28.

Blackman. R.C. Review of *The Magic Barrel. Christian Science Monitor* 15 May 1958: 11.

Bowen, Robert O. "The View from Beneath." *National Review* 2 Dec. 1961: 383-84.

Broyard, Anatole. Review of *Pictures of Fidelman. New York Times Book Review* 4 May 1969: 5, 45.

Catinella, Joseph. Review of *The Tenants. Saturday Review* 25 Sept. 1971: 36.

Cronin, Gloria. "The Complex Irony of Grace: A Study of Bernard Malamud's *God's Grace.*" *Studies in American-Jewish Literature* 5, ed. Daniel Walden (Albany: State Univ. of New York Press, 1986) 119-28.

Daniels, Sally. "Recent Fiction: Flights and Evasions." *Minnesota Review* 2 Summer 1962: 546-57.

Dickstein, Morris. "Cold War Blues: Notes on the Culture of the Fifties." *Partisan Review* 41.3 (1974): 30-53.

——. "The Tenants." *New York Times Book Review* 3 Oct. 1971: 1, 14, 16, 18, 20.

Ducharme, Robert. "Structure and Content in Malamud's *Pictures of Fidelman.*" *Connecticut Review* 5.1 (1971): 26-36.

Edel, Leon. "Narcissists need not apply." *American Scholar* 49.1 Winter 79-80: 130-32.

Elliott, George P. "Yakov's Ordeal." *New York Times Book Review* 4 Sept. 1966: 1, 25-26.

Elman, Richard M. "Malamud on Campus." *Commonweal* 75 (1961): 114-15.

Evanier, David. "Fanny and Duby." *National Review* 27 April 1979: 570-71.

Farber, Stephen. *"The Fixer."* *Hudson Review* 22.1 Spring 1969: 134-38.

Featherstone, Joseph. "Bernard Malamud." *Atlantic.* March 1967: 95-98.

Francis, H.E. "Bernard Malamud's Everyman." *Midstream* 7.1 Winter 1961: 93-97.

Frankel, Haskel. Interview with Malamud. *Saturday Review* 10 Sept. 1966: 39-40.

Freedman, William. "American Jewish Fiction: So What's the Big Deal?" *Chicago Review* 19.1 (1966): 90-107.

Friedman, Melvin J. "The American Jewish Literary Scene, 1979: A Review Essay." *Studies in American Fiction* 8.2 Autumn 1980: 239-46.

Gealy, Marcia Booker. "The Hasidic Tradition in the Work of Bernard Malamud." *DAI* 37: 963 A.

Geltman, Max. "Irrational Streams of Blood." *National Review* 1 Nov. 1966: 1117-19.

Gilman, Richard. "Dubin's Lives." *New Republic* 24 Mar. 1979: 28-30.

Glassgold, Peter. "Malamud's Literary Ethic." *Nation* 15 Nov. 1971: 504-05.

Gold, Herbert. "Dream to be Good." *Nation* 184 (1957): 350.

Goodheart, Eugene. "Fantasy and Reality." *Midstream* 7.4 Autumn 1961: 102-05.

Goyen, William. "A World of Bad Luck." *New York Times Book Review* 28 April 1957: 4.

Graber, Ralph S. "Baseball in American Fiction." *English Journal* 56.8 Nov. 1967: 1107-14.

Halio, Jay L. "Fantasy and Fiction." *Southern Review* 7.2 Spring 1971: 635-47.

Halley, Anne. "The Good Life in Recent Fiction." *Massachusetts Review* 3 Autumn 1961: 190-96.

Hartt, N.N. "The Return of Moral Passion." *Yale Review* 51 Winter 1962: 300-08.

Hassan, Ihab. "The Hopes of Man." *New York Times Book Review* 13 Oct. 1963: 5.

——. "The Way Down and Out." *Virginia Quarterly Review* 39 Winter 1969: 81-93.

Hays, Peter L. "The Complex Pattern of Redemption in *The Assistant.*" *Centennial Review* 13 (1969): 200-14.

Hicks, Granville. "American Fiction in 1958." *Saturday Review* 27 Dec. 1958: 11-12.

——. "His Hopes on the Human Heart." *Saturday Review* 12 Oct. 1963: 31-32.

——. "One Man to Stand for Six Million." *Saturday Review* 10 Sept. 1966: 37-39.

"Jewishness and the Younger Intellectuals: A Symposium," *Commentary* 31.4 April 1961: 306-59.

Kiely, Robert. *Rembrandt's Hat.*" *New York Times Book Review* 3 June 1973: 7.

Knopp, Josephine Z. "The Ways of *Mentshlekhkayt.* A Study of Morality in Some Fiction of Bernard Malamud and Philip Roth." *Tradition* Winter 1973: 67-84.

Korg, Jacob. "Ishmael and Israel." *Commentary* May 1972: 82-84.

Landis, J.C. "Reflections on American Jewish Writers." *Jewish Book Annual* 25 (1967-68): 144.

Leer, Norman. "Three American Novels and Contemporary Society: A Search for Commitment." *Wisconsin Studies in Contemporary Literature* 3.3 (1962): 67-86.

Lefcowitz, Barbara F. "The *Hybris* of Neurosis: Malamud's *Pictures of Fidelman.*" *Literature and Psychology* 29 (1970): 115-20.

Levin, David. "The Lives of Bernard Malamud." *The Virginia Quarterly Review* 56.1 Winter 1980: 162-66.

Lindberg-Seyersted, B. "Reading of Bernard Malamud's *The Tenants.*" *Journal of American Studies* 9.1 April 1975: 85-102.

Locke, Richard. "Malamud's Reach." *Saturday Review* 17 Mar. 1979: 67-69.

Malcolm, Donald. "The Groves of Academe." *New Yorker* 27 Jan. 1962: 105-07.

Maloff, Saul. "Loveliest Breakdown in Contemporary Fiction: Malamud's Lives." *Commonweal* 27 April 1979: 244-46.

———. "Schlemiel Triumphant." *Newsweek* 68.11 12 Sept. 1966: 108 B.

Marcus, Steve. "The Novel Again." *Partisan Review* 29 Spring 1962: 171-95.

Masilamoni, E.H. Leelavathi. "Bernard Malamud: An Interview." *Indian Journal of American Studies* 9.2 July 1979: 33-37.

Mesher, David R. "The Remembrance of Things Unknown: Malamud's 'The Last Mohicans'." *Studies in Short Fiction* 12.4 Fall 1967: 1-11.

Mott, Benjamin De. "Jewish Writers in America: A Place in Establishment." *Commentary* 31.2 Feb. 1961: 127-134.

Perrine, Laurence. "Malamud's 'Take Pity'." *Studies in Short Fiction* 2 (1964): 84-86.

Podhoretz, Norman. "Achilles in Left Field." *Commentary* 15 (1953): 321-26.

Pradhan, S.V. "The Nature and Interpretation of Symbolism in Malamud's *The Assistant*." *Centennial Review* 15 (1972): 394-407.

———. Prescott, Peter S. "A New Life." *Newsweek* 93. 12 Feb. 1979: 83-83A.

Ratner, Marc L. "Style and Humanity in Malamud's Fiction." *Massachusetts Review* 5 Summer 1964: 663-83.

Review of *Rembrandt's Hat*. *Publishers' Weekly* 26 March 1973: 69.

Roth, Philip. "Writing American Fiction." *Commentary* 31 (1961): 223-33.

Rubenstein, Roberta. "Search for Self." *The Progressive* 43 June 1979: 57-58.

Rubin, Louis D., Jr. "The Curious Death of the Novel: or, what to do about tired literary critics." *Kenyon Review* 28 (1966): 305-25.

Scholes, Robert. "Portrait of Artist as 'Escape-Coat'." *Saturday Review* 10. May 1969: 14.

Sharma, D.R. "*The Tenants*: Malamud's Treatment of the Racial Problem." *Indian Journal of American Studies* 8.2: 12-22.

Shenker, Israel. "For Malamud It's Story." *New York Times Book Review* 3 Oct. 1971: 20, 22.

Solotaroff, Theodore. "Bernard Malamud's Fiction: The Old Life and the New." *Commentary* 33. March 1962: 197-204.

Standley, Fred L. "Bernard Malamud: The Novel of Redemption." *Southern Humanities Review* 5 (1971): 309-18.

Stern, Daniel. "The Art of Fiction: Bernard Malamud." (Interview) *Paris Review* 61 Spring 1975: 40-64.

Stevenson, David L. "The Strange Destiny of S. Levin." *New York Times Book Review* 8 Oct. 1961: 1, 28.

Tanner, Tony. "Bernard Malamud and the New Life." *Critical Quarterly* 10 (1968): 151-68.

Turner, Frederick W., III "Myth Inside and Out: Malamud's *The Natural*." *Novel* 1 Winter 1968: 133-39.

Tyler, Ralph. "Talk with the Novelist." *New York Times Book Review* 18 Feb. 1979: 1 and 31-34.

Weales, Gerald. "The Sharing of Misery." *New Leader* 1 Sept. 1958: 24-25.

Wegelin, Christof. "American Schlemiel Abroad: Malamud's Italian Stories and the End of American Innocence." *Twentieth Century Literature* 19 (1973): 77-88.

Wershba, Joseph. "Close up." *New York Post Magazine* 14 Sept 1958.

Wershba, Joe. "Not Horror but 'Sadness'," *New York Post Magazine* 14 Sept 1958: M2.

White, Robert L. "The English Instructor as Hero: Two Novels by Roth and Malamud." *Forum* 4. Winter 1963: 16-22.

Wolff, Geoffrey. "Malamud's Biographer." *Esquire* 13 Feb. 1979: 17-18.

C. Bibliographies

Kosofsky, Rita Nathalie. *Bernard Malamud: An Annotated Checklist.* Kent, Ohio: Kent State Univ. Press, 1970.

Ristz, Donald. "A Comprehensive Checklist of Malamud Criticism." *The Fiction of Bernard Malamud*, ed. Richard Astro and Jackson J. Benson. Corvallis: Oregon State Univ. Press, 1977, 163-90.

INDEX

Aleichem, Sholom 191
Allen, John Alexander 169n
Allen, Walter 56, 73n, 74n
Alter, Robert 26, 34n, 95, 122n, 204n
Amos 13-14
"Angel Levine" 26, 195
Anna Karenina 66
Assistant, The 24, 25, 28, 34n, 51, 54-73, 79, 80, 126, 177, 192, 195, 198, 206
Astro, Richard 30n, 52n, 74n, 79, 92n, 94n, 150n, 169n
Avery, Everlyn Gross 204n
Axthelm, Pete 149n

Balakian, Nona 52n
Barth, John 79
Baumbach, Jonathan 29, 35n, 78, 79, 93n, 94n
Bell, Pearl K. 172, 182n
Bellow, Saul 11, 15-16, 19, 20-21, 23, 24, 31n, 32n, 33n, 200
Benson, Jackson J. 30n, 52n, 74n, 92n, 150n , 169n
Bewkes, Eugene G. 31n
Bible, The 184, 187
Binswanger, Ludwig 27

"Black Is My Favorite Color" 191, 196 97
Blackman, R.C. 192, 204
Blocker, Joel 33n
Blood Accusations: The Strange Case of Beiliss 96, 97
Blotner, Joseph L. 33n
Bluefarb, Sam 128, 151n
Boas, George 190n
Boroff, David 204n
Bowen, Robert O. 77, 93n
Bronowski, Jacob 11, 16, 31n
Buber, Martin 15, 18, 31n, 32n
Burgess, Anthony 79, 94n

Camus, Albert 16, 24
Candee, Marjorie Dent 34n
Carlyle, John 163
Catcher in the Rye, The 21
Catinella, Joseph 168n, 169n
Chute, Nevil 184
Clementia 188
Cohen, Sandy 29, 31n, 36n, 40, 53n, 93n
Craib, Roderick 169n
Crime and Punishment 56, 66

Dangling Man, The 20, 33n
Daniels, Sally 77, 93n
Davenport, Guy 127, 150n
Dev, Amiya 123n
Dickstein, Morris 154, 168n
Dimont, Max I 13, 30n, 31n, 96, 122n
Dostoevsky, Feodor 56, 72
Dreiser, Theodore 27
Dubin's Lives 28, 168, 170-181
Ducharme, Robert 29-30, 36n, 37, 142, 148, 150n, 151n

Edwards, Herbert W. 74n
Eigner, Edwin M. 99, 123n
Eisinger, Chester E. 33n
Eliot, George 170
Elliott, George P. 123n
Ellman, Richard 33n
Epstein, Joseph 189-90, 190n

Face of Violence: An Essay with a Play, The 11, 16
Family Moskat, The 23
Farber, Stephen 123n
Faulkner, William 16, 31n
Featherstone, Joseph 29, 35n, 100, 123n
Fiedler, Leslie A. 29, 35n, 37, 76, 92n
Field, Joyce W. 34n, 52n, 73n, 92n, 93n, 123n, 149n, 150n, 168n
Field, Leslie A. 34n, 52n, 53n, 73n, 92n, 93n, 123n, 150n, 168n
Fitzgerald, Edward W. 39, 53n
Fixer, The 28, 85, 92, 95-122, 126, 173, 206
Fixler, Michael 33n
Flower, Dean 172, 182n
Francis, H.E. 22, 35n, 56
Frankel, Haskel 27, 35n, 97, 122n, 123n, 124n
French Revolution 163
French, Warren 33n
Friedberg, Mauicer 122n

Friedman, Alan Warren 100-1, 124n
Friedman, Maurice B. 32n
Fromm, Erich 14, 18, 31n, 32n
Fuller, Edmund 17, 32n

Giles Goat-Boy 79
Gilman, Richard 170, 172, 182n
Gitenstein, Barbara 169n
God's Grace 28, 181, 183-190, 206
Gold 19, 52n
Goldman, Mark 128, 130, 150n, 151n
Goyen, William 56, 74n
Grebstein, Sheldon Norman 78, 79, 93n, 94n, 117, 124n, 126, 150n
Gwyn, Frederick L. 33n

Handy, W.J. 35n, 74n, 93n
Hardy, Thomas 170
Harper, Howard M., Jr. 126, 148, 149n, 151n
Hassan, Ihab 29, 31n, 34n, 35n, 39, 53n, 57, 74n, 92n, 168n
Hays, Peter L. 29, 35n, 37-38, 52n, 55, 56, 73n
Helterman, Jeffrey 33n, 123n, 126, 127, 149n, 150n, 199, 204n
Herzog 33n
Hicks, Granville 29, 35n, 39, 52n, 77, 93n, 122n, 124n
Hitler 27
Hoag, Gerald 114, 124n
Hoffman, Daniel 30n, 182n
Hoffman, Frederick J. 31n
Hollander, John 77, 93n
Horton, Rod W. 74n
Hosea 13
Hoyt, Charles Alva 52n
Humboldt's Gift 20
Hyman, A.E. 94n
Hyman, Edgar Stanley 78, 79, 93n, 94n

"Idiots First" 195-96
Idiots First 190, 191-92, 195-98, 199, 204n
Iyengar, Srinivas 191n

James, Henry 17
Jefferson, Howard B. 31n
Jung, C.B. 38

Kafka, Franz 98
Kakutani, Michiko 150n, 207n
Kazin, Alfred 29, 35n
Kellman, Steven G. 153, 155, 167, 168n, 169n
Kennedy, William 63
Kiely, Robert 205n
Klein, Marcus 40, 52n, 53n
Knopp, Josephine Zadowsky 18, 19, 32n, 101, 124n
Korg, Jacob 155, 169n
Kostelanetz, Richard 35n
Kulshrestha, Chirantan 32n

Landis, J.C. 18, 29, 32n, 35n
Lardner, Ring 38
Lawrence, D.H. 172, 173, 176
Lawrence, T.E. 163
Layman, Richard 33n
Leer, Norman 56, 74n
Lefcowitz, Barbara F. 135, 138, 151n
Leibowitz, Herbert 204n
Letting Go 22
Levin, David 192n
Lewin, Lois Symons 30, 36n
Lewis, R.W.B. 17, 24, 32n, 34n
Lincoln, Abraham 171
Lindberg-Seyersted, B. 167, 169n
Locke, Richard 172, 182n
Ludwig, Jack 73n

Madame Bovary 66
Magic Barrel, The 26, 34n, 190, 191-95, 199, 203n
Magician of Lublin, The 23, 101
Malin, Irving 33n, 93n, 150n
Maloff, Saul 124n, 172, 182n
Manor, The 23
Masilomani, Leelavathi E.H. 78, 93n, 169n
May, Rollo 16, 17, 31n, 32n, 52n, 205n

Meland, Bernard E. 123n
Mellard, James 37
Mesher, D.R. 128, 150n, 151n
Miller, James E., Jr. 33n
Moore Harry T. 52n
Mr. Sammler's Planet 33n
"My Son, the Murderer" 199, ?))

National Observer, The 28, 63
Natural, The 25, 28, 37-51, 54, 64
New Life, A 28, 73, 76-92, 178
New Testament, The 113-14, 187
Niebuhr, Reinhold 17

Olderman, Raymond M. 79, 94n
Old Testament, The 14, 114, 187
On the Beach 184
Our Gang 22
Ozick, Cynthia 154, 168, 169n

Passos, John Dos 153
Peretz, I.L. 191
Phillips, Robert 204n
Philo 14
Pictures of Fidelman, The 28, 122, 125-49, 154, 159, 170, 201, 205n
Pinsker, Sanford 79, 94n
Plimpton, George 33n
Podhoretz, Norman 37, 39, 52n
Pollitt, Katha 190n
Pondrom, Cyrena N. 34n
Popkin, Henry 204n, 205n
Portnoy's Complaint, 22
Power and Innocence, The 16
Prescott, Peter S. 171, 182n

Rahv, Philip 56, 74n
Ratner, Marc L. 63, 74n
Reading Myself and Others 33n
"Rembrandt's Hat" 201-02
Rembrandt's Hat, The 190, 191-192, 199-203, 204n, 205n
Richman, Sidney 34n, 35n, 52n, 53n, 56, 72, 73n, 74n, 75n, 79, 94n, 128, 191, 203n, 204n
Robinson Crusoe 184
Rosenfield 19

Roth, Philip 19, 21-22, 23, 25, 33n, 34n, 35n
Rubenstein, Robert 171, 182n
Rubin, Louis D. 93n
Ruotolo, Lucid P. 101, 124n
Rupp, Richard H. 39, 52n

Sabbath and Festival Prayer Book, The 15
Sachs, Nelly 19
Salinger, J.D. 11, 20, 23
Samuel, Maurice 96, 97
Sartre, Jean-Paul 122n
Satan in Goray 23
Schechner, Mark 11, 30n, 182n
Schwaz-Bart, Andre 19
Scott, Wilbur 32n
Seforim, Mocher 191
Seize the Day 20, 200
Seven Pillars of Wisdom, The 163
Shakespeare, William 70
Shenkar, Israel 168n
Sherman, Bezalel 13, 30n
Siegel, Ben 29, 33n, 34n, 36n, 52n, 56, 74n, 75n, 100, 123n, 150n, 167, 168, 169n, 203n
Silone 24
Simmons, Charles 52n
Sinclaire, Clive 190n
Singer, Isaac Bashevis 11, 19, 22-23, 101
Slave, The 23
Solotaroff, Robert 74n
Solotaroff, Theodore 19, 26, 32n, 34n, 94n
Stegner, Page 77, 93n
Steinbeck, John 153
Stern, Daniel 34n, 35n, 55, 73n, 92n, 123n, 154, 168n, 169n
Stetler, Charles 126, 149n
Stevenson, David L. 39, 53n, 79, 94n
Sullivan, Walter 126, 135, 150n, 151n

"Take Pity" 192, 193
"Talking Horse" 199, 202-3
Tanner, Tony 49, 53n, 74n, 91, 94n, 101, 118, 121, 123n, 124n
Tempest, The 184
Tenants, The 28, 149, 152-168, 170, 173, 196, 203
"The Bill" 192-93
"The Cost of Living" 195, 198
"The Death of Me" 195, 198
"The First Seven Years" 196
"The German Refugee" 195, 197-98
"The Jewbird" 196-97
"The Letter" 199
"The Loan" 192, 194-95
"The Magic Barrel" 195
"The Mourners" 194
"The Prison" 194
"The Silver Crown" 195, 202
Throeau, Henry David 171, 172, 173
Tolstoy, Leo 172
Towers, Robert 172, 182n
Trial, The 98
Troye, Chertian de 38
Twain, Mark 171, 173
Tyler, Ralph 182n

Ulanov, Barry 55, 73n
Unger, Leonard 74n
Updike, John 52n

Vickery, Olga W. 31
Victim, The 20
Vinson, James 33n, 168n, 169n

Waldmeir, Joseph 35n, 52n
Wasserman, Earl 37, 52n
Wershba, Joseph 27, 34n, 35n, 74n
When She Was Good 22
Whitman, Walt 197
Wiesel, Elie 19, 24, 34n
Williams, Daniel Day 100, 123n
Wisse, Ruth R. 148, 150n, 151n

Yeats, William Butler 127